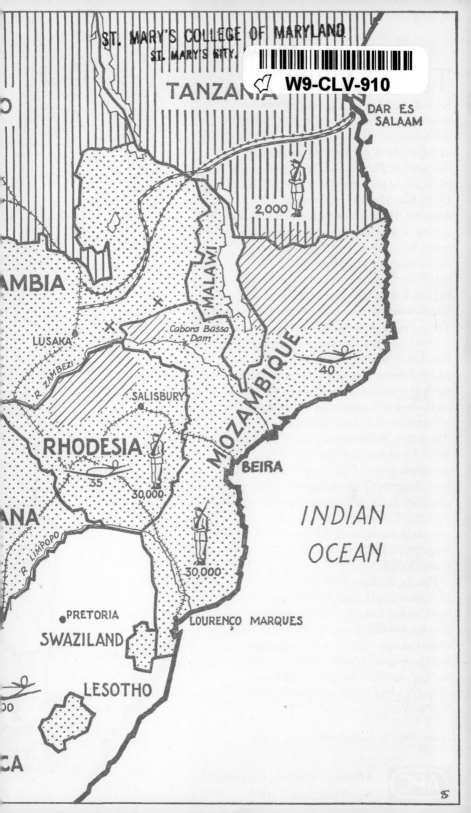

TANZANIA

DAR E.S SALAAM

2,000

AMBIA

MALAWI

LUSAKA

R. ZAMBEZI

Cabora Bassa Dam

MOZAMBIQUE

40

SALISBURY

RHODESIA

35

30,000

BEIRA

INDIAN OCEAN

ANA

R. LIMPOPO

30,000

PRETORIA

LOURENÇO MARQUES

SWAZILAND

LESOTHO

CA

THE HIGH PRICE OF PRINCIPLES

KAUNDA AND THE WHITE SOUTH

THE HIGH PRICE
OF PRINCIPLES

KAUNDA AND THE WHITE SOUTH

By
Richard Hall

AFRICANA PUBLISHING CORPORATION · NEW YORK

Published in the United States of America 1970
by Africana Publishing Corporation
101 Fifth Avenue, New York, N.Y. 10003

Library of Congress Catalog Card No. 74–106642

SBN 8419-0038-8

Printed in Great Britain
by Cox & Wyman, Ltd, London, Fakenham and Reading

Preface

At the Commonwealth Conference in London earlier this year, Lee Kuan Yew lectured African leaders around the Marlborough House table. If they wanted a "just solution" to the Rhodesian problem, their countries would have to find the discipline and durability for a war of attrition. The 150,000 white Rhodesians, even backed by 4,000,000 South Africans, could not be invincible for ever. But oratory alone was not enough. "In Southeast Asia, the Vietcong have demonstrated that given the tenacity, the capacity, the will to slog it out to the very end of time, even the world's mightiest military and technological power can be persuaded to negotiate a settlement."

The next day I was with Kenneth Kaunda, to whom the Singapore premier's remarks had offered almost a direct challenge. Before independence, Zambia had been known as Northern Rhodesia; in any war of attrition, it would become Africa's North Vietnam. Lee had warned that the Africans must be willing to pay a price for their beliefs. Geography dictates that the Zambians would pay most of all. However, everyone at Marlborough House knew that Black Africa was in no state, for the moment, to mount such an offensive – the remnant of its former militancy was hard pressed to hold the line against compromise. As if to illustrate this situation, on another floor of the Dorchester—where Kaunda was staying for the conference— was another president of diametrically opposed views: Hastings Banda of Malawi. There was a minimum of contact between the two. Banda has made it clear, again and again, that he wants no part in a confrontation to end racial inequality. Indeed, he has without qualms taken much financial and technical help from South Africa. When Kaunda called for the use of force to end the Rhodesian rebellion, Banda argued against it. Yet Zambia and Malawi are neighbours, with tight tribal links.

I asked Kaunda what he would do if his country fell into dire financial troubles through a slump in the price of copper, which provides ninety-five per cent of the export revenue. South Africa might well offer aid, as she had to Malawi. Would he accept, as Banda had done? Our conversation was taped and when I played it back later there was no mistaking, from the tone of his voice, how much that question had harassed Kaunda. He had said: "Honestly, I hope to God it does not happen. It would be a really serious challenge—obviously it would be—but I hope we get beyond that point with our rural development before we are overtaken by such things. I would find it very, very difficult indeed to use South African money. I hope it would be the last money I would have to use on earth. To sink to the depth of saying it was good enough, because we were in trouble!"

That dilemma was hypothetical, but trends in southern Africa in the past four years had already put Kaunda in an acute quandary. The position of Zambia has become increasingly hazardous, its policies crucial. So the first aim of this book is to tell, with as much significant detail as can be mustered, how it has happened – how the balance has shifted. At the time of Zambia's independence in October 1964, a group of liberal American journalists asked me, as a colleague on the spot, how long I thought it might be before Southern Rhodesia also became a Black State. "Three years," I said cautiously. It was taken as a very pessimistic forecast, and I was left feeling somewhat reactionary for having made it. Five years later, a far greater measure of pessimism is called for; my forecasts in this book are more wary still.

Originally I had thought of limiting myself to an analysis of Zambia's hapless involvement in the Rhodesian problem, and how this had affected her own economy and internal political development; moreover, why Kaunda—being the man he is—had grown so bitter about Britain's performance. I have still tried to keep this in the centre of the stage. But it also soon became plain to me that much of the minutiae of the Rhodesian affair since Ian Smith's UDI is intolerably tedious. Rarely can there have been an international crisis (if that is still the word) with so many non-events, so many non-people travelling to and fro, so many millions of words spoken inside parliaments and out, so much persiflage, logic-chopping and evasion. So I have skimmed over quite a lot. On the other hand, it grows more essential to consider Rhodesia in a wider context—especially in the light of South Africa's rapidly-progressing schemes for a *rapprochement* with the rest of the continent south of the equator. Moreover, it is obviously relevant that a growing disarray in the Organisation of African Unity has eased the path for this initiative from Pretoria. It sometimes seems that the countries of Black Africa are more fierce with one another, and with domestic political opponents, than they are towards the white-run south —or generally were towards the former colonial masters.

At the time of the 1965 Commonwealth Conference a memorable picture was taken of three senior African Leaders congratulating a new addition to the ranks, Dr Banda. The three around him were Sir Abubakar Tafawa Balewa, Premier of Nigeria (since murdered); Sir Albert Margai of Sierra Leone (detained without trial); and President Kwame Nkrumah of Ghana (deposed). By chance, I was in Lagos at the time of the first Nigerian coup. While I slept in a house just around the corner, Sir Abubakar was taken away to be shot and buried in a shallow grave. Two days later I slipped out on a plane to the Congo and from there telexed a report to London which ended rather tritely: "The image of Africa's happy giant has been smashed for good." Slightly more than two years later I was back in that part of Nigeria renamed Biafra, to see the most revolting displays of African inhumanity to fellow-Africans. To quote Lee Kuan Yew once again, in a letter to Kaunda: "Unhappy events have involved Black African governments, like the tragedies still being enacted in the Ibo territories of Nigeria. They do great damage to the cause of the Black peoples."

My own connection with Africa began well before the recent years upon which this book is focused. I was able to watch events rise to the crescendo of the sixties, and became actively involved in a minor way. Reactions had varied when in 1955 I suddenly took a job with a mining company in what is now Zambia. The foreign editor of the London newspaper I was working on said vaguely: "Oh, the Copperbelt. Isn't that the place where the natives want to massacre all the whites? Send us a piece if anything happens." Then as we were travelling on a train together, Alan Brien spent some time prophecying that I would be condemned to endless gin-drinking on the verandahs of fascist settlers. Before my plane took off, other friends warned of poisonous snakes and the sexual capacity of black women.

At that time, world interest in Africa politically was negligible. The Gold Coast had not yet become Nkrumah's Ghana and in the Central African Federation – which embraced my new milieu – Sir Roy Welensky seemed to have matters well under control. The black miners showed a proclivity for striking until their leaders were arrested and dispersed to bush restriction centres. This made little impact on the Copperbelt's 20,000 Europeans, who maintained a comfortable routine; underground, shift bosses spurred on their gangs with abuse and an occasional blow around the head. The British Commonwealth Secretary, Lord Home (later translated into Sir Alec Douglas-Home) visited the Copperbelt and provoked a flutter of excitement by talking to several hand-picked Africans in a district commissioner's garden. My responsibility was to edit two magazines, serving the mining town of Mufulira; it was understood that if any Africans happened to obtrude into photographs in the magazine for Europeans, they would not be named.

Shortly after my arrival, a servant looked up from scouring a saucepan and asked: "Where is Dr Banda? When is he coming back?" I was only dimly aware at the time of Banda's existence and could give no satisfactory answer. But the questions had also been a gambit. It later became clear to me that Hastings Banda was a legend in Central Africa and that his return would have messianic significance (although it was to turn out curiously). So the political possibilities grew more interesting and my two magazines gave the chance to look around on both sides of the racial fence.

However, the massacre failed to materialise, and after a holiday in Zanzibar I wrote an article about Arab–African rivalry on the island, working in an interview with a former stoker called Abeid Karume who was putting himself forward as the spokesman of the Africans. The foreign editor sent it back with a note explaining that Zanzibar was far too remote to concern the readers. Some years later, Karume came to power through a revolution in which 10,000 Arabs are reputed to have died.

By the time African nationalism was in full flood, I had left the Copperbelt, and moved to the capital Lusaka. There I spent two years running a string of rural newspapers as a colonial civil servant, and then launched a hectic weekly called the *African Mail*. It was notorious among the whites, sued by Welensky, snatched up by Africans and tolerated as a safety-valve by the Colonial Office. By this stage, Kaunda had emerged as the unchallenged leader of the mass of his people. It seemed remarkable then—as it often did later—that someone with rather old-fashioned missionary beliefs should rise to the top in the jungle of African politics and be able to command the loyalty of the Copperbelt toughs. Perhaps instinctively they knew they needed him, as he needed them. The five years of the *African Mail* were surfeited with excitements and tribulations. My wife was also involved with the paper and we lived very close to events. I had a curious status, one day being told I should be thrown in jail when the Federal Army took control, and the next being called to a white minister's office to say whether I thought Kaunda would accept parity in the legislature. Some of Kaunda's colleagues viewed me with suspicion, since I never joined a political party. It is true that they would have won anyway, without the help of white well-wishers. Independence was a watershed, and six months afterwards I switched to editing the national daily paper, the *Times of Zambia*. In 1968 I was finally able to hand over to an African editor, which had always been the intention.

So that is the background from which the book is written. Some people may find certain parts painful—for example, the account in Part Four of post-independence troubles inside Zambia. However, it seems that the time for cool appraisal has been reached. For information and advice on many points I am indebted to various quarters, but it seems better not to make any precise acknowledgements.

February, 1969.   RICHARD HALL

Contents

Contents

PART ONE

New Alignments in Southern Africa

CHAPTER ONE

The Zambian Outpost

Until the middle sixties, Zambia could be seen as the spear-head of Black Africa, pointing to the Cape. From Kenneth Kaunda's new republic, irresistible forces would sweep across the Zambezi River and beyond, to overcome the remnants of colonialism and white rule. It was an exciting vision, fanciful in retrospect but important to recall: at that time moral pressures appeared more real than military arithmetic or the influence of international finance. It was a matter of 250 million Africans against four million defensive whites, whose policies had been repeatedly condemned at the United Nations; there was a powerful illusion that mere numbers and distant resolutions created a tide of history.

Not until the overthrow of Kwame Nkrumah in early 1966 did the vision finally fade. The Ghanaian President had been the symbol of black militancy. Six months later came the assassination of Hendrik Verwoerd, the South African Prime Minister; he had generally followed a policy of white isolationism. Verwoerd's successor, Johannes Vorster, soon rejected the "laager" strategy, saying that a different wind of change was blowing. South Africa would take its rightful place on the continent and African countries would be helped to help themselves. This was a declaration of the "white counter-attack", using economic weapons but founded upon military confidence. With bewildering suddenness, Zambia found itself by late 1968 no longer a spearhead but an outpost.

The transformation came so dramatically because Black Africa had a false idea of its own potential. No real battle had been joined to try its muscles. In a score of countries, independence had been a gift – from metropolitan countries resolved to shed their imperial burdens. Britain, France and Belgium had yielded to world opinion, but were comforted with the hope of retaining their African markets while escaping from the tribulations of colonial government. The pro-consuls departed, leaving behind a motley of fragile states. The Scramble from Africa was more hurried (and in some ways more ignominious) than the Scramble for Africa in the closing decades of the nineteenth century.

Nominal nations, bounded by arbitrary lines on the map, possessed the trappings but not the means. In national assemblies there was the regalia of European democracy without the experience — even assuming the desire — to make the system work. Development plans were drawn up, despite an absence of skills to carry them through. Political philosophies, based on various concepts of African Socialism, were often undermined by bourgeois attitudes inherited by a new élite from its former white rulers.

This may sound too sweeping and too unkind. Certainly there have been achievements to set against the general failure. It is the unpredictable nature of African governments, with the capacity for bitter dispute regardless of the consequences, which has led to a loss of confidence. The leaders themselves now declare — so often that it almost seems masochistic — that Black Africa is "in a mess". It will take a long time, and still more tumult, to put it right.

Yet to be condescending about African folly and incompetence is not enough. The main indictment must be served upon those who so casually handed over sovereignty. Neglect of education for the indigenous peoples was widespread in colonial times and it is to the credit of the new states that they have made desperate efforts to set this right. The reasons why so many African countries were flung into independence with a pathetic handful of graduates and almost no people with technical and managerial skills are various: sometimes it was simply indolence and a reluctance to spend money; there was also a fear of producing Africans able to ask awkward questions or to challenge the settlers for their jobs and trade. Writing in 1759, Samuel Johnson put into the mouth of an imaginary Red Indian chief the kind of accusation which might well be made by twentieth-century Africans: "Either they promised protection which they never have afforded, or instruction which they never imparted. We hoped to be secured by their favour from some other evil, or to learn the arts of Europe, by which we might be able to secure ourselves. . . . Their treaties are only to deceive and their traffic only to defraud us."

From self-interest alone, Europe's failure to teach Black Africa to stand on its own feet was unwise. Belgium would have had more profit from an independent Congo if she had cared to produce an enlightened cadre able to steer the country away from disaster. Britain's commercial interests in Nigeria would have been better served if, from the time of Lord Lugard onwards, the tribalism which was to produce civil war had been seriously tackled rather than sustained to ease administration. For their part, the French were languid in development and created an intelligentsia more loyal to Paris than to its own home territories. The Germans had shown, during their two decades of colonialism, a mixture of ruthlessness and efficiency unmatched by the other powers – but it is idle to speculate how this might have stimulated through rivalry the rest of Africa, had the First World War not intervened.

It is equally idle to suggest that the nationalist leaders should have seen that they were not prepared for freedom and so abandoned their demands. Human nature is not like that, and in any case the Africans were encouraged by external events and influences. Clement Attlee had set a pattern in India in 1947, by erasing the very symbol of imperial might. Moral considerations apart, a weakened Britain could not hope to hold on to its empire in the postwar world. Pursuing global influence, the Soviet Union dwelt constantly at the United Nations upon the sins of colonialism; by the middle fifties, the United States could not ignore such a challenge if it hoped to stay in the contest for the allegiance of the "Third World". At the height of the Suez crisis, Vice-President Richard Nixon said revealingly: "For the first time in history, we have shown independence of Anglo-French policies towards Asia and Africa which seemed to us to reflect the colonial tradition. This declaration has had an electrifying effect throughout the world." The European countries were urged by Washington to give up their African colonies – and potential leaders were wooed and aided. The Central Intelligence Agency became extremely active on the continent.

Time was clearly short. On a visit to Central Africa, the then Archbishop of Canterbury, Dr Fisher, told a white audience: "There would be no problem if you had 250 years, but you have not." Sophisticated replies to questions about preparedness were devised. Hastings Banda said that nobody could learn to play tennis without being given a racket. Kwame Nkrumah declared: "Seek ye first the political kingdom and all other things will be added unto you." A widely-quoted dictum was that it was preferable to sleep under one torn blanket of your own than to be smothered in a dozen provided by other people – nothing was as important as dignity and self-respect.

So freedom for Africa could not be refused. There was a deluge between 1958 and 1964. Surveying the outcome, progressive academics at Oxford, the Sorbonne and Harvard tend to blame the very ease with which power was acquired. They say that if Black Africa was denied its revolutions before independence, such cathartic experiences must come afterwards. Only when the colonial structure is genuinely riven to the foundations, will the constructive energies of the people be released. A similar diagnosis has also been made by Chou En-lai, who said in 1964 that Africa is "ripe for revolution".* This phrase has remained popular among students at Africa's new universities, to the chagrin and alarm of the national leaders, who fear that they are rearing a generation which harbours dangerous thoughts. Quite often, 1972 is suggested as the year for Africa's "second revolution".

For those with romantic leanings, the idea of making a fresh start through revolution is always appealing. "Bliss was it in that dawn to be alive, but to be young was very heaven," said Wordsworth of France in 1789. Yet for Africa, revolution might not be the patent medicine. Few of its countries yet possess the healthy economic and administrative base on which to build a new order; although marxists concede that it is sometimes possible to shape a classless, socialist society without

* See Chapter 14, p. 216.

passing through the capitalist stage, this makes several assumptions in the case of Africa. In spite of constant efforts to promote African Socialism (the most coherent interpretation undoubtedly being that of Julius Nyerere in Tanzania), it would be rash to accept that there is a definite ideological trend – indeed, the military coups have been consistently rightist. Moreover, internal differences based upon tribalism will not yield easily to calls for unity and nation-building, while class structures are emerging to make the problem more complex.

Algeria is a case in point. Although the Arab states of the Mediterranean littoral have more in common culturally with the Middle East than with Black Africa, the Algerian war of independence was part of the same historic processes which involved the rest of the continent. The country was subject after 1962 to the intrinsic weaknesses, produced by colonial rule, which have shown themselves farther south. The struggle and the purpose were described by Frantz Fanon, theorist of the Algerian Front de Liberation Nationale: "The naked truth of decolonisation evokes for us the searing bullets and blood-stained knives which emanate from it. For if the first shall be last, this will only come to pass after a murderous and decisive struggle between the two protagonists." Yet the death and torture in Algeria has led to no more success than the painless transfers of authority in many other countries.

The fading of optimism about Black Africa since 1965 has coincided with a diversion of interest among the great powers. The Soviet Union has become more preoccupied with its war of ideas against mainland China and with its difficulties in the Warsaw Pact countries of Eastern Europe. Apart from an involvement in the Nigerian civil war, Russia has taken few initiatives on the continent. (Its support for Egypt in the Middle East conflict can only be regarded as connected with Africa in strict geographical terms.) Soviet diplomats tend to make cynical jokes: "They say Africa for the Africans – well, they can have it." In countries like Tanzania where the German Democratic Republic has a foothold, the Russians appear anxious that the Germans should make the running and accept the limelight.

Such efforts as the Soviet Union chooses to make in Africa are largely dictated by fear of giving the Chinese too much advantage. On this point, they are at one with the United States. The Russians compete with the Chinese in supplying arms to the guerrilla movements in southern Africa, while the Americans limit themselves to making funds available through various agencies. It is the prospect of Chinese domination of the Congo which has made the United States maintain a high level of activity there and shore up the military regime, for the Congo borders on nine other African countries and has vast mineral resources. The Russians have never been allowed to operate in the Congo since their embassy was closed after the overthrow of Patrice Lumumba in 1961.

Yet the American effort in Black Africa was markedly scaled down after the growth of the Vietnam dilemma and the concentration upon domestic problems in the United States. Vexation over racial issues has produced a swing of sympathy towards South Africa and Rhodesia, who in many American eyes appear to be contending with a similar form of black militancy. This is allied to a new interpretation of Black Africa in some official Washington circles. It is contended that the "gamble has not paid off", that the continent will decline into a condition like that of South America after Simon Bolivar, run by military juntas and only likely to deserve serious consideration following several decades of obscurity.

Black Africa has found that as it becomes relegated to the side of the world stage, the aid so acutely needed to maintain development is harder to come by. This in turn makes it impossible to fulfil the promises given at the time of independence, and the political dangers are increased. The tactic of playing off one power against another is no longer effective – in the early sixties an African leader could bring the Americans scurrying forward with grants virtually on the strength of one pro-communist speech. But in 1966, when the Chinese offered to build a railway from Dar-es-Salaam to Zambia, there was no counter-offer from the West, despite the vast geo-political significance of the project. Desultory efforts in London to set up a consortium came to nothing and, by the end of 1968, hundreds of Chinese surveyors were busy in the heart of central Africa.*

Private investment is equally elusive in Black Africa. Companies aim to bring into a country as little as possible, raise local loans and make large profits. A twenty per cent return is generally viewed as the minimum worth considering for investment between the Sahara and the Zambezi. This evokes charges of profiteering and neo-colonialism from African politicians, so that the investors take fright and try to extricate their capital even faster. Countries which do best, both with governmental aid and private investment, are those which are willing to commit themselves politically to the former colonial powers. Thus the Ivory Coast is financially favoured by France because of the close relationship between Felix Houphouet-Boigny and ex-President de Gaulle; the conservative nature of Kenya, its agreement with Britain for military and naval liaison, as well as Kenyan backing for British policy in Nigeria, have gone hand-in-hand with financial generosity by the former colonial power.

Yet most African countries have been unwilling to compromise their newly-granted freedom. The analogy of the man under his one torn blanket holds good. Foreign policies which from the outside may appear quixotic and unreal, reflect an angry determination to stay non-aligned. It is repeatedly declared that Africa's votes in the General Assembly are not up for auction to the highest bidder, although there is an admission that the going rate has fallen with the withering of UN authority.

The Manhattan arena had seemed to Africa in the early sixties the place where the world's conscience could be captured; there, nations were equal regardless of colour – and regardless also of material strength. Only slowly was the frailty of idealism in the face of power acknowledged. Frustrations became more acute with the realisation that neither could effective action come through the Organisation of African Unity, and that its violent discords were shaming the continent.

* See Chapter 14.

CHAPTER TWO

Allies and Enemies

The political environment in the closing months of 1968 imposed upon Zambia the need to make agonising reassessments. This need was recognised most clearly by Julius Nyerere of neighbouring Tanzania. Although Tanzania was by no means as exposed as Zambia, it showed an anxiety to display a total commitment. This derived from Nyerere's intense beliefs and his loyalty to Kaunda, who much relied upon their friendship. It might also have been reinforced by the knowledge of how extensively Tanzania had gained from Zambia's use of emergency supply routes through Dar es Salaam since the end of 1965, when sanctions against Rhodesia began; there was a psychological unease at having profited by the difficulties facing Zambia which would be placated by stressing an eagerness to shoulder more of the Pan-African burden.

Nyerere made a speech of startling frankness in Zambia in September 1968. He encapsulated the whole dilemma by saying that the first priority was to survive in freedom, for nations could be legally independent but unable to determine their own policies. They could have flags and guards of honour for their presidents – but all these were a chimera, if the price was the acceptance of help from political enemies. "From our own history we know that a destitute man can sometimes get a good meal, clothes and shelter by selling himself into slavery. But once he is in the power of the master these good things may, or may not, continue. . . . It is the same with countries. Once a nation has sold its freedom for economic assistance, or once it has accepted the domination of external forces, it is lost."

As Nyerere spoke, Kaunda was on the platform listening

carefully. The Tanzanian leader has a high repute in Africa for acumen and foresight. Nyerere went on to urge a realistic understanding that although independence had seemed at the time a triumph, attempts to build a nation took hard work, persistence and time. But even while the effort was being made, it was undermined from the south by "fascists and colonialists". These were people trying to divide and rule the new states. They would then laugh while they "ground an African face in the African dirt".

Nyerere largely discounted the possibility of a direct military attack from the south, since Black Africa was far more vulnerable economically. But if it came, what then? "A frontal attack would force us back, however brave our soldiers and airmen. If this happens, we have recently been provided with an example of a different kind of national resistance – the determined non-military resistance of a united people who refuse to be controlled by an occupying power. What the Czechoslovak people can do, the people of Zambia and Tanzania could do too."

The idea that Zambia might be militarily overrun had been discussed privately by diplomats for some months. Not until Nyerere's speech was it mentioned openly. The Soviet invasion of Czechoslovakia had sharpened the disquiet, making it clear that if an attack occurred, the Western powers would be unlikely to lift a finger to help.

Men like Nyerere and Kaunda had in 1956 been too little concerned with world affairs to fully absorb the message of Hungary. Now they had a devastating lesson in *realpolitik*; it was suddenly very lonely in southern Africa. Admittedly, South Africa was no rival to Russia in the table of armed might, but if there was an invasion it would be rash to expect more from Britain or America than expressions of sympathy and speeches in the Security Council. It was a world in which might was right, in which Stalin's jibe at the Pope could be re-phrased: "How many divisions has the UN?"

Quite apart from the implications for southern Africa, both Zambia and Tanzania were appalled at the Soviet suppression of the Czechs and made protests to the Kremlin. However difficult their own position might be, they would not

easily accept help from the Russians after this show of imperialism. Both Kaunda and Nyerere sent messages of sympathy to
Dubcek. So with Russia untouchable, a foe to all their ideals,
where could they look? In a discussion on what he would do if
war broke out along the Zambezi, Kaunda also dismissed the
Chinese – for quite another reason: "If I asked Chairman Mao
for help, the big western powers would be fighting on the side
of South Africa. Then Zambia would be the battlefield for a
world war. We would be heaping hot embers on our heads."
In the last analysis, therefore, no alternative existed but the
Czech methods to which Nyerere had pointed. At that time,
they seemed to offer some chance of success.

In Pretoria, capital of South Africa, the suggestion that an
invasion of Zambia could ever be contemplated was dismissed as
a calumny. It was also interpreted as an effort by Nyerere to
stir up emotions in Kaunda's Cabinet and to distract attention
from Black Africa's own troubles. However, there had been
reports in the South African newspapers in mid-1968 that the
army was drawing up plans for "Israeli-type strikes" against
guerrilla holding camps in Zambia, and Vorster had once said
he might himself hit Zambia so hard that Zambians would
never forget it. Michiel Botha, Minister of Bantu Administration, threatened that Zambia would get "the worst hiding of
its life" if it ever attacked South Africa. Sir de Villiers Graaf,
leader of the opposition United Party, joined in with the
observation that Zambia and Tanzania were risking "unfortunate and unpleasant consequences" by giving refuge to
guerrillas operating against Mozambique, Angola and Rhodesia.
Sir de Villiers played upon the popular theme of Israeli
readiness to cross the frontier and retaliate; he did not think
that any fairminded person could blame them.

Ten days after Nyerere's speech, Vorster gave his own gloss
on the Central African scene. He said he was "going to do his
utmost" to persuade Zambia to oppose Communist infiltration,
in the manner which Malawi and the three former High
Commission territories – Botswana, Lesotho and Swaziland –
were so resolutely showing. In East Africa there were more than
4,000 diplomatic representatives and staffs from Communist
countries. The Chinese had a good foothold in Nyerere's Tan-

zania and a dangerous vacuum existed in the Indian Ocean since Britain's decision to withdraw her forces from the Far East.

Vorster told his predominately Afrikaner audience at the congress of the Transvaal National Party: "If I can save southern Africa from Communism and its terrorist activities, I shall have done more than my duty." In his emphasis upon Communism, Vorster was playing on a responsive chord. Since the late fifties, all South Africans had been inculcated with the idea that they were the targets of an international conspiracy directed from Moscow and Peking. (Furthermore, official propaganda has spread the idea abroad, to the United States in particular. There has grown up a considerable lobby in Washington which supports South Africa as a bastion of the free world, *apartheid* notwithstanding.) However, Vorster's talk of influencing Zambia received a hostile retort from Kaunda, who told him to put his own house in order. "Vorster can talk until doomsday, but we shall not abandon our principles."

As usual, Vorster's weakness when dilating on the new "outward-looking policy"* which he had encouraged was a lack of finesse, a revealing turn of phrase. It was remarkable enough, of course, how far he had gone – this former Nazi sympathiser who was held in detention during the 1939–45 war. As Minister of Justice, Police and Prisons he well earned a name for ferocious legislation and for his use of the ninety-day detention clause; he played a major part in the smashing of all African political parties in South Africa. Yet on January 10, 1967, only four months after replacing the assassinated Dr Verwoerd as premier, Vorster took the almost incredible step of welcoming to South Africa the leader of an independent Black state. Chief Leabua Jonathan of Lesotho was photographed with Vorster, both of them unsmiling and self-conscious – which was scarcely surprising. A few weeks later, in a speech at Bloemfontein University, Vorster said: "African states need leadership. We are not settlers – we are part of Africa and the most developed state in Africa. We therefore have a duty."

* See Chapter 16.

The real credit for master-minding the *verligte*, outward-looking policy towards Black Africa must go to Dr Hilgard Muller, Minister of Foreign Affairs. He is a man of beguiling charm. Unlike Vorster, who has only once ventured outside South Africa (and that on a cruise to Buenos Aires), Muller is widely-travelled and enlightened. He studied at Oxford as a Rhodes scholar and spent several years in London as his country's ambassador. Until 1964 he was regarded by most other Afrikaner politicians as hopelessly liberal, as having too much in common with the English-speaking intellectuals with whom he was inclined to mix. But Muller was to become an invaluable asset to the white redoubt, by singing his siren song of "co-prosperity" across the waters of the Zambezi.

For Muller, the moment to take the initiative came after Vorster and Chief Jonathan had shaken hands and the skies had not fallen. The Boer farmers of the *platteland* were assured that this was simply the old *voortrekker* method – to negotiate with native chiefs on a basis of equality. Admittedly, some might have remembered the fate of Piet Retief at the hands of the Zulus when he went to parley – or with more pleasure the retribution that followed. But the appeal to folk history was powerful and it came at a moment when white South Africans had lost their fear of the Black states. This fear had been at its apogee in the early sixties, after the spectacular savageries of the Congo. Several hundred white refugees from Katanga had fled as far as Johannesburg and Durban, some to settle permanently in South Africa; they told blood-curdling stories to justify their flight. This was the time when the Afrikaners felt in danger of being swept off the end of the continent, which was their only home.

In 1960, the South African defence budget was only £20,000,000. By 1965, it was £100,000,000. Moreover, in the Congo a few hundred mercenaries – the greater part of them South African – had shown how easily the white will could be imposed upon an African country of 15,000,000 people (perhaps more, if anyone were to count them). Even Dr Hastings Banda had said in December 1965 that ten mercenaries could "whip 5,000 so-called African soldiers".

Then in July 1966, the South Africans were released from a

worry which had been hanging like a sword of Damocles for four years. The International Court of Justice side-stepped a challenge to say whether South Africa should continue to govern South West Africa; it declared that the applicant states, Ethiopia and Liberia, had no legal right to raise the matter. This pathetic judgement came after the Court had been listening to arguments since 1962. In Black Africa there was incredulity and severe depression, but the triumphant South African advocates flew home from The Hague to a heroes' welcome. Had the World Court decided positively, pressure at the United Nations on Britain and America to impose sanctions – or even threaten war – to make South Africa relinquish control of South West Africa, would have been overwhelming. As it was, the United Nations descended into farce, by renaming South-West Africa "Namibia" and appointing a multi-racial group to administer the territory. The group had no shred of hope of being allowed to do so; after several members had travelled to Zambia with the declared intention of flying on to Windhoek in a chartered plane to plant the United Nations flag, their resolve melted when it was announced from Pretoria that they would not be allowed to land. The whole affair, which had shortly before seemed a threat to the fundamental authority of the whites in southern Africa, faded completely away.

The clearest exposition of the Muller strategy, based upon the secure position of South Africa after its World Court success, was given in May 1968 during a parliamentary debate upon the Foreign Affairs vote. The debate was opened by Jaapie Basson, a relatively liberal Afrikaner regarded by many of his compatriots as traitor. His speech was peppered with sarcasm, but also revealed the extent to which progressive white opinion in South Africa had already been captivated by the idea of contacts with African states; despite a nagging awareness of the government's real motives, the new policy had given a feeling of liberation from the "Verwoerd *laager*". Basson warmly praised Muller and his staff, whom he described as labouring night and day to "overcome the handicaps under which South Africa suffers". He mentioned the growth of commercial links with neighbouring countries and said: "We believe the time has come to leapfrog our immediate neighbours and try to make friends with African states farther afield." Basson suggested that South Africa could become an uncommitted country, forming its own little world next to the Third World.

Other MPs followed with praise of Muller, a Dr Bodenstein saying: "I want to take this opportunity to congratulate the Hon Minister and his department on the large-scale break-through which has already been made to the African states." (The word breakthrough is widely used in describing the new policy.) Dr G. F. Jacobs urged that Madagascar should be "drawn in" as soon as possible; he applauded President Banda as being calm, moderate and responsible. The relationship with Malawi was also commented upon by parliamentarian W. M. Holland, who spoke from experience of living in that country. He described how at the time of independence he had feared that South Africans had "wasted their intellects" in trying to improve the natives there. Now he knew it was not so. An Afrikaner, Louw Pretorius, had just been appointed chairman of the Malawi Censor Board, which showed how much faith was placed in South Africans.

In his reply, Muller ignored references Basson had made to £300,000 voted for the secret Special Account and a further amount of £200,000 cryptically provided for "assistance to and co-operation with foreign countries". But he offered other facts; for example, in the previous year there were 136 occasions when ministers from African states had made friendly contacts while visiting or passing through the republic. Every time, there had been gratitude for the treatment received. "The time has come when more and more African states and statesmen who have come to know us better are helping to rectify the distorted image of South Africa abroad." This remark was received with satisfaction by an audience which a few years before would have viewed as impertinence any attempt by a representative of a Black State to be officially received in South Africa; no member of the Broederbond demurred at Muller's reference to "African statesmen".

After talking in general terms about his hopes for friendship with the rest of the continent, Muller turned to Zambia – "one of the most important states in southern Africa". He said more in sorrow than in anger that Kaunda must reconsider his attitude, and it was possible to descry his confidence that such a change could be engineered. Muller explained that Kaunda understood "very well" where he stood with South Africa: he had been repeatedly advised against encouraging terrorists, he knew that the SA Defence Force was not aggressive, but also that it could hit back very hard if that became necessary.

Kaunda had been given terms for peaceful co-existence. "But I think it is high time he begins to realise he is sounding a discordant note in southern Africa, where good neighbourliness is being practised. . . . If Dr Kaunda wants to play the role of a statesman in southern Africa – and I believe that he is capable of doing so – he should abandon the methods of Nkrumah and should take his cue from other African leaders who are in co-operation with us." This was gentle and persuasive, but contained an apparent miscalculation in the sharp reference to Nkrumah. Although Kaunda had admitted after the Ghana coup of 1966 that Nkrumah had made mistakes, he revered him as a spiritual liberator of Africa; diplomatic relations between Zambia and Ghana were broken off after the coup and Kaunda was still in 1968 referring defiantly to "President Nkrumah". On the other hand, Muller may have felt that there could be a certain force in the advice to stop behaving like a president whose overthrow was widely believed in Africa to have been encouraged by external forces.

Muller was speaking of a man he had never met, but one compatriot would have left him with no illusions about the character and quality of Zambia's leader. Sir Richard Luyt, the new Vice-Chancellor of Cape Town University, had been Chief Secretary in Northern Rhodesia in the years when the country was being prepared for independence. He had struck up a close friendship with Kaunda. There had been so much rapport that at one time when Luyt was going on leave, the United National Independence Party had thrown a dinner party for him. Kaunda had made a speech expressing the hope that "our friend Dick" would have a good time in Britain; Luyt had looked a little awkward, but managed to keep it from his hosts that he was not going to Britain at all, but to his home in the Cape. Promoted after his success in Zambia, Luyt had

moved on to British Guiana with a knighthood, to become its
last Governor. When Guyana was created. Luyt returned to
South Africa and renewed his old friendship with Hilgard
Muller; these two notable Afrikaner intellectuals had been at
Oxford together.

It was Muller who had made a public apology when a group
of South African policemen crossed into Zambia at the start of
1968. But exchanges were not always so courteous, and his
opposite number in Zambia, Foreign Minister Reuben
Kamanga, said he was very happy to see two-thirds of the
delegates walk out of the General Assembly when Muller got
up to speak. "We are not prepared to take South Africa's dirty
hand in friendship," said Kamanga. However, in Pretoria
the rising intensity of such utterances was held to be a proof
that the moment of seduction was near at hand. Behind the
scenes, far more significant exchanges were in train.

Series of visits to Lusaka were made in 1968 by South African
businessmen, the chairmen of powerful companies with branches
in Zambia. They had interviews with members of the Cabinet,
including Kaunda, and dropped hints that their country was
able to offer financial and technical assistance. They mentioned
that South Africa had just set aside £2,500,000 for direct
bi-lateral aid to friendly developing countries, scarcely dis-
guising that they were speaking with official inspiration. Sometimes these visitors astounded their listeners by showing a
detailed grasp of the difficulties within the Zambian administration and the most sensitive points of the economy. Such
knowledge did not come merely from a reading of the extensive
coverage of Zambia in South African newspapers. A regular
supply of intelligence had always gone southwards from Lusaka
to the industrial and business headquarters in Johannesburg.
There were few secrets which Zambia could keep.

Confronted by the obvious South African determination to
win him over, Kaunda could not ignore the statistics which
showed how great was Zambia's dependence on the south.
In 1964, the year of independence, imports from South Africa
had amounted to £16,000,000. Four years later they were
more than double, and it was equally significant that the bulk
of imports from other countries outside Africa had to reach

Zambia through Capetown and Durban, or through the Portuguese-controlled ports of Beira, Lourenço Marques and Lobito. During the long, exhausting sanctions campaign against the Smith regime in Rhodesia, Zambia had been able to reduce its imports from the rebel colony from £35,000,000 a year to less than £12,000,000. Yet imports from South Africa had risen by almost precisely the same amount; indeed, some of the extra South African supplies were simply the normal Rhodesian goods, re-packed with new labels in Johannesburg.

But the economic factors could be explained away as an inheritance from the past. Crucial was Zambia's political ability to defy the blandishments from South Africa. Would it agree to co-exist, or would it cling to the Pan-African ideals which had been so vital in the early sixties? At the start of 1968, the national council of the United National Independence Party had met in Lusaka to pass a resolution which said: "Liberation of Rhodesia, South Africa, Angola and Mozambique from the yoke of colonialism is a course to which the council and the whole nation are fully committed." This was more than histrionics, for guerrillas had well before begun operating from Zambia into the Caprivi Strip, South-West Africa, Rhodesia, Angola and Mozambique. In Lusaka there had been set up a Liberation Centre, where more than a dozen freedom-fighting movements had their headquarters; it was supervised by a representative of the president.

The one point at which the guerrillas operating from Zambia could always penetrate directly into territory ruled by South Africa was along the 100-mile common border of the Caprivi Strip. This is a sandy and desolate projection of South-West Africa reaching to the Zambezi above the Victoria Falls. As early as 1966, a landing ground capable of taking large jet aircraft was built in the Strip only a few miles from the Zambian border, and Kaunda protested that this was an aggressive move. The South Africans intensified military patrols and the Zambians had the satisfaction in August 1968 of capturing two Afrikaner policemen armed with sub-machines who had wandered across the ill-defined boundary; the two were taken to Lusaka for trial and heavily fined.

Two months after that incident came the first admission

that South Africa was having difficulty in the Strip. A nationalist organisation called the Caprivi African National Union, "having strong ties with Zambia", was stirring up the local populace. Details were given in Cape Town by Lourens Muller, Minister of Police and the Interior, who said the Caprivi inhabitants were "badly disposed towards the white man". Lourens Muller had been promoted to the South African Cabinet in 1968 as one of Vorster's *verligte* protégés. After explaining the Caprivi Strip situation, he spoke with enthusiasm on the lines laid down by his namesake, Foreign Minister Hilgard Muller: "It is essential that the goodwill of black countries south of the equator be won, so that they may serve as buffer states against pressure from our enemies north of the equator." The equator traverses Africa through the Congo, Uganda and Kenya; it is well to the north of Zambia.

But if Zambia were to change, it could only follow the policies of neighbouring Malawi. There, Hastings Banda had no truck with guerrillas and had willingly thrown in his lot with the white-run countries to the south. Banda had taken decisive steps in March 1967, when he sent ministerial goodwill missions to South Africa and Portugal. These missions signed agreements on trade and communications, to the chagrin of several other Black states. One of the sharpest critics was Zambia, and in his customary manner Banda hit back during a speech to the Malawi Parliament. In a clear reference to Kaunda, he said: "As for my critics in neighbouring countries, I treat them with utter contempt, because they are physical and moral cowards and hypocrites. . . . While they are decrying South Africa, they are doing so on stomachs full of South African beef, mutton and pork. . . . They are doing so while allowing South African financiers and industrialists to invest heavily in their mines, industries and agriculture."

Banda went on to propound an argument close to that used by Hilgard Muller. South Africa was a fact, it was "here to stay", so the African countries had to learn to live with it. The politics of bluff and bluster had failed and a dialogue would have to be opened with Pretoria. "What then is the solution to the problem of South Africa, the problem of apartheid? I do not know. I have no answer." This remark summed up the opposing attitudes of Banda and Kaunda. For the latter, the solution was straightforward – to end discrimination between the races. Kaunda could not say how this would come about, but it must: "Apartheid defies God." Banda also is prone to invoke the Almighty, being an elder of the Church of Scotland – and was educated at the Livingstonia mission beside Lake Malawi. But he prides himself on being a realist, even claiming that by contact he can persuade the South Africans to modify their internal racial policies.

In financial terms, this has paid off for Malawi. Banda's plans for moving his capital from Zomba in the extreme south of Malawi to the more central town of Lilongwe were condemned by an economic team from Britain. The team said the idea was wasteful. So the South Africans were invited to make a study and Vorster sent up one of his leading advisers, Dr L. S. Rautenbach. This time the response was favourable and Pretoria went further – it offered Malawi a £4,700,000 loan to help build the new capital. Private investment followed and Banda could boast an economic upsurge in a country which three years before had been called a "rural slum". Moreover, Malawi completely ignored the sanctions campaign against Rhodesia which cost Zambia almost £20,000,000 a year for three years. Close ties with the Portuguese had produced an agreement to build – with South African finance – a railway linking Malawi to the Mozambique port of Nacala on the Indian Ocean.

Six months after sending a goodwill mission to South Africa, Banda announced that he was opening diplomatic relations with what he called the "Jericho of apartheid". The first representative of Malawi was a white civil servant, with a black understudy. Kaunda said nothing about this development, but there was widespread comment elsewhere on the continent. In Guinea, Radio Conakry thundered: "The greatest African traitor, Hastings Banda, has once more shown his disgusting cynicism." But in post-Nkrumah Ghana a government newspaper editorialised: "The Vorster regime has been pursuing a policy of 'outgoingness' to Africa. They believe that establishing diplomatic relations with Black African countries will bring more understanding and perhaps a change in their own attitudes towards Africans. Perhaps Dr Banda has lighted a torch that might blaze the way even earlier than his detractors think." But there was an official denial that Ghana — which even in the time of Nkrumah had done a considerable undercover trade with South Africa — was thinking of following Malawi's lead.

Less than three weeks after the announcement, Banda went to Kenya to open the Nairobi Agricultural Show. He was introduced by President Jomo Kenyatta, who said: "I and Dr Banda were planning to rid our continent of colonialism at a time when those others were lying in their mothers' wombs." He did not identify "those others". It was a notable show of solidarity between two ageing, conservative leaders who had been regarded, before their countries were given independence, as the ultimate in bloodthirsty extremism. Earlier in the year, Kenyatta's Vice-President, Joseph Murumbi, had resigned to become chairman in Kenya for the Rothmans cigarette company, owned by Dr Anton Rupert — a leading South African exponent of the new policy towards Black states.

The next step in the breakthrough to Malawi came in August 1968, when Foreign Minister Muller made an official visit with a large entourage. The party was entertained at a banquet, taken to beauty spots and agricultural projects, and assured that South African tourists would always be welcome. Before flying home, Muller repeated his well-tried phrases about good neighbourliness and invited Banda to make a State visit to South Africa at his convenience. He also gave Malawi assurances of military support if ever it were needed.

The week after Muller's departure, Banda gave vent to his exuberance by claiming large parts of southern Tanzania and eastern Zambia. He said that the boundaries of Malawi were artificial and that all the land around Lake Malawi must be surrendered to him. The already touchy relations between Banda on one side and Kaunda and Nyerere on the other became still more strained. At a meeting of party officials, Kaunda said: "Dr Banda may depend on South African and Portuguese support — I depend on my people. If South African and Portuguese soldiers enter Zambia, they will not get out."

For Kaunda, the breakdown of relations with Malawi

and Banda's increasing commitment to the South African "sphere of co-prosperity" created a further sense of isolation. Earlier in the year, Zambia and Malawi had exchanged goodwill missions and there was discussion about the setting up of diplomatic relations. Now all thought of that was abandoned. Instead of Zambian diplomats, Banda had South Africans in Zomba – including a high-ranking military attaché. By 1969, experts loaned from Pretoria were helping to control some of Malawi's key institutions; one was the broadcasting service, audible in part of Zambia. In February, a new director of the Malawi information services began work; he was David van der Spuy, from the South African information department. The Air Malawi services to Johannesburg were stepped up to cope with a growing traffic.

In 1958, when Banda had returned home after forty years' absence in America, Ghana and Britain, Kaunda had regarded him as an African saviour. There had admittedly been some disillusion in 1963, when Banda had kept Kaunda and several of his colleagues waiting in the rain for almost an hour outside the gates of his house when they called to pay their respects, and then treated them with condescension when the guard had let them in. Kaunda had been prepared to forget this, but the events of September 1968 finally convinced him that Banda was a maverick in whom no trust could be placed. When Malawian exiles arranged a demonstration in Lusaka and displayed posters saying that Banda was a "black foreigner", there was no attempt to disperse them.

Yet the two countries could not disengage easily. Their political relationship had been close since the last decade of the nineteenth century and both had been members of the Central African Federation. Tribes such as the Chewa and Tumbuka straddled the 400-mile border. Kaunda's own parents came from the Henga and Tonga areas along the northern shores of Lake Malawi.

Facing different ways, thinking on different lines, Zambia and Malawi had by 1969 come to epitomise the struggle in southern Africa. They might be frozen in their positions indefinitely. Yet a change was always possible, either through internal upheaval or by a subtle erosion from outside.

CHAPTER THREE

The Character of Kaunda

In a speech in Washington in 1967, the Foreign Minister of Portugal, Dr Franco Nogueira, said he would not attempt to defend colonialism: "Many of its features are to be deplored. Economic exploitation of one people by another, race segregation and discrimination, denial of human rights and suppression of individual freedom – all these should be rejected and condemned." Coming from the representative of a country which has clung more resolutely to its colonies in the postwar years than any other, this was a somewhat surprising assertion. Of course, Dr Nogueira had an escape hatch: in his view, these strictures could not be applied to the Portuguese colonies, which in any case were constitutionally an integral part of the homeland. He went on to admit that Portugal's stand was misunderstood by the new African nations, who were "not prepared to sacrifice themselves for interests, ideals and principles which are entirely alien to them". Perhaps the word "sacrifice" was not exactly intended by Nogueira, and "dedicate" might have been more apposite.

Whatever value may be placed upon the ideals and principles underpinning Portuguese colonialism, it was clear that Nogueira – coming, after all, from a country with 450 years experience of Africa – well understood the quandary of the Black leaders. "There is no doubt that the African nations have an increasing feeling of deep frustration, struggling against forces which are not entirely clear to them, against myths they were led to accept as sacrosanct, against interests which are not their interests. There is no doubt that the African nations feel they are being used as tools in the conduct of policies which do not help them and which are not meant to help them." Nogueira later expanded his ideas in a book.

It is the need to discover an identity which has made independent Africa so argumentative and vociferous, a trait which has done much to alienate outsiders. There is a desperate need to demonstrate equality. Colour is inescapably a large part of the problem: in a white-dominated world it makes an African more different than, for example, a Chinese or an Indian. But beyond that, there is a matter of culture. When the white man took over Africa, its peoples could not write or keep records, they had not invented the wheel. These are clichés, but they are clichés which Africans have not been allowed to forget, and have not allowed themselves to forget. In recent years there have been determined and worthwhile efforts to rehabilitate African culture. Its music and sculpture have won acceptance. But that has not been enough.

There is the profound frustration mentioned by Nogueira, the fear that if Africans are no longer hewers of wood and drawers of water, they are still tools of outside forces – victims of the neo-colonialism about which Kwame Nkrumah wrote so passionately. This is a political and economic liability, of course, but what stings more sharply is the implied racial subservience. How can it be answered? One way is to match the whites on their own terms, to develop, start industries, grow rich. But this is a heartbreaking prospect, for the leeway is so enormous that at the current rate of progress it will take, according to the UN Economic Commission for Africa, more than 340 years for African incomes to reach the level in America now. Moreover, this involves a complete submission to outside standards. To imitate, even to imitate successfully, is an admission.

For the Japanese or the Indians, such a course is tolerable, because they can carry forward with them the grandeur of their past. When Pandit Nehru stood beside Winston Churchill at an Old Harrovian dinner, to sing "Forty Years On", he did so with an assurance derived from the knowledge that India had advanced civilisations when the Ancient Britons were covered in woad. For Africans, there is no such confidence.

They were taught by white masters to despise their own past, to reject and forget it.

So if Africa cannot stand comparison in terms of gross national products and incomes *per capita*, if it cannot even flaunt its past, what claims can it make for respect? Africans passionately believe that they can offer ideas – an entirely fresh perspective on the purpose of life – notwithstanding their own temporary problems. They argue that those who have not been able to climb aboard the twentieth-century express may be better placed to see where it is going and to notice that nobody is properly at the controls.

The African disquiet about modern civilisation, a fear of being enmeshed in a system which de-humanises, is far from new. Before Zambia became independent, Kaunda made a speech at Fordham University in the United States, during which he remarked: "We believe both the East and the West are failing mankind. We see far too much emphasis placed on material development, which in fact is very quickly leading to the eclipse of man as the centre of all human activity. Can they recover from this, or is there going to come out of Africa a new ideology to help our fellow men in these two camps? I should point out that if we ourselves in Africa are not careful, we might also find ourselves slaves to the machine."

Early in 1967, Kaunda began to codify and promote as a national philosophy for Zambia his ideas of man's rights and duties in society. This must be related to the numerous attempts to define African Socialism, a phrase which became popular among nationalists in the early fifties. According to the needs of a particular country and to the inclinations of a particular leader, African Socialism has been used to describe systems ranging from Marxism to liberalism. Its vagueness was a great irritation to the leading Soviet expert on African affairs, the late Professor I. I. Potekhin. As recently as 1965 a booklet condemning this ideological heresy was distributed widely by the Novosti Press Agency; it ended with the admonition that Africa should "follow the correct road to socialism based on Marxism–Leninism and proletarian internationalism".

One common element which can be found in most of the interpretations of African Socialism is the desire to retain in a modern world the traditional values of the Black races. Leopold Senghor, President of Senegal and poet of négritude, said in a lecture at Oxford in 1961 that African society was "community-based" and spiritually free. In Dar es Salaam, Julius Nyerere also laid stress upon the communality of traditional African life, explaining socialism by the Swahili word *ujamaa* – which can best be translated as "togetherness" or "brotherhood". Nyerere explained that in tribal days there was a socialist attitude which gave a sense of security; now men should regard themselves as belonging to a family which extended beyond the tribe and the nation, to all mankind.

Kaunda has been keenly influenced by Nyerere, but it would be wrong to suggest that his own brand of African Socialism – which he calls "Humanism" – is merely derived from *Ujamaa*. There are marked differences between the intellectualism and grasp of doctrine shown by Nyerere and the earnest high-mindedness of Kaunda. Without question, Kaunda sees Humanism as unique, as his own offering to the world.

It is possible to disentangle three main threads in Kaunda's thinking. Like Nyerere he believes that African society must not lose sight of its traditional values, especially the extended family system; he regards himself as a socialist, although not in any very doctrinaire way; and he is deeply religious. It is the last aspect which is crucial and which sets him apart from other African leaders. Only by constant reference to the way in which religion dominates him can Kaunda's actions be fully understood. Without his faith and conviction that God has imposed a duty upon him he could not go on, since he is not an instinctive leader. With it, he cannot give up. Even when he does not refer to God specifically, his speeches are shot through with a fundamentalist attitude to good and evil. It is in such terms that he interprets international affairs.

In an address to his United National Independence Party in April 1967, Kaunda declared himself on the situation in southern Africa: "Let me mention once again that we were only a year old when evil men, determined to do what is wrong, took over control of Rhodesia illegally. . . . Needless for me to say to you that they have been backed by people of equal minds from many quarters of the world; near to us they

have got champions in the like leadership of Vorster and
Salazar who, together with them from that day of illegal declaration of independence up to now have tried to squeeze the
life out of this young republic. There is no denying that these
are powerful forces, in that they have got almost everything
that makes a modern state strong and lack only the one important and Godly thing: the foundation of their government is
not the people as a whole. Nevertheless, this world is still
crude and in many quarters might is very difficult to distinguish
from right, and so the unholy trio — helped as I said earlier by
many other sinister forces in various parts of the world —
have gone all out to try and portray Zambia as a new state on
the verge of collapse." Such language is rarely heard today from
political leaders, yet its tone is ironically reminiscent of the
speeches by the previous generation of Afrikaner politicians,
who saw South Africa as serving God's will in a hostile world.

Kaunda's early years explain his religious intensity, which
has come down to him from the Scottish missionaries who
went to Central Africa in the nineteenth century. He speaks
with a voice which had almost died out before the First World
War. Kaunda's father was born beside Lake Malawi at Bandawe, which until the coming of the missionaries had been a
centre for the Arab slave trade to Zanzibar. He went from
Bandawe to the famous training centre called Livingstonia,
after the Scottish explorer, and was prepared there in the
1890s for a life of teaching and evangelism. The missionaries
gave him the biblical name of David, which also was Livingstone's Christian name.

The men who taught David Kaunda were possessed by
evangelistic fervour. They were inspired by the message of
Livingstone himself: "I go back to Africa to try to make an
open path for Christianity. Do you carry out the work which I
have begun!" In overcoming the slave traders and defying the
physical hazards of Central Africa, the first missionaries
suffered great loss of life. They were utterly dedicated and had
behind them enthusiasts like James Stevenson, an Ayrshire
businessman who gave most of his fortune for the building of a
missionary road along what is now the Zambia–Tanzania
border. The Livingstonia mission was described as "an institu-

tion at once industrial and educational, to teach the truths of the Gospel and the arts of civilised life to the natives of the country".

After his training, David Kaunda was sent westward to the country of the powerful Bemba tribe in what had shortly before been delineated as Northern Rhodesia. The White Fathers were establishing missions among the witchcraft-ridden Bemba and the Church of Scotland was determined, within its means, to put up a challenge to the Church of Rome. David Kaunda based himself at Chinsali, and began to spread the simple but stirring message he had learnt at Livingstonia. He also ran village schools, at which the children were taught selections from the Bible.

Nearly ten years after David Kaunda's arrival, white missionaries followed to establish a permanent station at Lubwa near Chinsali. There was some conflict between the African evangelist and the men who now took charge and it is not without significance that David Kaunda was one of the sponsors of a Native Welfare Association based on another mission at Mwenzo, farther north. A district commissioner, Moffat Thomson, wrote a memorandum about the association in which he remarked that educated natives were starting to discuss Europeans, the government and their own positions. "They do not consider they are receiving from life what they believe they are entitled to."

It was a period in which African dissent was generally expressed through religion and the area where Kaunda's family lived was a centre of ferment. The Watch Tower movement was gaining many converts and the few educated Africans were prone to set themselves up as messiahs. One of the most famous of these figures was Tomo Nyirenda, who had been educated at Livingstonia. Nyirenda called himself Mwana Lesa (Son of God) and began a savage campaign of witch-finding among the neighbouring Lala tribe. He was ultimately hanged for murder. But David Kaunda remained loyal to the Church of Scotland and was ordained. He ran his home on severe Christian principles and held daily services for his children, of whom Kenneth was the youngest. All the children said prayers in turn. Although in a lonely part of

Africa, the household was like many which could have been found in Britain in the middle of Victoria's reign. Living in a strange tribe, the family clung tightly to its faith.

Kenneth Kaunda was born in 1924, when his parents were in their middle age. He was highly-strung and afflicted by a stammer, but he was also energetic and bright. His mother, Helen, remarked when he became President: "As he grew up we thought he would follow in his father's footsteps and become a minister of religion." Kenneth Kaunda was already attending the Lubwa school when his father died. Life became hard and to earn money for fees he had to clean drains and wash dishes at the home of the white minister in charge. Kenneth Kaunda grew up on the mission, was trained as a teacher and became a Scoutmaster.

By the late forties, Kaunda was married and teaching in the Copperbelt town of Mufulira. He was already caught up in politics, but never lost the uplifting ideas absorbed in his early days. The first political incident in which he was involved happened when he went into a Mufulira shop to buy a book. Two white miners threw him out into the street for having the temerity to walk in through the door rather than wait to be served at a hatch reserved for Africans. The book he had wanted was called *Talks for Boys*, by Arthur Mee. Even by 1947, Mee had generally come to be thought pious and old-fashioned.

From 1950, when Kaunda first became a party official, until 1964, when he was elected the Head of State, his religious enthusiasm varied considerably. In the early fifties, much of his attention was devoted to political theories and he turned from reading the Bible to leftwing magazines sent from abroad. The possession of a journal called *The African and Colonial World*, edited by Krishna Kumria, earned him a two-months' jail sentence. In 1957 he made his first trip to Europe and for seven months was a guest of the Labour Party in Britain. From this experience Kaunda acquired not only clear ideas about political organisation (he was to tell his followers later: "The European rules not because he is white, but because he is better organised"), but also made strong friendships inside the British Labour movement. These friends included Barbara Castle and James Callaghan. He wrote to them often.

On March 10, 1959, Kaunda posted to Callaghan a copy of a letter sent to the Governor, Sir Arthur Benson. In his letter to the Governor, Kaunda had said: "It is not often remembered in certain circles that so-called agitators can only succeed where there are serious grievances and that no amount of governmental gangsterism, or any other, has ever succeeded in keeping any determined people from achieving their political aspirations." Such language was far removed from the world of Arthur Mee. In a covering note to Callaghan, beginning "Dear James", Kaunda said: "Terror is mounting daily here. You never can predict what will happen!" As it turned out, Kaunda and his lieutenants were arrested forty-eight hours later.

The faith which Kaunda placed in British socialists at that period was to survive for almost a decade. This feeling of closeness to the Labour Party was shared by other African leaders, who had been befriended while in Britain by the Fabians and the Movement for Colonial Freedom. At the time of the 1964 general election, which was to bring Labour back to power for the first time since 1951, Kaunda was visiting Dar es Salaam. To hear the results come in, he sat until the small hours of the morning with Nyerere and Milton Obote, the President of Uganda, around Nyerere's shortwave radio. "At the news of every Labour victory we cheered, and when the Tories won we groaned," he says. This faith in the Labour Party goes a long way to explain the strength of Kaunda's reaction to Harold Wilson's handling of the Rhodesian rebellion.

Another significant influence upon Kaunda in his years of political struggle came from India. The granting of independence to India was seen by Africans as a precursor of their own freedom, and some progressive members of the Hindu community in what was Northern Rhodesia made donations to nationalist funds. In London in 1957, Kaunda visited the Indian High Commission and was afterwards offered a ticket to New Delhi. He made the journey in 1958 (and was to go back again in 1961, when he was welcomed by Nehru). The writings of Mahatma Gandhi had a powerful appeal – and it seemed, moreover, that civil disobedience and non-violent

opposition to authority were the best tactics in striving for the
break-up of the Central African Federation and national
independence. This conviction took possession of Kaunda
during the nine months he spent in restriction and jail in
1959.

His first smuggled letter to close followers after being restricted
had little of Gandhianism about it: "You know, comrades, that
the British will always pat stooges on their backs, but at the
bottom of their hearts it is the rough guys they have both
respect and consideration for." (The new party which Kaunda
had been chosen to lead six months before by the militants
was called the Zambia African National Congress. It had been
banned as being a threat to law and order.) But when he
emerged from prison early in 1960 to take over the leadership of
the United National Independence Party, which had been
formed in his absence, Kaunda had adopted a different tone.
He gave the party four watchwords: "Discipline, patience,
loyalty and non-violence."

Although Zambia achieved independence with very little
bloodshed, Kaunda was later forced to admit that non-violence
had its limitations. Talking to African students during a visit
to Sweden in 1968, he said that African freedom fighters had
only one course of action open to them – "organise and fight".
Yet the teaching of Gandhi had seemed to him invested with
an all-embracing significance: "It accords with the teachings
of all the world-known religious leaders, and those of the
people who might be termed leaders of progressive thought."
Gandhi's philosophising about the sacred nature of man is
echoed in Kaunda's "Humanism", while his asceticism has
also been matched: Kaunda has never drunk alcohol, coffee
or tea, he does not smoke and refuses to eat red meat.

Through the varying moods of his political apprenticeship,
Kaunda remained a Christian. He says that life in prison was
bearable because "I felt God's hand was guiding me", and one
of his favourite recreations was singing hymns in Bemba. But
it was not until he became President of Zambia that he returned to the religious fullness which had surrounded his child-
hood. This was due in part to the need for a spiritual and mental
bastion to help withstand the strains of office. It was derived

as well from the shock of the Lumpa uprising, in the middle of 1964. More than 700 people died in a series of battles between the fanatic Lumpa Sect followers of "holy woman" Alice Lenshina Mulenga and security forces, as well as between the Lumpas and UNIP groups. It was appalling enough for Kaunda, the devout believer in non-violence, to be taking over control of the country in the middle of such gruesome events. What was worse, he was also closely connected personally.

Alice Lenshina was born at Kasomo, four miles from Kaunda's own birthplace at Lubwa. They were the same age, and Alice had attended services at the Lubwa mission church. When Alice set up her own sect in 1954, after claiming to have risen from the dead, Kenneth Kaunda's elder brother, Robert, was one of her first disciples. Then in the early sixties, clashes began between Kaunda's own political followers and the Lumpa adherents. It was after these intermittent disturbances, which Kaunda tried to stop, that the police and troops forces were ordered in. Police fought their way into the huge brick-built church at Kasomo which was the headquarters of the Lumpa sect. Pictures taken inside the deserted church after the attack showed a long trail of blood in the aisle. The killings lasted for agonising months and once they had begun there was no going back or hope of reconciliation. The Lumpas had become crazed and desperate, reverting to obscene witchcraft rituals which they believed would make them immune to bullets. Among the UNIP heirarchy there was a bitter hatred of the sect, for having—as Kaunda put it—"left a blot on Zambia's record".

Alice Lenshina gave herself up and was held first in jail at Mumbwa near Lusaka, and later restricted to a remote part of Barotse Province, nearly 1,000 miles from Lubwa. The scattered remnants of her followers fled in twos and threes to the Congo and established themselves at Mokambo on the Copperbelt border. This was only nine miles from Mufulira, where Kaunda had lived as a young schoolmaster. Gradually the Lumpa settlement in the Congo grew, till it contained nearly 20,000 people—one of the largest refugee groups in Africa. As late as August 1968, four years after the uprising, the Lumpas rejected all appeals to them to return to Zambia, in

spite of an amnesty and the offer of financial help for resettle-
ment. Only in January 1969, when plans were announced to
settle them permanently deep inside the Congo, did some drift
back into Zambia.

Following independence, Kaunda developed a close friendship with the Reverend Colin Morris, a young and brilliant
Methodist. Morris had arrived in the Copperbelt in the fifties
and quickly established a reputation for pugnacious liberalism.
Many of his white congregation were offended by his views
and on two occasions his church was broken into and desecrated.
By 1964, Morris had written several books, had dabbled in
politics and been elected president of the United Church of
Zambia, which embraced all the non-conformist denominations.

Kaunda and Morris had known one another well for some
years before the Lumpa disturbances, and had produced a
book called *Black Government?* in 1960; but it was the role
Morris played in the disturbances which brought them much
closer together. Unarmed and accompanied only by an African
clergyman, Morris had walked far into the bush from Lubwa
in search of Alice to persuade her to surrender. After she had
been detained he had a long series of meetings with the Lumpa
matriarch in an unsuccessful effort to bring her back to orthodox Christianity. During their meetings to discuss the Lumpa
problem, Kaunda and Morris began an intensive discussion of
religious topics. Another book was produced by the two, called
A Humanist in Africa, taking the form of an exchange of letters
in which Kaunda expressed his ideas on the needs and problems
of a new nation.

Humanism was put forward by Kaunda as the national
philosophy two months after Julius Nyerere's Arusha Declaration, which was not only the signal for large-scale nationalisation in Tanzania but also laid down the country's policy of
"Socialism and Self-reliance". Undoubtedly, both Nyerere and
Kaunda had been profoundly influenced by the French
agronomist and author, Professor René Dumont. In the
previous year, Dumont's book *L'Afrique Noire est Mal Partie*
had finally appeared in English as *False Start in Africa*. Kaunda
invited Dumont to Zambia to survey the country's agriculture.
But although both the Arusha Declaration and the first essay

on Humanism contained echoes of Dumont, there was a marked divergence in the approach to national affairs.

Nyerere's thoughts were knife-sharp and aimed always at specific problems, whereas Kaunda's dwelt at length on the whole purpose of life. He made it plain that he believed people would do better and work harder if they could be taught that it was right to do so. The development of the country was to have that concept as its mainspring. Material advancement based upon the profit motive was not enough.

Humanism has been promoted energetically in Zambia. A series of pamphlets with such titles as "A Guide to the Implementation of Humanism" and "Ten Thoughts on Humanism" have been given massive distribution. Villagers throughout the country have been lectured upon it by party officials, school children have been offered prizes for essays about it, student groups debate it and civil servants promise to do their work on humanist principles. In July 1968, during his first visit to London for three years, Kaunda expounded upon Humanism to distinguished audiences. In April 1969, he set up a Ministry of National Guidance to advance the cause.

One paragraph has been repeatedly quoted by Kaunda. He regards it as the essence of his thinking:

"This high valuation of MAN and respect for human dignity which is a legacy of our tradition should not be lost in the new Africa. However 'modern' and 'advanced' in a Western sense this young nation of Zambia may become, we are fiercely determined that this humanism will not be obscured. African society has always been man-centred. Indeed, this is as it should be; otherwise why is a house built? Not to give man shelter and security? Why make a chair at all? Why build a factory? Why do you want a State ranch? For what else would there be need to grow food? Why is the fishing industry there? We can go on asking these questions. The simple and yet difficult answer is 'MAN'. Simple in the sense that it is clear all human activity centres around MAN. Difficult, too, because man has not yet understood his own importance. And yet we can say with justification and without any sense of false pride that the African way of life

with its many problems has less setbacks towards the achievement of an ideal society. We in Zambia intend to do everything in our power to keep our society man-centred. For it is in
this that what might be described as African civilisation is em-
bodied and indeed if modern Africa has anything to contribute
to this troubled world, it is in this direction that it should."

Away from official duties, Kaunda likes to read the Bible and
discuss the meaning of his favourite passages with friends. He
derives solace from the Psalms, from verses such as: "He is my
rock and my salvation: he is my defence: I shall not be moved."
He often astounds his visitors, and a typical reaction was
displayed by René Dumont, a renowned sceptic. Until he
went to Zambia and met Kaunda, Dumont's experience of
African leaders had been almost entirely limited to those in
the francophone countries. In the journal *Esprit*, he published
in September 1967 an article entitled "Kenneth Kaunda et le
'socialisme zambien' ". Dumont wrote: "I have encountered,
in my whole life, only one Head of State who truly seeks to live
as a Christian: he is an African, a black, President Kaunda."
He quoted Kaunda's exposition of the man-centred society and
his praise of Gandhi, Bertrand Russell and Teilhard de Chardin.
In their conversations, Kaunda explained that the Africans,
being a pre-scientific people, saw no conceptual cleavage
between the natural and the supernatural. After the mutal
philosophising, Dumont went off to examine the state of
Zambian agriculture and his article admitted that he found
many things to criticise. In the final paragraphs, Dumont
returned to the character of Kaunda. He warned that the
"good nature" which made the Zambia leader unwilling to deal
severely with farmers who frittered away loans might easily
be taken as a sign of weakness.

More recently, Kaunda has tended to say that he no longer
regards himself as a Christian, but as a "Godman". He explains
that God is all-embracing and cannot be limited by Christianity. "I cannot see God saying to me: 'I'll accept you because
you are a Christian, and I won't accept this fellow because he is
a Hindu, or a Moslem, or a follower of Confucius." Although
such remarks may somewhat loosen the bonds with his mis-

sionary upbringing and the simple Christianity brought by his father from Livingstonia, the religious fervour has in no way lessened. Moreover, he believes that he can persuade the mass of the people through the precepts of his Humanism to be altruistic, to progress through brotherly love. It is not an idea with much support from economic planners and development experts, who see the only reliable approach as exploiting self-interest.

The recurrent question is how Kaunda has reconciled his religiosity with his political actions. It is sometimes contended that he operates on two levels, that he does not allow his right hand to know what he is doing with his left. Kaunda insists that there is no dichotomy, even going so far as to claim that there has never been any issue of "outstanding importance" where he has been called on to take a decision that goes against his principles. He argues that the world is an imperfect place, that man is striving upwards, and that politics is the highest instrument in this struggle.

Talking privately, Kaunda comes to the heart of the matter when he says that the first essential for a young country is that it must "remain standing". When his domestic political behaviour over the years is viewed in perspective, it can be seen that this has been his overriding consideration. The ultimate calamity would be tribal warfare and the end of the nation's fragile administrative structure. Like most African countries – and more than most – Zambia is not a natural entity; there is no rational basis for its being as it is. But Kaunda had no option except to struggle for its independence as it stood and then try to make it work. Time is what is most needed and sometimes it has to be bought. Kaunda maintains that tribalism was far more acute when he was a child and tells stories of inter-tribal fights with sticks and stones at his school. But most Zambians have continued to think tribally, and act tribally in politics.

Kaunda is a highly emotional man, which is why he sometimes weeps in public. He can become so excited that he momentarily loses control and this most often happens when he is confronted with a situation which seems to threaten the unity of the country. The most consistent danger to the cohesion of Zambia has come from the province of Barotseland,

D

which has a long history of attempted secession. In the general election of December 1968 this trait re-asserted itself in dramatic style and the United National Independence Party lost control of all the main Barotse seats. Kaunda's alarm at this outcome was too strong to be concealed. At his first public appearance after the election there was a tense and bitter atmosphere; it was known that he was fighting off demands from within the Cabinet that a one-party state should be created immediately by legislation. Kaunda did not mention his pre-election forecasts that a one-party state would be achieved democratically at the polls. Instead, he railed against the opposition candidates who had won the Barotse seats, accusing them of having "misled, cheated and tricked" the voters. He threatened that all civil servants who had supported the opposition would be sacked. Suddenly he announced that all opposition MPs who had businesses would lose their trading licences. Kaunda turned, waved his arms at the Minister of Commerce and Industry, Justin Chimba, and shouted: "If you renew these men's licences, you will be sacked yourself." The incident was shown on Zambia TV. When lawyers pointed out denial of the licences would be illegal, the threat was quietly dropped.

In dealing with the squabbles among the Cabinet and among senior officials of his party, Kaunda tries to act as a mediator and works for a consensus. His methods have been far removed from those of more dictatorial African leaders, such as Milton Obote of Uganda. At the height of one bitter tribal contest within the Cabinet, Kaunda forecast: "They will soon exhaust themselves." As it turned out, he was far too optimistic. Whatever the longterm dangers of using a loose rein, however, Kaunda has shown increasing political adroitness over the years since independence. He maintains what almost seems like a game of musical chairs for top political, diplomatic and civil service jobs, regardless of the high price in terms of efficiency; the value of this tactic is that it gives factions little chance to crystallise.

Although Kaunda occasionally remarks that no man is indispensable, he clearly regards it as his first duty to stay in power. Even before the 1968 general election it had become certain that if Kaunda should give up the Presidency, his successor would be the Vice-President, Simon Kapwepwe. There was no other credible contender. Kapwepwe's enormous following in the northern half of Zambia was only equalled by the hostility towards him in the south. In such a situation, Kaunda has never been able to risk an irretrievable alienation of any group which might split the ruling party. The Copper-belt has needed most careful handling and its more strident political figures have been allowed to get away with statements and actions of startling extremity. Kaunda regards this as "letting off steam" – although the damage to Zambia's image in overseas newspaper reports has often been considerable. Sometimes he has found it necessary to appease political ambitions by creating jobs with resounding titles, such as the appointment of "district governors" throughout the country. Early in 1969 this innovation was proving awkward, for many of the incumbents recalled the gubernatorial grandeur of colonial days – and began acting accordingly by closing down the local courts where political opponents held office.

It is easy enough to be critical of Kaunda's performance, of actions or omissions which looked at in isolation have seemed deplorable. He has had to tolerate atrocious lapses of behaviour by some of his associates, although his own moral standards are puritanical. But his priority has never changed – to "keep the young country standing". Always less certain was just how far he might go in applying this yardstick to foreign affairs. Amid the intrigues of southern Africa he often looked like a youth leader who had wandered into a gangsters' den to deliver a lecture on clean living and honest behaviour. Yet in Pretoria it was decided that Kaunda's character was more subtle than that – when it came to the push he could accommodate to political realities; by the end of 1968, there was an openly-stated belief that "Zambia was in the bag". Whatever the value of that judgement, there could be no doubt that since the moment of Zambia's independence Kaunda had served a hard apprenticeship in international affairs, and been exposed to some rare displays of political deviousness.

PART TWO

Born Unfree – The Zambian Background

CHAPTER 4

"Africa's Second Chance"

Zambia was carried to nationhood upon the dying gusts of the "wind of change". Harold Macmillan produced that phrase early in 1960, during a speech in Cape Town at the southern tip of Africa. Kenneth Kaunda had, at the time, just emerged from his second spell of imprisonment and was building up the bravely-named United National Independence Party. When Zambia's independence was finally attained almost five years later, the climate was altering within Africa; so were the attitudes of the outside world.

October 24, 1964, was chosen with care by Kaunda as the date upon which the Protectorate of Northern Rhodesia would be transformed into the Republic of Zambia. It was the sixth anniversary of the founding, under his guidance, of the country's first African party with a programme of uncompromising nationalism. It was also United Nations Day. But in retrospect, the date can be recognised as having another significance. It was the end of an era – an era which had started when the Gold Coast became Ghana in March 1957. In seven years the whirlwind had swept through thirty countries, to the wide river which formed Zambia's southern boundary and from which it took its name. There it died.

Across the Zambezi was the British colony of Rhodesia, self-governing for forty years, and with power always firmly in white settler hands. Early in 1964 the premiership had been assumed by a man almost entirely unknown outside Rhodesia. He was a wartime fighter pilot named Ian Smith, who quickly showed his mettle by arresting all the leading African politicians in the country. In his first public statement as Premier, Smith (then aged forty-four) declared: "I cannot see in my lifetime that the Africans will be sufficiently mature and reasonable to take over. . . . If we ever have an African majority in this country we will have failed in our policy, because our policy is one of trying to make a place for the white man." His Minister of Justice, Clifford Dupont, had earlier put it more succinctly: "We can and will halt the wind of change." Such utterances were then publicly dismissed in Black Africa as reckless defiance by reactionaries who would soon be swept from office. Kaunda assured Britain in July 1964, that his country could be used as a base if troops were thought necessary to put matters right in Rhodesia. Yet behind the African façade of confidence, there was mounting anxiety. It was hard, moreover, to promote a credible African government-in-waiting in Rhodesia while the contending nationalist parties fought among themselves with far more hatred than they displayed towards the settlers. When Kaunda privately urged Duncan Sandys, the British Commonwealth Secretary, to transfer power to the African leadership in Rhodesia, he received the bleak response: "Which leadership?"

At the time when Sir Roy Welensky was still the Premier of Central Africa, nationalists like Kaunda and Banda had had one immediate political objective: to end the federation of the two Rhodesias and Nyasaland. They regarded the partnership policy as a device to perpetuate white control which must be overthrown as a prelude to independence. But Julius Nyerere put forward a different strategy. In a conversation with Kaunda in the early sixties, he argued that it might be a dire mistake to dismantle the Federation — because once this had been done, there would be less hope of an evolution to majority rule in Southern Rhodesia. The whites would create a political Maginot Line along the Zambezi.

It is possible now to push further the Nyerere thesis, which was in strict accord with the principles of Pan-Africanism. It can be said that the destruction of Federation meant the abandonment of Rhodesia's 4,000,000 Africans. After the federal bonds had been cut, the chance of hauling Rhodesia into the community of independent black states slipped away.

In 1960, the year of the wind of change, a commission had been set up by Britain under the late Lord Monckton to examine the workings of Federation. One of the commission's main recommendations was that without delay there should be parity between the races in the Federal parliament in Salisbury; as matters stood, Africans occupied only twelve out of fifty-nine seats in the assembly. Had such an advance been achieved there could have been no going back and the next step would have been clear.

Ian Smith and many other white Rhodesians shared, without knowing it, the opinion of Nyerere about the end result of Federation. As the Monckton Commission observed: "In Southern Rhodesia there is a large volume of European opinion hostile to Federation. Many believe it will bring about a too rapid increase in the political power of Africans, both in the Federation and all three territories."

But it was the 1961 constitution which really alarmed the settlers – even though Joshua Nkomo and his nationalist colleagues also rejected it as unfair to Africans. The constitution was worked out under the umbrella of Federation by Duncan Sandys and Sir Edgar Whitehead, then the colony's premier. Ian Smith resigned from the ruling Federal Party, for which he was Chief Whip in the Federal Assembly, in protest at what had been agreed by Sir Edgar and at the intention to repeal the Land Apportionment Act. Much later, when he himself had become Premier of Rhodesia, Smith gave a droll explanation for his resignation in 1961: "Racialism had been introduced into our constitution for the first time in our history." But the Rhodesian Front party which Smith helped to found after his resignation put matters rather differently. Its programme condemned the 1961 constitution for allowing the possibility of "premature African dominance"; Sir Edgar Whitehead had forecast majority rule within fifteen years – which the British Labour Party for its part condemned as far too long a time.

Notwithstanding the extent to which future events were casting their shadows before them, the Africans of Southern Rhodesia never made any complaint that they were being sold down the Zambezi. They could still feel, in the early sixties, that the force of nationalism was invincible, that it would drive on to the Limpopo and thence to the Cape. It seemed then that independence for the northern territories would advance their own cause. In any case, they would have had no hope of persuading the African leaders in Lusaka and Blantyre of altering their aims. The smashing of Federation had become an article of faith and if Joshua Nkomo had questioned it he would only have reinforced suspicions that he was a "moderate" – the term of greatest obloquy because Welensky used it in a complimentary way about Africans who belonged to his party.

Hastings Banda was until 1963 the doyen of nationalists in Central Africa. He was regarded by whites as being an ogre, the ultimate in extremism. After his arrest in 1959, he was kept in prison at Gwelo, Southern Rhodesia for more than a year – while Kaunda was for a shorter time jailed in Salisbury. The decision of Iain Macleod, the Colonial Secretary, to release Banda, was strongly resisted by Welensky, who sensed that this spelt the doom of Federation. The collection of the little doctor at dawn from a Rhodesian airstrip had a conspiratorial air. But Banda had relished his imprisonment, telling the white civil servant who was sent from Zomba to escort him back:

"It was the best turn the British ever did for me."

The white Federationists would not have opposed Banda's demands so strenuously in the early sixties if Nyasaland could have been dealt with in isolation. They had not wanted it in the first place when Federation was being devised in 1950–1. It was forced on them by the Conservatives, who said bluntly: "No Nyasaland, no Federation." Nyasaland was a drain on the British Treasury, needing transfusions of more than £2,000,000 every year to keep it going, and the burden could be off-loaded by merging it with the Rhodesians. In effect, this meant that Nyasaland would be sustained by the wealth of the Northern Rhodesian Copperbelt – which was also the prize which Southern Rhodesia had in view, for their economy was frail in the early fifties.

To take the prize, Sir Godfrey Huggins accepted as a liability the homeland of Banda (who at the time was working unconsidered as a general practitioner in Brondesbury Park, London). But when the consequences of that decision were faced a decade later, Nyasaland could not be dealt with in isolation. The domino theory had to operate. That was why Harold Macmillan's acquiescence in the discussion by the Monckton Commission of the principle of secession from the Federation seemed to Welensky the ultimate betrayal. It meant that he could not hold Northern Rhodesia, which was what really mattered. At the end of 1963, R. A. Butler acknowledged that Nyasaland could secede. A few months later, with far more reluctance, he granted the same right to Northern Rhodesia – although refusing to make any promises about white-run Southern Rhodesia.

But for the "falling domino" effect of the acceptance that Nyasaland should opt out, the obstacles facing Kaunda and his lieutenants in their pursuit of power would have been much greater. The protectorate status of Northern Rhodesia had never been so clearly defined as in Nyasaland. Since the latter kept its own police force within the Federal structure, so did the former. Federal troops could only operate in the northern territories at the request of the Colonial Office. But whereas Federation put both territories on the same footing constitutionally, their relationships with South Rhodesia were historically very different. Nyasaland had no common boundary with Southern Rhodesia – to reach it from Salisbury meant a journey across Mozambique. Its white population numbered less than 10,000 and most of these were plantation managers or civil servants – there were very few urban settlers on the pattern of Southern Rhodesia. In contrast, Northern Rhodesia had a long common boundary and its settlers, numbering more than 75,000, lived mainly in the tightly-knit communities in the towns.

Essentially, whereas Nyasaland then had stronger ties with the British possessions of East Africa, Northern Rhodesia had social, political and economic affinities with Southern Rhodesia and South Africa.

White miners on the Copperbelt considered that they were in a province of South Africa and acted accordingly; their trade union was for some years only a branch of the miners' union on the Reef. They commonly spoke Afrikaans among themselves and in their contacts with the local Africans employed in Chikabanga, a master-servant patois of South African origin whose slang title is "Kitchen Kaffir".

Such traits went back a long way. Boer farmers from the Transvaal had trekked northwards in the early 1900s, following the advance of the railway across the Victoria Falls, to settle in areas suitable for maize production. For the first quarter of the century, Northern Rhodesia was effectively controlled from Salisbury. Sir Drummond Chaplin, Administrator of Southern Rhodesia, was ultimately put in charge of Northern Rhodesia as well for economy reasons.

Then in 1922, the settlers in Southern Rhodesia agreed to vote upon the idea of amalgamation with South Africa. Five months before the referendum took place, General Smuts wrote from Pretoria to Winston Churchill, then Colonial Secretary, saying: "I will be prepared to consider the Government of the Union of South Africa taking over Northern Rhodesia and relieving the Imperial Government of the burden." Smuts had already made known his terms for absorbing Southern Rhodesia. The possibility was considered by Churchill, but the obstacle was the need to reach agreement with the British South Africa Company on its compensation claims for mineral and land rights in Northern Rhodesia. Churchill wrote back to Smuts: "The short time at our disposal did not permit of any progress in that direction." The truth was that the British South Africa Company would have settled for around a mere £250,000, but the British Treasury was too tight-fisted.

The Southern Rhodesia referendum showed the settlers voting by 8,774, to 5,989 against amalgamation with South Africa. So for want of 3,000 votes in Salisbury and £250,000 in London, lands covering more than 400,000 square miles and stretching to Lake Tanganyika slipped from Smuts's grasp. From then on, proposals for the amalgamation of the two Rhodesias gathered momentum – with added enthusiasm in the south when the Copperbelt orebodies were discovered. This idea had first been suggested in 1915 and the map in an official guidebook of 1924 shows the two Rhodesias with no hint of a dividing boundary. In the late thirties, Britain sent out a commission under Lord Bledisloe to examine the basis for amalgamation. Bledisloe was both gently liberal and very cautious (he was nicknamed Lord Bloodyslow) and came out in favour of doing nothing on the political level while fostering economic ties across the Zambezi.

So the door was left open. In 1943, Roy Welensky moved in the Northern Rhodesia legislature that amalgamation should be carried through immediately. The whites in the north wanted amalgamation because it would give them greater security, but the Colonial Office could not ignore the advice of its administrators: unless Southern Rhodesia was willing to liberalise its native policies, any merger would be an abandonment of Britain's pledges to protect the Africans of Northern Rhodesia. The political leaders in Salisbury quickly made it clear that they were not willing to meet this objection.

In the end, the settlers of the Rhodesias achieved federation, which they saw as a stepping-stone to dominion status. Welensky has claimed that federation was an invention of the British Government: in fact, it was conceived by a pressure group called the United Central Africa Association set up in Salisbury early in 1948. Economically, Southern Rhodesia did very well out of it, for the fiscal arrangements allowed her to diversify and strengthen her economy to an extent which was to be crucial in the late sixties. The Copperbelt was the milch cow and Northern Rhodesia suffered a net loss in the years 1953–63 of nearly £100,000,000 – the bulk of which was used to develop Southern Rhodesia and the rest to prop Nyasaland. As though this were not enough, when the £280,000,000 Federal debt was divided up at the end of 1963, Northern Rhodesia was saddled with £96,000,000 – for which it had relatively little to show in the way of assets; it was more than five times the territory's national debt in 1953.

The ten years of semi-amalgamation had kept the north almost entirely at the mercy of Southern Rhodesia in a variety of ways. Salisbury controlled all telecommunications and its flight headquarters directed the movement of aircraft as far north as Lake Tanganyika. The collection of statistics essential for the running of government were centralised in Salisbury. The jointly-owned railways had their administrative headquarters and repair workshops in Bulawayo. The banks and almost all major companies were run from main offices in Southern Rhodesia, and many of these were in turn directed by headquarters in South Africa.

Then there was the £80,000,000 Kariba hydro-electric scheme. Kaunda told a meeting of the Organisation of African Unity in July 1964: "There was talk of building a dam on our Kafue River before the imposition of the Federation of Rhodesia and Nyasaland. Soon after the federal imposition, the Kariba dam was built instead, on the Zambezi River which forms the boundary between Zambia and Southern Rhodesia – the result was power installations were built in Southern Rhodesia; although we own the dam jointly, we depend on them for power." He summed up the position in these terms: "Our economy has been planned in such a way as to depend on copper alone, while we were made a cheap dumping ground for South African and Southern Rhodesian goods."

The economic ties with the south were to be quaintly epitomised a few weeks later, when it was learnt that a gold lamé evening gown had been ordered through a Bulawayo firm for Mrs Betty Kaunda. The dress was to be made in Johannesburg for the Zambia's "first lady" to wear at the independence ball. It was said to have been ordered by an anonymous well-wisher. When the facts reached the newspapers the golden dress was hurriedly cancelled.

It was the economic advantages which had made the Salisbury politicians so reluctant to loosen their political hold on the north, which essentially meant the line-of-rail area through Lusaka and the Copperbelt. Over the years, various formulae for keeping this control had been aired.

In 1959 the Dominion Party led by Winston Field produced a "Central African Alliance" plan, which would have combined Southern Rhodesia with the financially worthwhile parts of Northern Rhodesia in an independent dominion. The rest of the Federation would then become African-run, and supported by grants from Britain and Rhodesia. Field explained the scheme to Hastings Banda and reported that it had been enthusiastically received. (Years later, Roy Welensky was to admit to close friends: "I misjudged Banda. I might have come to terms with him.")

In January 1962, Ian Smith told the Federal Assembly: "If popular opinion means anything, it looks as though we might be left with a new federation – Nyasaland out and the two Rhodesias together." It can be assumed that when he mentioned popular opinion, his interpretation of the phrase was somewhat limited. Sixteen months later, Smith was to be at the Victoria Falls break-up conference as deputy premier and minister of the Treasury for Southern Rhodesia. He argued with skill on the apportioning of the Federal debt, and helped to persuade Butler that Southern Rhodesia should acquire almost all the military equipment in Central Africa. When they accepted that there was no prospect of keeping the Rhodesias together on their own terms, Smith and his colleagues saw to it that they took home most of the spoils.*

Yet there was another element in Salisbury which had long maintained that with Nyasaland out of the way, Northern Rhodesia could have been "contained" by the intelligent use of security forces. They proposed that Kaunda and his principal party officials should be kept indefinitely in restriction camps (a technique which from 1959 onwards was being developed in Southern Rhodesia). The rest of the population could then be firmly disciplined. Among the advocates of the policy was Robert le Quehen, head of Welensky's security branch.

It was conceded that this might involve establishing a 100-mile *cordon sanitaire* across the waist of Northern Rhodesia from the Congo to Mozambique and virtually abandoning the vast and unproductive area beyond it. This would also reduce by 1,000,000 the number of Africans to be disciplined; if they wished, they could join up with Tanganyika or Nyasaland – and good riddance, for the Bemba of the north were notoriously obstreperous. The parts which mattered, including the mines south of the Congo border, would be left in white hands.

The credibility of the scheme was somewhat damaged at the start of 1963 when the United Nations finally managed to overthrow Moise Tshombe. He was a firm ally of Rhodesia, and Katanga under his control would have provided a backrest, as it were. Welensky had even suggested that Katanga would join the Rhodesias – in economic terms, an excellent

* See p. 99.

exchange for Nyasaland. Moreover, with Tshombe in place of Banda, there would still have been a persuasive multi-racial air. A prominent settler said: "We would become the Ruhr of Africa." The fury among Salisbury's hierarchy at UN action in Katanga amounted almost to hysteria; the emotion is quite apparent in Welensky's memoirs. Yet Tshombe was merely an African, and every other black leader on the continent was viewed with contempt. The fervent support for secession in Katanga (at precisely the time when secession from the Central African federation was being just as fervently opposed) only becomes explicable when the visions in Salisbury – fostered by financiers in Brussels and London – are understood.

So looked at in the perspectives of Central Africa, the emergence of Zambia, and its escape from white political control must be accounted a close call. If Welensky had been able to hold on a little longer, if Tshombe's gamble had succeeded (as it so nearly did) – an entirely different pattern could have been developed. It might in the end – after a fierce struggle – have brought about the downfall of white rule in Southern Rhodesia by overstraining its resources. Nyerere would have been proved right. On the other hand, while disarray elsewhere on the continent grew worse, outside support could have grown fast enough to sustain the old order in Central Africa.

As it was, by the middle of 1964 events in various parts of Africa were lending support to the arguments of Smith and his supporters in the British Conservative Party, that Rhodesia was defending order and Christian civilisation against chaos and Communism. This line found increasing favour in the United States. After the assassination of John Kennedy in November 1963, the new administration was revealing a preference for "stable" regimes, with less regard to their political nature. The Congo had been a calamity from the start, its unceasing troubles offering an apparent proof of black inadequacy. The US felt keenly disillusioned over the Congo, which had nearly ruined the United Nations and had soaked up billions of dollars in aid with no visible improvement.

The start of 1964 in Africa had been especially discouraging to liberal well-wishers in Britain. A brutal coup had taken place in Zanzibar on January 12, only five weeks after the Duke of Edinburgh had attended the island's independence festivities. The Sultan, Seyyid Jamshid bin Abdulla, was ousted by a self-styled field-marshal called John Okello, who made numerous blood-curdling radio broadcasts before being removed himself by Abeid Karume. When Karume assumed the presidency, the Chinese and East Germans gained a dominant influence in Zanzibar – it was viewed as a "second Cuba" and the Americans were ordered to remove their satellite tracking station without delay.

On the East African mainland, the Zanzibar revolution was followed by a wave of army mutinies in Tanganyika, Kenya and Uganda. British marine commandos went ashore in Dar es Salaam to restore order for Nyerere. Troops were airlifted from Britain to Nairobi and Kampala to overcome resistance there. Sir Alec Douglas-Home, Prime Minister at the time, said it seemed very likely that the troubles had been "stirred up by Communists" – an echo of the developing theme. In letters to Sir Alec and Duncan Sandys, the Rhodesian Government was making great play with the "Communist direction and finance of our African nationalists".

The offer of a loan from China was the pretext for a Cabinet upheaval a few months later in Malawi. Only eight weeks after his country had become independent, Banda replaced six of his senior ministers for approving of what he called a "naked bribe" from the Communists. There were street fights in Zomba, intimidation in the villages and a flight of refugees across Malawi's western frontier into what would shortly become Zambia.

But even more damaging for Africa's image than the disturbances on the eastern side of the continent was the pattern of dictatorship revealing itself in Ghana. After all, Kwame Nkrumah was the cynosure among African leaders and his country was the pace-maker. As early as 1961, political purges had begun in Ghana and these increased in intensity after Nkrumah had been wounded in an assassination attempt during August 1962. However, internal troubles did not deter "His Messianic Dedication" – as Nkrumah was called in the government-owned Accra newspapers – from pronouncing upon

E

international affairs. In August 1963, he told his national assembly that for Britain to grant independence to Rhodesia under minority rule would be a "travesty of morality and justice".

In November 1963, Ghana was saddled with a new law which made it possible, at presidential discretion, to keep a person in preventive detention for ten years; previously, the limit had been five years. The following month, a special court which had been trying two ex-ministers on charges of complicity in the assassination plot gave its verdict. The accused were acquitted – although immediately re-arrested and put back in detention. Nkrumah showed his anger at the verdict by dismissing Ghana's Chief Justice, Sir Arku Korsah, who had been president of the special court. The incident caused an outcry in London, where the sixty-nine-year-old Sir Arku was much respected in legal circles. The International Commission of Jurists observed: "The action sets a highly dangerous precedent for the future ordered development of Africa."

Worse was to follow in 1964. It began with yet another attempt to assassinate Nkrumah and the detention of several senior police officers. Shortly afterwards there was the arrest of Dr J. B. Danquah, a venerable lawyer who had once been Nkrumah's mentor and later his political opponent. Danquah died a prisoner. Then came a referendum to make Ghana a one-party state: it was won by 2,770,000 votes to 2,500, but many observers claimed to have seen widespread intimidation. Next Nkrumah sacked four more judges and a tight censorship of outgoing press cables was imposed. When a mob attacked the United States embassy in Accra, the Americans threatened to cancel their £10,700,000 aid for the Volta Dam project. By this stage it was common knowledge that Ghana had run down the £190,000,000 in reserves it had been handed at the time of independence to around £45,000,000; there was a balance of payments deficit of £40,000,000 a year.

All these facts created the image of a reckless and undemocratic country, dominated by a desperate bully with illusions of grandeur. Although the Congo was in an appalling muddle, nobody had been very optimistic from the start. Yet Ghana vied with Nigeria for being regarded as the most sophisticated and evolved country in Black Africa. If it had slid down so far in seven years, what hope was there for the rest? Political scientists began speculatively to stand on its head the stock argument of anti-colonialists that it was morally right to give independence on a basis of majority rule. They began to suggest that it could also be morally wrong, if the maturity to cope with it was lacking. Zambia was yet to be tested.

As guests for the independence celebrations converged upon Lusaka, somebody coined an expression about Zambia: "Africa's second chance." It might be able to succeed where others were failing.

The new country was fortunately endowed with its copper mines. In terms of export earnings measured against population, Zambia would be far richer than any other "wind of change" state. Elsewhere in Africa the promises the politicians had made before they reached office were provoking dangerous expectations; foreign aid could never bridge the gap. But Zambia had only 4,000,000 people and a revenue of at least £100,000,000 a year as long as the copper market stayed healthy. The real economic difficulty would be to spend so much money without creating inflation.

Of course, there were sceptics. While they acknowledged Kaunda's charisma, they wondered whether he was firm enough to control certain of his lieutenants, or to damp down the tribal rivalries among them. Others remarked that copper was not merely Zambia's greatest strength, but also its weakness: if prices slumped – as they had done in the late fifties – there was nothing else to fall back on and the country would quickly become an international pauper. Then there was the appalling shortage of qualified Zambians to fill key posts, because after more than half a century of colonial rule there were only forty graduates, and less than a thousand men and women who had found opportunities to complete secondary education.

Far more ominous, however, than any of Zambia's internal frailties, was the inability of Britain to control events in Rhodesia. It was not merely that the government in Salisbury refused to accept the principle of majority rule; it was also edging towards a position where it openly spurned any kind of colonial status. Britain had only once granted independence to a minority government – and that was in 1910 to South Africa; a repetition was not tolerable in the sixties, especially when Rhodesia's whites numbered 240,000 and the Africans 4,000,000.

Whispers that the white Rhodesian politicians might take independence, if it could not be given, rose to a clamour at the start of 1964; even in the days of Federation there had been unfulfilled threats by Welensky that he might "go the whole hog".* The predecessor of Ian Smith, the rather gentle farmer Winston Field, was forced from office for his lack of grit in pursuing sovereignty. All he had won from the British Government was an agreement that it would stop calling Rhodesia a colony in public.

By October 1964, Smith had made his mark as a very different character. Angered at Sir Alec Douglas-Home's refusal to have him at the Commonwealth Prime Ministers' conference, he said: "If anyone still believes there is much hope of negotiating independence from Britain on the lines we want, he is indulging in wishful thinking." The Selukwe butcher's son was completely unmoved by the British tactics of alternating sternness with cajolery. In his exchanges with Sir Alec he adopted a patronising tone and conceded nothing during the London talks to which he led a Rhodesian delegation in September 1964. As though to underline the position early in October, Smith dismissed the commander of the Rhodesian forces, Major-General John Anderson. It was known that Anderson, in spite of being a South African, could not be relied upon to disown the Queen in the event of a unilateral declaration of independence. There were rumours that Smith might decide to catch Britain on the hop by seizing independence on October 24, the day when Zambia would come into existence.

What if UDI happened? The railway which brought in nine-tenths of Zambia's imports and carried all its copper went through Rhodesia. The turbines and switchgear of the Kariba Dam, which supplied the Copperbelt's power, were on the Rhodesian bank. At the break-up of Federation, its power-

* See Chapter 7.

ful force of Canberra bombers and Hunter fighters had been allocated to Rhodesia despite the protests of Kaunda; in desperation he had asked for the Alouette helicopters "for crop spraying", but was told amid condescending smiles that one could not use military helicopters for such a purpose. So Zambia would be very helpless if Rhodesia decided to use her as a hostage. Smith seemed quite capable of it — and Britain had not made it clear how she would react to a UDI.

But such speculations were put aside in the exhilarating atmosphere of the last days before October 24. Independence only comes once and it is a very special feeling. Almost every building in Lusaka was decked out with the green, black, red and orange colours of the Zambian flag. The green stood for the natural resources of Zambia, the black for the majority of its people, the red for the freedom struggle and the orange for copper. In every town and village there would be dancing and drumming. The Rhodesian-born governor, a shy man called Sir Evelyn Hone, was preparing for his final appearance in plumes and epaulettes. He would hand over Government House, with its peacocks on the lawns, and the Union Jack would never fly there again. When Sir Evelyn had assumed the governorship, in April 1959, Kenneth Kaunda had just begun a ten-months stint of restriction and imprisonment. Yet the two men were now close friends, their understanding deepened by mutual anguish three months before independence, when they had together directed the bloody campaign to quell Alice Lenshina's Lumpa sect.

Kaunda put out an independence message, full of sentiments inevitable at such a moment: "We are proud that our independence has been achieved without bitterness, and with the greatest goodwill on all sides. We know that we have many problems to face in the future, but I am confident that the spirit of unity, tolerance and co-operation which prevails in our homeland today will enable us to surmount every difficulty." There were expressions of gallantry towards the Princess Royal, who had been despatched from London to represent the Queen — a function she had performed two years earlier at the independence celebrations of Trinidad and Tobago. Yet there was one representative from Britain whose presence had been in doubt until only nine days earlier. He was Arthur Bottomley, the new Commonwealth Secretary. In the general election of October 15, the Labour Party had been narrowly returned to power.

CHAPTER 5

Bottomley Behind the Tent

The day Arthur Bottomley moved into the Commonwealth Office in October 1964, there were several files arranged neatly on his ministerial desk; they had been left by Duncan Sandys, who had realised that he might not be coming back after the general election. One bore a red tag to show that it needed urgent attention. The subject was the fate of the mineral rights of the British South Africa Company, in what was to become Zambia within ten days. As Bottomley began studying the file, he realised he was destined to be in at the death of a financial colossus whose money-spinning formula had no parallel anywhere in the world. When the Zambian constitution had been drawn up four months earlier, the Conservatives had inserted — in hope rather than expectation — a clause defending the mineral rights. But the British South Africa Company had to go, and everyone knew it. Kaunda had already said that immediately after independence he would hold a referendum to alter the constitution, if there had been no settlement by then.

The whole bizarre situation went back to Cecil Rhodes. In October 1889 he had been granted a royal charter by Queen Victoria for his British South Africa Company, which as a result was commonly known as Chartered. Rhodes had obtained treaties with chiefs in Central Africa and these gave his company complete rights over all minerals in the region. Rhodes died young, but the rights remained. In South Rhodesia, Chartered sold them for £2,000,000 in the early thirties — by which time it was clear the company had struck it rich in the "black north". The wealth of the Copperbelt had become known by 1928 and a royalties agreement was made with the mining groups to which Chartered had granted concessions.

The agreement worked well, paying the company £160,000,000 gross and more than £80,000,000 net in little over thirty years. It was certainly a handsome return on the outlay at the turn of the century. Matters had also worked well for the British Treasury, which collected about £40,000,000 in tax from Chartered after Northern Rhodesia became a Colonial Office responsibility in 1923; the total outlay on the protectorate from Britain in the same period had been £5,000,000.

But it was not merely the loss of money which made Chartered so intolerable to the nationalists. The company epitomised the economic and political tentacles stretching up from the south. Lord Malvern, formerly Sir Godfrey Huggins, had until recently been the resident director – resident not in Lusaka, but in Salisbury where the company maintained a ponderously impressive office block in Jameson Avenue. Malvern had been the principal architect of the Central African Federation and had devised the concept of racial partnership as the "rider and the horse" – the horse being the Africans. Not surprisingly, Chartered had been ardent in support of the United Federal Party, which had a majority in the Federation's parliament; it gave £5,000 a year to the party and was ready to help its more important members in a variety of ways.

In Lusaka, capital of the country which provided the wealth, Chartered had maintained only a few sleepy offices. Apart from taking part in prospecting for new orebodies which might still further inflate the royalties, the company had no function north of the Zambezi except to ensure that every penny was safely garnered. It was not even permitted for Africans to dig sand from a river bank without making a payment to Chartered; some remote villagers who earned a few pounds every month by selling locally-produced salt were subjected to the company's attentions after a government information officer had written a report applauding their initiative. But the bulk of Chartered's income was derived, of course, from the copper mines. The complicated sliding-scale formula ensured that some royalties would be forthcoming even if metal prices were so low that the producers were not making any money themselves.

The first serious effort to question the basis for the mineral royalties had been made in the thirties by a colonial governor, Sir Hubert Young. From Lusaka he had initiated a long series of exchanges with the Colonial Office in London about the validity of the original agreements by which Chartered laid claim to rights over the Copperbelt area. He was convinced that the royalties were being taken on false pretences. (Some information about Sir Hubert's researches had become available by the time of Zambia's approach to independence, but the full details only became known in 1968 when access to official files in London was allowed.) Sir Hubert's interest in the topic had been aroused by a legal dispute between Chartered and Paramount Chief Yeta of the Barotse. The Governor made his first approach to the Colonial Office in March 1936 by letter, and followed it up in person when he went on leave at the end of the year.

He had a cool reception. The idea of challenging the rights of Chartered did not appeal to the Colonial Secretary, William Ormsby-Gore. He was connected by marriage to Dougal Malcolm, the president of Chartered, and the two were friends; moreover, Ormsby-Gore had been parliamentary under-secretary for the Colonies in 1923 when an agreement had been made confirming the company's position. Before going back to Lusaka, in April 1937, Sir Hubert had written again to Ormsby-Gore, saying that he "wanted the matter resolved". Before asking for another interview, he outlined his views in detail.

Young made it clear where his sympathies lay: "I cannot believe that it is either necessary or desirable to give way to the company on this point, to the permanent detriment of the native interests. . . ." He spoke of "the facts that I have with the greatest difficulty elicited" and concluded: "I grant you that I was under the impression that the concessions and certificates together covered the whole of Northern Rhodesia, but that was because I and my predecessors had been led to believe that this was the case."

His letter was the subject of urgent and anxious study in the Colonial Office. The comments in the files made it clear that the officials were deeply vexed with Sir Hubert for having delved into such a delicate matter. They also knew how strongly he felt, and one commented that care had to be taken because the Governor might go to the extent of resigning. There was also a fear that the explosive discoveries he had made could somehow find their way in Lusaka into the hands of members of the all-white legislature, who had several times before shown their resentment at Chartered's grip on the country.

In his reply to Young, Ormsby-Gore began: "The first point of importance is that I am not prepared to question the claim of the British South Africa Company to own the minerals throughout Northern Rhodesia." He went on to reject Sir Hubert's arguments, but admitted: "I agree with you that some of the company's actions in the early days were dictated by their commercial interests, rather than by the interests of the territory which they were administering." It was now clearly hoped that Young would drop the whole matter, but he refused and submitted – "in justice to myself" – an official despatch embodying his arguments. This went to the law officers of the Crown, a step which Ormsby-Gore had earlier refused to consider.

By the autumn of 1938, the legal opinion had been given. There was now a new Colonial Secretary – Malcolm Mac-Donald, a former Labour MP and son of Ramsay MacDonald. (By an odd turn of events, Malcolm MacDonald was to be much involved in Zambia's relations with Britain thirty years later.) In December 1938, MacDonald sent a despatch to Lusaka containing the law officers' findings; these dismissed Young's contentions on grounds which were later proved entirely false. The despatch was published "to answer the growing volume of complaint and criticism" – although Sir Hubert's long debate with the Colonial Office was unknown to the public and his arguments were not given. At the last moment, a solitary reference to Young and to one of his assertions was removed from the despatch.

All this passed off quietly, for the tiresome Governor so bothered about native interests had been given a new appointment – far away in the West Indies. Shortly before Mac-Donald's despatch was released, one senior civil servant in the Colonial Office wrote a comment in the file: "It is clear that most of the arguments so tenaciously put forward by Sir Hubert Young would have little chance of being successfully sustained in the court of law. He has, in fact, wasted a good deal of everybody's time and it is perhaps as well that he himself is no longer in Northern Rhodesia to receive the news which we shall now have to send."

For most of the war years, the Chartered question rested in abeyance, although in 1944 it was mentioned in the legislature by a former engine driver who was making his way in politics. Roy Welensky was brushed aside at that time, but kept pressing the point, and in the late forties there was discussion about buying out the mineral rights; a sum of between £5,000,000 and £6,000,000 was confidentially suggested by Sir Andrew Cohen, an official of the Colonial Office. Ultimately, Welensky won what appeared to be a great victory. An agreement was signed by which Chartered's mineral rights would expire in 1986. Earlier, the company had regarded Welensky as a near-Communist agitator, but after the agreement had been signed relations were to become most harmonious.

Profits apart, the directors remained imbued with a *mystique*. Chartered was a company, but also more than a company. It was the custodian of a great imperial duty. It had actually ruled and administered much of Central Africa for a quarter of a century. The police in Southern Rhodesia were still called the British South Africa Police – and proud of it. Chartered felt paternalistic about the Rhodesias, founded by the company's founder and named after him. In 1953, Sir Dougal Malcolm wrote in an article marking the centenary of the birth of Rhodes: "And what is to be the future of Rhodesia, with what is still a comparatively small European population deeply wedded to British parliamentary institutions, but surrounded by a mass of millions of native Africans, still politically unconscious for the most part but affording a field for the activities of a small African intelligentsia, which may look for the future of their people elsewhere than to the true British South African tradition?"

What, indeed. Sir Malcolm did not attempt an answer, but said the situation called for another Rhodes, "a man capable of visualising a great objective".

When Sir Malcolm died, his place was taken by Lord Robins, who although American-born was a traditionalist *par excellence*. His statements made plain that since Chartered had given Federation and Sir Roy Welensky the nod of approval, any criticism approached heresy. In the early sixties, when everyone else had recognised the Federation as a lost cause, Lord Robins was still defending it sternly in his reports to the Chartered shareholders. Perhaps at the age of seventy-seven he was not as capable of making adjustments as was Harry Oppenheimer, the overlord of the vast Anglo American Corporation with which Chartered had close financial ties. Anglo American had given money to the United Federal Party, but withdrew in good time; Chartered kept on to the bitter end. While Anglo American contributed to African education on the Copperbelt and ploughed back a tolerable amount of its profits, Chartered took out its royalties as swiftly as possible and used them in South Africa, Southern Rhodesia and Canada. By 1962, the company had investments worth £55,000,000 of which only about one-sixth were in Northern Rhodesia — and that almost exclusively in the mines.

The first hint from Chartered that it feared for the survival of its rights — which were due to expire in 1986 — was given in February 1961. The *African Mail* had complained that despite exchange control, the company was still allowed to remove its royalties from Central Africa because it was registered in London.

This provoked the company into preparing a rejoinder, which was published throughout Central Africa as an advertisement. It gave a somewhat tendentious account of Chartered's record. Some of the statements were far from the truth: "The company was largely responsible for developing the Copperbelt. . . ." Others were vague: "The company has made substantial investments in activities outside the mining field. . . ." Finally there was direct reference to the criticism: "It has long been a doctrine of leftwing politicians and journalists that no private enterprise should be allowed to make substantial profits."

Chartered's public relations officer in Salisbury also made an angry reply which described the newspaper's attitude as "part of the softening-up process in a campaign now being developed in certain quarters to deprive the company of its legal rights". The remark was a desperate tactical error, for its defensive tone greatly encouraged the critics of Chartered. Up to that moment there had been nothing like a campaign, but one quickly flowered in the knowledge that the company felt vulnerable. It was put about that the country might lose another £100,000,000 in royalties before Chartered bowed out in 1986 – a great deal for an under-developed territory with a *per capita* income of £25 a year. The estimate of £100,000,000 was full of imponderables, for copper is one of the most erratic of commodities; however, it was a good, round figure.

A year later, the Chartered directors were really alarmed. The Federation was near to collapse and it was clear that the "native Africans" of the north were to be given independence – already they were in virtual political control.

Lord Robins had not lived to see the appalling moment, and his position was taken by a kindly but indecisive old man called Paul Emrys-Evans. He did his best to accommodate to events. Lord Malvern was pensioned off as resident director in Salisbury and his place taken by Sir Frederick Crawford, a former Governor of Uganda reputed to have liberal inclinations. The company began offering scholarships for Africans and organised a short story competition. It also loaned £2,000,000 for African housing (at six per cent).

In March 1963, Emrys-Evans was still putting up a front, protesting at criticism of Chartered and talking as though the rights were inviolate. But he could see they were not. By September of that year he was making secret approaches to discover what the selling price might be.

The Chartered directors were under heavy pressure by this time from Harry Oppenheimer. He wanted an amicable settlement quickly, for a public wrangle might damage the interests of Anglo American; there was also the twenty per cent holding of Anglo in Chartered – Oppenheimer realised that to win maximum compensation for the rights it was vital to act before Northern Rhodesia was given full internal self-government after the general elections scheduled for the following January. So in response to the appeals from Emrys-Evans,

the British official still holding the territory's finance portfolio
flew to London in October. The proposals he was to make had
been put to the African ministers, including Kenneth Kaunda,
and had received their approval. The offer was generous:
£50,000,000 spread over until 1986 in equal yearly payments
of £2,250,000, tax free in London. Emrys-Evans was typically
hesitant and asked if there was any proof that an African
government would honour the payments. Would the British
Government guarantee them in case of default? An observer
from Whitehall who was present at the talks hurried off to the
Treasury. When he returned, it was known that the proposal
for a guarantee had been rejected. Then Oppenheimer weighed
in with a scheme devised by Anglo American and the other
big Copperbelt company, Roan Selection Trust: they would give
the guarantee themselves. It was both ingenious and practical,
but Emrys-Evans could not agree. The talks petered out.

Three months later, Northern Rhodesia had an African
Cabinet and it was accepted that independence was only a
matter of months away. In the excitement of the general elections, which had significantly strengthened Kaunda's position,
the "BSA affair" had momentarily slipped from view. In any
case, the talks in the previous October had been conducted in
great secrecy and only a handful of people knew about them.
Now there was an African Minister of Finance, Arthur Wina,*
to take decisions. Ironically, Wina came from the Barotse
tribe, whose treaties with Cecil Rhodes had given Chartered
its historic claim to the country's mineral rights. Wina was at a
loss on the subject, as were his ministerial colleagues. Chartered
appeared to have so much legal backing and so many friends in
high places in the British Tory administration, that to take
issue with the company could even mean a withdrawal of the
promised independence. One of the more fiery members of the
Cabinet urged that the £50,000,000 should be raised immediately and paid to the company to "finish the whole
business".

At this point, a long and detailed study of Chartered was
made available from a private source. It was circulated around
the Cabinet and the revelations about the frail foundations

* For Wina's subsequent career, see Chapter 13.

upon which the mineral rights had been based produced a dramatic change in attitudes. The idea of paying £50,000,000, or anything like it, was jettisoned. Kaunda commissioned a London firm of economic consultants headed by the Hon Maxwell Stamp to make a full investigation.

The following month, Emrys-Evans visited Lusaka and announced publicly that he was willing to start negotiations. But his offer fell on stony ground, for the team of investigators was ransacking government archives for evidence against Chartered. In London, the company's directors hurriedly launched a campaign to arouse support in the City. Financial journalists speculated with a strange unanimity that £50,000,000 was a suitable "golden handshake". Kaunda was said to be thinking in terms of three years' revenue, which at the current level of payments would add up to at least £18,000,000, and probably far more.

In May, the independence conference was held in London and on the day before it opened there was another secret meeting to discuss the future of Chartered. Harry Oppenheimer convened it – and this was to be his last attempt to extricate Emrys-Evans from his predicament. Kenneth Kaunda was there with Arthur Wina and facing them sat the Chartered directors. But nothing was achieved, for Kaunda was polite yet deliberately vague. He could not discuss the matter then, but only after the independence conference was completed. Perhaps he could invite everyone to Lusaka in the following weeks. His strategy was plain: to avoid any showdown on the issue until the day of independence was settled. There was also the prospect of a general election in Britain which might bring the Labour Party back to power; Kaunda knew he could rely upon their support; whereas the *éminence grise* of the Conservative establishment, Lord Salisbury, had been a director of Chartered until a few years before.

Week after week slipped by. Emrys-Evans sent a succession of pleading messages to Lusaka, but the Cabinet remained unapproachable. Arthur Wina had clustered around him several young white economists of radical tendencies. They were overjoyed at the way events were turning out in this confrontation with a capitalist dinosaur. It was the fulfilment of undergraduate dreams. At the end of August, with a bare two months to go to independence, Wina announced solemnly that there were now grave doubts about Chartered's legal right to mineral royalties. He implied that if any compensation were to be paid, it was Britain's task because she had confirmed the company's position in earlier years. The game was now growing ruthless.

More time was quietly dissipated. At the start of September Kaunda sent a letter about Chartered to Sir Alec Douglas-Home, but the latter was totally engaged in preparing for his general election fight. Central Africa was proving intolerably tiresome at such a moment, for Ian Smith was in London and a whole week was taken up with talking inconclusively to him. In mid-September, Wina arrived for what he called "decisive discussions" on the mineral rights. He announced blandly that Zambia's independence, now five weeks away, might have to be delayed; but everyone knew that this was not possible. To make the situation even more difficult, Wina refused to talk to the Chartered directors. He was only willing to discuss the situation with British ministers and officials. This in itself showed how far the Zambian policy had hardened since Kaunda's stone-walling operation with Oppenheimer and the Chartered representatives a few months before.

But worse was to follow. Wina was asked how much Zambia would pay for the mineral rights – which by this time were providing Chartered with almost £1,000,000 a month net and had more than twenty years to run. The answer came without hesitation: nothing. The Zambians denied all responsibility, and if Britain wanted to pay compensation, that was her affair. After all, the British Treasury and the Chartered shareholders had been the principal beneficiaries of the royalties. However, the Zambians were willing to make a gesture of goodwill. They would contribute £2,000,000. It was a drop of £48,000,000 in ten months.

This was such a staggering piece of effrontery that it commanded some respect. Then Chartered named its price: £15,000,000. It represented a major retreat and had no more logic than any other figure that had been, or might be, pulled out of a hat. The mineral rights were simply worth what could be got for them, and in Chartered's latest balance sheet they were merged into concessions and land rights throughout Central Africa, with a total value of £841,000. As the cards were laid on the table, Britain put forward its negotiator. He was Lord Dilhorne (formerly Sir Reginald Manningham-Buller), the Lord Chancellor. Perhaps fortunately for the Zambians, Duncan Sandys was away at the Malta independence celebrations in mid-September and Dilhorne could best be spared from the election campaign.

Lord Dilhorne found the whole matter somewhat bewildering. He told Wina that £2,000,000 was a derisory figure and he sympathised with Emrys-Evans, who was a former Conservative MP. But if the Africans would not reach a gentlemanly agreement, it was hard to see what might be done. The Treasury was adamant – it would no more provide £13,000,000 to bridge the gap, than it was willing earlier to guarantee the £50,000,000. After all, the 1950 agreement limited Britain's responsibility to so long as it had control of N. Rhodesia. In reply to questions from a journalist, the Lord Chancellor said: "Her Majesty's Government have not the slightest intention of stating their thinking." That was a somewhat grand way of confessing that he did not know what to do next. The Zambians proceeded to pile on further agony by releasing a White Paper, the result of the long months of research. Written in a style which contrived to be both elegant and fierce by a former *Financial Times* staff man who was part of the Wina entourage, the document indicted both Chartered and Britain through a close examination of events from 1890 onwards. Emrys-Evans described the White Paper as "propaganda".

As Zambia's independence day grew ever nearer, the City of London watched from the sidelines with scandalised fascination. But it had already prepared for the way matters might go. The yield on Chartered shares had for some time been above twelve per cent, twice covered by earnings, proof enough that the City expected the royalties to be cut back or eliminated. The Zambians had a strong publicity campaign moving for them, organised by the Maxwell Stamp organisation in alliance with friendly Fleet Street journalists. The Chartered directors

F

were now isolated, for Oppenheimer and Sir Ronald Prain, the RST Chairman, had washed their hands of the affair. A show of loyalty towards Chartered – whose directors they in the main despised – could prove very expensive in post-independence years.

There was, however, another point of view: if the Zambians managed to railroad Chartered, it might encourage them at some future date to feel that they could safely nationalise the Copperbelt mines, in which there was investment worth more than £300,000,000. It was true, of course, that the way Chartered's treaties with Lewanika and other chiefs had been acquired might not be too savoury. But much of the history of the richest companies built up in the British Empire's heyday did not bear too close a scrutiny, if you wanted to be moralistic. The more knowledgeable supporters of Chartered pointed out that if Rhodes had not acquired the Central African region for Britain, it would have fallen to the Portuguese. In which case, Kenneth Kaunda and his friends would not now be in a position to argue about anything.

But such analyses solved nothing. Dilhorne never managed to bring Emrys-Evans and Wina together, but interviewed them separately in a panelled chamber of the House of Lords. Britain hinted that it might go along with Zambia on a pound-for-pound basis. There was no advance from Wina on £2,000,000 and Emrys-Evans refused to consider a mere £4,000,000. There were now slightly more than three weeks to independence and as the debonair Wina boarded his plane for Lusaka he forecast that immediately after the celebrations the expropriation would be put in train. With his departure a letter was circulated to Chartered's shareholders in which Wina said he was sorry for them. He added: "The action which we are compelled to take is hurtful and unpleasant. We hope it will not result in permanent harm to the relations between Zambia and Britain."

A week later, Chartered dropped its asking price by £7,000,000. The directors' hope was that the Zambians would double their offer to £4,000,000 and Britain would produce the other half. A brief message came back from Lusaka: "Ask the British Government." But the Conservatives were in the last week of their administration; there was no time for such matters.

And so it was that Arthur Bottomley came to Lusaka, to the heat and the bunting, among guests from more than sixty countries. He felt elated, for he had long been interested in colonial affairs and was impressed by Kaunda. He, too relished the significance of the moment, as the first Labour Commonwealth Secretary to attend an African independence festivity. The only obstacle to his full enjoyment was the Chartered business. But he had read the files Duncan Sandys had left behind and he had a mandate from Harold Wilson. This was to tell the Zambians that Britain would give them £2,000,000 to add to the like amount they had already offered. Then the Zambians could pass the lot on to Chartered. Bottomley had met the company's directors in London and with much anguish they had agreed. Emrys-Evans had also flown out to Lusaka, so that the deal could be signed and sealed. As soon as he was off the plane, Bottomley went into discussions – and received a rude shock.

The Zambians would not accept Britain's £2,000,000. They insisted that this would be contrary to their declared position that Britain must accept responsibility. Their own £2,000,000 was nothing more than a gift. At once, complications became apparent, for if Britain paid its share direct to Chartered, it might well be liable to heavy tax unless there was a special Act of Parliament.

Bottomley felt out of his depth. He announced that he was flying straight back to London in his Comet to receive further directions from his premier. Then somebody suggested that he might try telephoning. Wilson calmed Bottomley down. The Zambian position should be accepted and if Chartered had to pay tax, that was just their bad luck. The Commonwealth Secretary would have to tell Emrys-Evans that there was no option but to accept with what grace he could muster.

By now it was only a matter of hours to the midnight ceremony at which the Union Jack would be lowered and the colours of Zambia hauled up in its stead. The job had to be done by then. Bottomley went from his telephone conversation with Downing Street to a garden party in the grounds of

Government House. More than 1,000 people were there, but after Bottomley had exchanged greetings with a few of his closest friends he button-holed Emrys-Evans and drew him behind a tea-tent. The tired and dispirited chairman of Chartered protested bitterly at the prospect of not even receiving all the pitiful £4,000,000. The Commonwealth Secretary had nothing else to offer. Around them was the rattle of cups and the carefree chatter of other guests. Emrys-Evans asked for a chance to think and as the garden party ebbed away an emergency conference was set up in a room of Government House. When it was dusk, somebody pointed out that there was little time left for everyone present to change and dress for the evenings festivities in the Independence Stadium several miles outside the capital. With minutes to go before the meeting broke up, Emrys-Evans caved in.

Later that evening, as 1,200 tribal dancers were performing under arc-lights in the stadium, one of Wina's radical economists arrived, bearded and wearing sandals. Beside the main stand he found a huddle of journalists discussing their stories for the next day's papers. It had been a very orderly and uneventful independence so far; even the sale of beer had been banned to remove any risk of unbridled behaviour.

The economist drew from his pocket a piece of crumpled blue paper. On it, hand-written were the terms of a statement prepared by a group of officials. "The basis of an agreement has been reached. . . ." A few more undramatic phrases pronounced the death-warrant for the dream of Cecil Rhodes, for the company which had ruled a region seven times the size of Britain. Soon afterwards, Zambia was born. A flame was lit on a hill overlooking the stadium and £5,000 worth of fireworks were let off. In the centre of the fireworks was a vast set-piece, reading "Kaunda".

In Lusaka, the last visible reminder of the British South Africa Company was soon afterwards erased. It was an equestrian statue, commonly known as "The Rider and the Horse", which had been presented by the company in 1960 to adorn a wide expanse of grass outside Lusaka's High Court. The statue was a copy of a work called "Physical Energy", created by Victorian sculptor G. F. Watts. The founder of Chartered had much admired the original and a plaque upon the plinth in Lusaka bore the words "In Memory of Rhodes". Not long after independence the statue was hauled down, while a crowd cheered. Some wit had suggested that it might have been allowed to stay with the rider painted black and the horse white, but the idea did not appeal. "Physical Energy" was taken on a lorry across the Zambezi to Salisbury, and there set up again.

CHAPTER 6

The Financial Fetters

It had been a famous victory over the British South Africa Company and the ghost of Cecil Rhodes. The Zambians adopted the royalties system as it stood (despite promises that the formula would be changed to encourage mining expansion) and the millions that had formerly flowed into Chartered went straight to the government coffers. But although Chartered had lost the battle, it retained the wealth it had built up over the years – investments worth £70,000,000. These included Copperbelt holdings of more than £10,000,000, at market values, comprising twenty-three per cent of the Anglo American share of the mines.

The company lingered on in a twilight existence for several months until its most powerful director – Harry Oppenheimer, the chairman of Anglo – took effective control. Chartered was merged with the Central Mining and Investment Corporation and Consolidated Mines Selection Company, both of Johannesburg. Emrys-Evans was allowed to remain as chairman of the new and far more powerful organisation, entitled Charter Consolidated, and was moved into Anglo American's London offices in Holborn Viaduct. He was given little to do and spent much of the time composing letters to *The Times* on southern African affairs. Oppenheimer became chairman after a discreet interval and Emrys-Evans died quietly a little later.

To underline the new relationship, a place on the Anglo board was given to Sir Frederick Crawford, who had been the resident director of the British South Africa Company in Salisbury; Sir Frederick also joined the board of Bancroft mine in Zambia. (Some time later he was to be a centre of

controversy when the British Government seized his pass-
port on the ground that he had aided UDI.)

The secrets of the £500,000,000 Oppenheimer empire have
long been a compelling subject for economists and financial
journalists. Charter Consolidated was now to provide Anglo
American with a London-based company having powerful
links to the political and City of London establishment –
members of the old BSA board had included Lord Salisbury
and Sir Charles Hambro, doyen of merchant bankers. The
BSA dowry included investments in Britain, the United States
and Canada worth more than £20,000,000. Charter Consolidated would ease the penetration of areas where Anglo American's direct South African connections could be embarrassing
and would improve the possibility of support from bodies such
as the World Bank. Through Central Mining, Charter was
given an intimate relationship with powerful transatlantic
interests, represented by Charles W. Engelhard. Already,
Engelhard was much involved in South Africa and sat on the
board of Anglo American. He now joined the board of Charter
Consolidated.

By an odd coincidence, Charles Engelhard had been present
at the Zambian independence celebrations, although he took
no visible part in the discussions over the fate of the mineral
royalties. He had been chosen by the State Department to
lead a goodwill mission on behalf of the United States. The
involvement of Engelhard in South African big business did
not escape notice in Lusaka and the US diplomatic mission told
Washington that the choice was singularly inept. However,
Engelhard was a supporter of the Democrats and had contributed handsomely to party funds. His leadership of the
team for Lusaka was widely thought to be a recognition of
these services.

While the Anglo American-Charter Consolidated financial
network controlled the Zambian Anglo mines, it also had a
considerable stake in the Roan Selection Trust properties on
the Copperbelt. This was reflected in a thirty per cent holding
of the issued share capital of Mufulira mine, which produced
the bulk of the RST output; both Oppenheimer and his deputy
chairman, Sir Keith Acutt, were directors of Mufulira. Anglo

also had identical holdings in two smaller RST mines, Chibu-
luma and Chambishi. RST itself was dominated by United
States interests — forty-six per cent of its shares being held by
American Metal Climax (AMAX) of New York. Threads also
led back to South Africa from AMAX, which had a substantial
holding in the Palabora copper mine of the Northern Transvaal
and the Tsumeb mine in South West Africa.

One of the more curious aspects of the American involvement
was that Engelhard had acquired in his own country a reputation for liberalism. President Lyndon Johnson called him "a
humanitarian of the first order"; he accompanied Johnson on a
trip around the world. Also seen in the same light were the two
senior directors of AMAX, Harold and Walter Hochschild;
they had always been closely involved with the African-
American Institute of New York, publishers of the magazine
Africa Report, and had taken a great interest in organising
scholarships for African students to attend universities in the
United States.

The Zambians were well aware of the power these mining
groups had over the economy. In the year of independence,
copper amounted to ninety-two per cent of the country's
exports, contributing fifty-three per cent of the total government revenue and supplying forty-seven per cent of the net
domestic product. It had often been pointed out by men such
as Sir Ronald Prain, chairman of RST, that without its copper
industry Zambia would be one of the poorest parts of Africa,
but because of it, it was the richest.

Yet the role of the mining companies did not stop there.
Between them they had supplied a quarter of the capital for
the £80,000,000 Kariba Dam, from which the Copperbelt
drew its power supplies. Anglo largely owned the Wankie
colliery in Rhodesia which exported to Zambia the 1,000,000
tons of coal it needed every year for the copper smelters and for
the railways and minor industries. The Oppenheimer empire
also extended into quite different fields, controlling Northern
Breweries, which had a monopoly of bottled beer production in
Zambia; this company was an offshoot of South African
Breweries, into which Anglo had moved earlier. Both of the
copper companies were shareholders in the Ridgeway, Lusaka's

leading hotel. Other associations were less apparent – for example, Anglo had a holding in South Africa in Stewart and Lloyds, the steel company, which in turn had branches in Zambia. Sometimes the relationship was reversed, as with the Old Mutual insurance company. The Old Mutual was the leader in its field in Zambia, having branches in every town. It was a South African concern, with a Brigadier George Werdmuller as chairman. The Old Mutual enjoyed a major investment in Anglo shares, which it had bought in the early sixties to help stabilise the South African economy during the Sharpeville shootings.

Likewise, banking was largely run from the south. The first commercial bank in the country had been opened in 1906 at Kalomo by the Standard Bank of South Africa. Another was the Netherlands Bank of South Africa. The main rival was Barclays DCO. All of these organisations in Zambia were directed from Salisbury, and ultimately Johannesburg; their senior staffs were transferred freely between the three countries.

The main chain of bookshops in Zambia was a subsidiary of the South African company, Central News Agency; the chain handled the distribution of the daily newspaper, the *Northern News*, which was owned by the Rhodesian Printing and Publishing Company – in turn a subsidiary of the South African Argus Group. This was a pattern repeated in chemists shops, department stores, travel agencies and garages.

When new companies appeared around the time of independence, to establish themselves in the current aura of goodwill, they almost invariably reflected the traditional economic trends. Typical was the Rothmans cigarette company, which quickly won a large share of the Zambian market. The chairman of Rothmans, Dr Anton Rupert, studied at Stellenbosch University, where one of his professors was Hendrik Verwoerd, later to become South African premier. By 1964, the millionaire Rupert was known as a progressive, outward-looking Afrikaner. The Rothmans factory in Lusaka was opened with a flood of publicity and the leading Zambian politicians were the guests of honour.

Another South African company, Hume Pipes, entered the Zambian market to make engineering bricks and sewer pipes in association with the Industrial Development Corporation and Anglo American. Hume Pipes is part of the Rand Mines group of companies, of which the chairman is Charles Engelhard. Charter Consolidated also has a fifteen per cent interest in Hume Pipes.

One of the few South African organisations which fell a victim to Zambian independence was the Witwatersrand Native Labour Association, commonly known as WENELA. Engelhard is one of its directors. For many years, WENELA had recruited labour in the country, mainly in Barotse Province, for the South African gold and coal mines. Thousands of men were taken on every year for nine-month contracts. Although the decision meant a loss of earnings for the Barotse people, who had few employment opportunities, the Zambian authorities banned the system as degrading and politically repugnant and ordered WENELA to close its offices in the country. Significantly, President Banda refused to take the same step in Malawi, where WENELA recruitment was on a far larger scale than in Zambia.

Probably the most dynamic new arrival in the middle sixties was the London and Rhodesia Mining and Land Company (Lonrho), which at that time had its main interests in Rhodesia and South Africa. Lonrho had a fifty-one per cent interest in the Beira-Umtali pipeline, which had been built with the financial aid of South Africa's Industrial Development Corporation. The pipeline supplied crude oil for the refinery at Feruka near Umtali, which produced the petrol needs of Rhodesia and Zambia.

The driving force behind Lonrho was its new joint managing director, Roland Rowland, widely regarded as a protégé of the British financier Harley Drayton. A large part of Drayton's interests were in South Africa. Before independence, Lonrho had been invited by Kaunda to look into the possibility of building a railway between Zambia and Tanzania, but later the speed of the company's expansion caused it to be viewed with suspicion.

The first series of take-overs by Lonrho was of Heinrich's Syndicate, whose main profits came from the brewing of African-style maize beer. On the hard-drinking Copperbelt, a fortune had been made in ten years by a German-born South African, Max Heinrich, who also had a variety of other interests in Johannesburg and Durban. After digesting Heinrich's Syndicate, Lonrho went on to buy the *Northern News* (which it re-named the *Times of Zambia*), and simultaneously acquired construction companies, garages, a large road transport organisation and an amethyst mine. For a considerable time during this expansion its operations were run from Salisbury. After UDI, Lonrho hastened to cut these links, and as it spread northwards through Africa as far as Ghana and Nigeria, the Rhodesian interests became only a small percentage of its total assets. Yet the name ensured that the company would not be allowed to forget its origins. More fortunate was Charter Consolidated, the progeny of the British South Africa Company: it was able to exploit larger copper deposits in Mauritania at the invitation of President Moktar Ould Daddah – even being discreetly helped from Johannesburg by the expertise of Anglo American.

In tracing the South African links with the Zambian economy, it was often hard to distinguish them from the Rhodesian links. During the ten years of the Central African Federation, many companies had set up subsidiaries in Rhodesia to be inside the tariff barriers created to protect Federal industries. By 1963, South African assets in the Federal area were officially estimated at £170,000,000. In 1964, Zambian imports from Rhodesia were £30,000,000 and from South Africa, £16,000,000 and the total was considerably augmented by re-exports from those countries. Most of the remaining imports from Britain and other sources outside Africa were ordered through agents in South Africa and Rhodesia and almost without exception the supply line was the railway from the south.

Faced with these economic realities, the Zambian leaders naturally had feelings of helplessness. At a meeting of the Organisation of African Unity calling for a boycott of South African goods, Kaunda pointed out that every village store in Zambia had goods on its shelves with South African labels. He said: "Economically, we are in very bad shape." The signs were visible everywhere. On the breakfast-tables of Zambia, the cornflake packets were printed with Afrikaans as well as

English; the newspapers carried advertisements for holidays in South Africa; the cinemas showed newsreels from Johannesburg. But such things might not matter so profoundly, perhaps.

What did matter was that in the ten years leading to independence, £260,000,000 had been sent abroad by the coppermining industry alone in dividends, interest and royalties. This, from a country of 4,000,000 people – of whom less than 1,000 had been given the opportunity to complete a secondary education in the seventy-four years since Chartered had promised, in its first treaty, to provide "civilisation and schools".

PART THREE

The Rhodesian Climax and Kaunda's Dilemma

CHAPTER 7

Talking Towards UDI

After Arthur Bottomley's debut as Commonwealth Secretary at the Lusaka independence celebrations in October 1964, it was expected that he would go on to Salisbury before returning to London. The Rhodesian capital was only forty minutes away in his RAF Comet, and Bottomley was anxious for a quick meeting with Ian Smith. But Bottomley could not go, because Smith would not agree to the terms imposed from London by Harold Wilson. These were that the Commonwealth Secretary must have access to the detained nationalist leaders, Joshua Nkomo and Ndabaningi Sithole.

Wilson had appeared to begin strongly on Rhodesia. Ten days after he had moved into Downing Street, an emphatic message was sent to Smith pointing out that any illegal declaration of independence would "bring to an end" relationships between Rhodesia and Britain. The new Labour premier listed the other consequences for the colony. A UDI would: "Cut off Rhodesia from the rest of the Commonwealth, from most foreign governments and from international organisations; would inflict disastrous economic damage upon her; and would leave her isolated and virtually friendless in a largely hostile continent."

This went no further than a message sent by Duncan Sandys to Winston Field in the previous February. The difference was that Sandys never made his statement public. Wilson did, after a flurry of messages between London and Salisbury. He had asked Smith for a "categorical assurance forthwith" that there would be no illegal declaration, failing which the warning would be released to the press. The assurance was not forthcoming, which was hardly surprising since Rhodesia was only a few days away from a referendum in which the electorate (almost exclusively white) was being asked whether it wanted independence from Britain.

Wilson was hoping to make flesh creep in Rhodesia, and Smith well understood it. He may have been a little flustered by the tactics of his new British adversary, for his first message was couched in terms far less imperious than those he had been using in exchanges with Sir Alec Douglas-Home. But to his followers he maintained an imperturbable front. When the referendum was held on November 5, the electorate showed its confidence in Smith by 58,076 votes to 6,101. The first round in the Wilson-Smith contest had ended; the former had displayed clever footwork, but the latter had landed the only solid punch.

Moreover, Smith was methodically planning ahead, especially on military aspects. The removal of the dignified Major-General John Anderson from his position as Rhodesian Chief of Staff had passed almost unnoticed in Britain. His place had been taken by Brigadier Rodney Putterill, a close friend of Smith. Like his predecessor, Putterill was a South African by birth, but he had lived in Rhodesia since he was thirteen. The new army chief was no intellectual, but he was tough and aggressive – a sporting enthusiast who had played rugby for Rhodesia in his younger days. Smith and Putterill had agreed between themselves that independence had to be taken and that the Rhodesian forces could "make a fight of it" if the need arose. Putterill began to shuffle around his senior officers, advancing those he felt he could rely on and pushing into corners from where they could exert less influence the men likely to have qualms about disloyalty to the Queen. Training was stepped up and detailed plans made for defence against any sudden airborne invasion. Several officers were sent on courses in Britain and entrusted with a double task: to find out whatever they could about military intentions towards Rhodesia, and to foster sympathy for the "white African" case among friends in the British Army.

Smith had known where he was going for some months. In July 1964, his Finance Minister, John Wrathall, had announced that spending on the army and air force would be more than

doubled, from £2,500,000 to £5,900,000. In the course of his
Budget speech, Wrathall paid thanks to Britain for a gift of
£4,000,000. He explained that this would provide a "solid
base" for dealing with future problems.

For a country of its economic size, Rhodesia was strongly
armed. It had four infantry battalions with ample artillery, and
armoured car and parachute groups. There were eight terri-
torial battalions to call on, together with 22,000 reservists for
the para-military British South Africa Police – which itself had
a strength of more than 5,000 men. The air force had two
fighter squadrons (Hunters and the obsolete Vampires), two
Canberra bomber squadrons and various helicopters and
trainers. By African standards it was a powerful array. The
weakness might lie in the army, since most of the troops
were black; if they refused to obey orders in the event of
UDI, the game would be up, for the white forces alone
could not hope to defend Rhodesia's 150,000 square miles –
about three times the size of England. But no Africans
held commissions and "educated natives" who might hide
dangerous thoughts were not encouraged to join the
army.

The prospect of a military encounter with Britain was
nothing new. Threats of a "Boston Tea Party" had for years
been a stock-in-trade of Rhodesian politicians, to be brought
out whenever there were serious political quarrels. Ian Smith
had been an obscure young back-bencher in the Federal
Assembly in August 1956, when Lord Malvern had explained
the need to consolidate economically, because "when we are
strong enough we do not care". Nobody would then be able
to stop Rhodesia doing what it liked. Malvern had been quite
precise: "We have complete control of our defence force. I
only hope we shall not have to use it as the North American
colonies had to use theirs, because we are dealing with a stupid
government in the United Kingdom."

Sir Roy Welensky was to come much nearer than words in
February 1961, during a conflict with Iain Macleod over the
Northern Rhodesia constitution. He heard that British forces
were massing in Nairobi and that reinforcements were standing
by at Lyneham in Wiltshire. Welensky sent a Canberra to

G

Nairobi on a "training flight" to spy out the ground and after-wards – his suspicions confirmed – had discussions with his staff officers. According to his memoirs, the scheme in Salisbury was to put the radio beacons out of action, lay oil-drums and logs across airfield runways, and open fire on the RAF Comets and Britannias as they were about to land. All this was no secret in Lusaka. The white territorials were mobilised and prepara-tions made to arrest the Governor, Sir Evelyn Hone, and the Northern Rhodesian judges. Welensky quickly had 7,000 white troops lined up. The only explanation which nervous Colonial Office officials could give was that the deposed Con-golese premier, Patrice Lumumba, had escaped from prison in Katanga and might cause civil commotion if he fled across the border; in fact, it was already rightly assumed that Lumumba had been liquidated by Tshombe.

The sabre-rattling had put Northern Rhodesia in a state of high excitement. The *African Mail* rushed out an emergency edition, with a front-page editorial headlined "Don't try it, Sir Roy!" The Governor flew back from constitutional talks in London and immediately began countermanding Welensky's orders for troop movements. The African nationalists sensed that if their followers engaged in rioting they would play into Welensky's hands; urgent and effective calls for calm were made repeatedly.

The British Government gave assurances that it did not intend to launch a military intervention, and Sir Roy suddenly retreated from the brink when he realised that Sir Edgar Whitehead, premier of Southern Rhodesia, would not co-operate with him. But in the Federal Assembly there were headstrong speeches by several back-benchers on the last day of February 1961. John Gaunt, who was later to be a Cabinet colleague of Ian Smith, used the "kith and kin" argument and forecast that British officers would refuse to fight against white Rhodesians: "Rather would they follow the example of their predecessors in 1914 at the Curragh, who resigned their com-missions rather than risk spilling a brother's blood." Gaunt made a call, which was warmly received, for a unilateral declaration of independence. A former wing-commander called Dudley Wightwick said he did not advocate revolution, but argued that Rhodesia might have to "take its future into its own hands". The government had enough powers to act, but if any attempt was made to remove those powers by force, "that would be another matter".

Although Welensky's nerve had failed, the thoughts of a UDI smouldered on in Salisbury. It was the reason why the group around Smith was so determined at the Victoria Falls conference in mid-1963 to acquire the military equipment of the expiring Federation. It took some months for the world at large to realise the significance of what "Rab" Butler had done. In October, the national executive committee of the Labour Party passed a resolution deploring his action. In the same month, Kenneth Kaunda announced that he was having "serious second thoughts" about the Rhodesian air force and demanded that the planes should be taken over by Britain rather than given to Rhodesia. He received a bleak retort from London.

Both Kaunda's appeal and Labour's protest had been sparked off by a resolution in the UN Security Council calling on Britain "not to transfer to its colony of Southern Rhodesia the armed forces and aircraft as envisaged by the Central African conference". The resolution had been sponsored by Morocco, Ghana and the Philippines and gained the support of countries as diverse as Norway, Brazil and Nationalist China. The United States and France abstained from voting – and Britain used her veto for the first time since the Suez Crisis of 1956. Subsequently, Harold Wilson was to claim that the Tories had sold the pass on that day (September 13, 1963), thus making it impossible to use force after he came to power.

Yet it has been argued that Sir Alec Douglas-Home considered sending troops into Rhodesia in 1964, shortly after Ian Smith became premier. In his book *Rhodesia and Independence* Kenneth Young says that for a fortnight "British troops were on instant stand-by in Aden to fly in to Salisbury if there was a UDI". In fact, this is entirely without foundation. The Conservatives never considered force. At Duncan Sandys' regular Monday morning meetings with his junior ministers when he was Commonwealth Secretary, not once was the possibility discussed. The repeated offers from Kaunda that Britain could use his country as a military base were ignored. The Suez humiliation remained too strong in Tory minds. It was one thing to use troops in a trouble-spot where British power was still acknowledged, but quite another to take an initiative and establish a new military presence.

So there was a quiver of surprise when Labour's Arthur Bottomley arrived back in London from the Zambian celebrations and said that the use of force against Rhodesia was not being considered "at the moment". It was clear that Bottomley, already exhilarated by his role as a principal gravedigger for the British South Africa Company, had been profoundly influenced in Lusaka by Kaunda's militancy. This was the first time in forty years that a British minister had ever hinted that it might be on the cards to fight the white Rhodesians. The new Commonwealth Secretary also said he sympathised warmly with Rhodesia's black nationalists, observing that "like all people who are struggling to get their rights, if you are not allowed to do it by lawful means sometimes other methods have to be employed". Duncan Sandys had never talked in those terms.

As soon as they had a chance, the Conservatives tackled Wilson in the Commons. Douglas-Home said magisterially that he hoped such language would cease. He spoke up strongly for the white Rhodesians: "I must ask the government to be sympathetic and to remember that these people, who are our kith and kin, are faced with one of the most desperately difficult problems that has confronted anyone." Wilson's careful answer made it clear that he was vexed with Bottomley's lack of discretion, although he threw in a passing reference to the way his Commonwealth Secretary had succeeded in the Chartered affair. The speech contained conciliatory references to Smith; there was no mention of military intervention.

This did not pass unnoticed in Salisbury. By the end of November, Smith was again using his old confident language in letters to Downing Street. On December 15 he accused Wilson of trying to intimidate and blackmail him: "It is with regret that I have to record that during the short tenure of office of your government in Britain there has been a drastic deterioration in relations between our two governments."

He had now taken the measure of the situation. Labour possessed a majority it could count on one hand and was grappling with the economic woes inherited from the Conservatives. Most important, Wilson might be cleverer than Douglas-Home, but he was no tougher. The Duke of Montrose, Rhodesia's Minister of Agriculture, told a political meeting in Salisbury that Wilson was beginning to regret his threats, which he could not implement. By the middle of January, Smith was no longer bothering to hide his intentions: "If you persist in standing in the way of our just request I shall have no alternative but to take such steps as may be necessary. . . ." Buoyed up by his 58,000 referendum votes, he wrote as might the leader of some major power.

Wilson had little to offer in reply, except to say that he looked for a peaceful transition to majority rule. This was exactly what Smith was determined to avoid, so that their exchanges had a completely unreal quality. Smith flew over to London – as did Kenneth Kaunda – at the end of January 1965 for the funeral of Sir Winston Churchill. After the service in St Paul's there was a meeting at which Smith agreed to a visit by Bottomley and Lord Gardiner, the Lord Chancellor. The two men spent ten days in Rhodesia and were grudgingly allowed to meet Joshua Nkomo. Nothing came of their trip, but Bottomley was notably more cautious on his return. He made a prepared statement in the Commons, in which he said he had emphasised to Smith that force would not be used. In reply to a string of questions by Duncan Sandys, he even went as far as to promise that the Rhodesian constitution would not be altered without full agreement from Salisbury. In a letter at the end of March, Wilson underlined the "no force" promise – apparently in the hope of mollifying his opponent. In the event, the effect was quite different.

The day after receiving the letter, Smith announced that there was to be a general election. Now he had it in writing that there was no likelihood of British troops descending on Salisbury, he wanted to remove any defiance from within his own parliament. The end result was beyond doubt and the Salisbury correspondent of *The Observer* was able to forecast on April 3 that UDI would happen "within the next six months", after the season's tobacco crop had been sold. It was to come in six months and one week.

As the restricted electorate prepared to vote, India announced that it was closing its diplomatic mission in Salisbury. The chargé d'affaires, K. N. Gaind, sent a message to the Governor, Sir Humphrey Gibbs, explaining that the Government of India saw the election as a possible step towards a unilateral declaration of independence. After reciting how the "minority settlers' government" was "persisting in the determination of its illegal objectives", the message said that the closure was to mark Indian disapproval and to show "solidarity with the people of Southern Rhodesia" – meaning, of course, the majority. Despite a request by Sir Humphrey, Gaind refused to inform Smith that he was withdrawing. On the telephone, the British High Commissioner, Jack Johnston,* told Gaind: "You're making a mistake – there won't be a UDI."

Smith had, by this time, marshalled white opinion so efficiently that the Rhodesian Front obliterated all opposition from the fifty "A" roll seats; eighteen months before, they had scraped into power by capturing thirty-five seats. The party was not interested politically in the fifteen "B" roll seats – which were designed in the 1961 constitution for Africans – and so put up no candidates; a string of black nonentities was elected, each collecting a handful of votes from close friends and relatives. The most effective opponent left in the Salisbury parliament after May 1965 was one defiant radical, Dr Aarn Palley, who was returned from the "B" roll by an African township on the edge of the capital. Surveying the outcome, Smith said: "It seems to me that this is the real Rhodesian nation that has emerged."

While Smith was working implacably towards his goal, Wilson was bracing himself for the Commonwealth Conference which was due in mid-June. The conference showed every sign of being acrimonious, for the Afro-Asian leaders were growing irritated with Great Britain's fear of taking issue with 230,000 whites – of whom 160,000 were women and children. If the British themselves found it hard to accept their country's

* Johnston always made it plain that he disliked and despised Smith. Later he was knighted.

new position as a second-rate power, the rest of the Commonwealth was simply uncomprehending. Here was the nation which in the thirties had still ruled the mightiest empire the world had ever seen, which in the forties under Churchill – so lately departed – had defied Adolf Hitler; here it was, being made to look ridiculous by a tiny minority in Rhodesia. But Wilson was quite decided on what he had to do at Marlborough House: to avoid any commitment to action.

As a first step he briefed Johnston in Salisbury on his intentions, with instructions to explain these to Smith. He was going to "keep the temperature down and the ground clear for negotiations". As far as possible, the scheme for a Commonwealth peace mission to Vietnam (a patently futile project) would be used to divert attention and consume the time of the conference. Wilson's tactics were largely successful and he even managed to delay until late in the evening the final debate on the communiqué to be issued. Only one Head of State proved awkward – Julius Nyerere of Tanzania; he dissociated himself from the section on Rhodesia, declaring afterwards that the British premier had refused to give any assurance that before independence was granted there would be "a majority of adults of all races on the voters roll". Kenneth Kaunda was more conciliatory, perhaps because it was his first Commonwealth Conference. Although he made it clear that his fears about Rhodesia were acute, he did not formally dissent from the wording of the communiqué.

Yet Wilson could not prevent the emergence of some sort of recommendation. This was for a constitutional conference, to be held within three months if negotiations with Smith brought no results. The Rhodesian Government should be called on to attend, and to release detainees so that all shades of political opinion might be represented. If Smith resisted the idea, then Britain should suspend the constitution, appoint an interim government and arrange free elections. The communiqué merely said that Britain "undertook to take account of these views".

In Salisbury, Johnston had been urging Smith to keep silent while the conference was in progress. Now Wilson hastened to explain how well he had done in keeping the temperature down at Marlborough House. Even before the conference ended, he dashed off a telex message to Salisbury, thanking Smith: "I am grateful for your own forbearance at this time and your understanding of the difficulties which I have been facing here." He then gave a watered-down account of the suggestion for a constitutional conference, but stressed that he had refused to be deflected from his own aims.

Smith was not at all impressed. He wrote back after seeing the full text of the communiqué, to say that a constitutional conference was completely out of the question. He would not attend one and if Britain went ahead with the idea, it would be viewed as interference in Rhodesia's internal affairs. The three terse paragraphs of his letter ended: "I am willing at all times to receive suggestions from you and to listen to what the British Government has to say on Rhodesia, but, frankly, I am not interested in what the other members of the Commonwealth say about our affairs, and what they do say will not turn us from what we consider to be the right thing to do in the interests of our country." A few days later, Smith said the Commonwealth was an unholy alliance; the more its members talked, the more he was determined to win. He dismissed Zambia's renewed offer of her territory as a military base as "laughable".

Everything now seemed to be going in his direction, for in the first week of July he had been encouraged from several sources. The Duke of Edinburgh had told a meeting in Edinburgh that it was best to use patience – a "few years here or there" did not matter, as long as a bloodbath was avoided. On the way back from London, Dr Hastings Banda had given a press conference at Salisbury airport and said emphatically that Britain could not, and should not, try to use troops. In the Commons, Bottomley was pressed on the issue by Nigel Fisher, a radical Tory who had been a junior minister in the previous government. Fisher had said that it was agreed by everyone that force could not be used, so there was really no way in which Britain could suspend the Rhodesian constitution and appoint an interim government. Bottomley was only slightly indiscreet this time: "No one goes to war without first trying peaceful means."

Encouragement of a different kind had been provided by the Congo. Premier Moise Tshombe was locked in a power struggle with President Kasavubu, while the Congolese army was still trying to overcome the rebels north and south of Bukavu. Ever since the previous November, the time of the "Stanleyville massacre", world opinion had swung more and more against Black Africa. The Stanleyville incident had revealed an abyss of mutual animosity and distrust between the West and the new nations. The Belgian-American-British decision to fly in paratroops seemed fully justified in white eyes and the shooting of hostages a proof of black savagery. The hysterical condemnations of the operation in the speeches of African delegates at the United Nations only added insult to injury. But in African eyes, the intervention at Stanleyville was only proof of Western duplicity and double standards. It was undertaken to rescue a handful of whites, whereas in Rhodesia there were 4,000,000 Africans denied basic freedoms for whom no such action was contemplated. Moreover, there were some African leaders who discerned another purpose: the landing effectively destroyed Christophe Gbenye's "revolutionary government" in Stanleyville, and buoyed up the hated Tshombe, creature of the Union Minière and big business generally. The operation left a deep scar of humiliation. The almost contemptuous ease with which it had been carried through made Africans wonder how real was the independence which the white man had bestowed.

When the news of Stanleyville had come through, Kaunda was on a world tour. Asked in Dublin for his reactions, he was immediately anxious, saying that this could set a precedent for intervention in Black Africa. One day the South Africans might copy the pattern, to embark on a military violation of Zambia's sovereignty. It was a prophetic remark.

The year 1965 was to be the heyday of the mercenaries in the Congo. Recruiting agents were busy in Johannesburg and Salisbury. Major Mike Hoare became an international figure and the mercenaries a legend for swashbuckling prowess — which those who knew them felt was ludicrously exaggerated. But the political significance of the mercenaries was pinpointed by William Harper, the Rhodesian Minister of Internal

Affairs, while he was opening a church fête at Marandellas. Threats by African countries that they might start a war across the Zambezi were confidently described by Harper as poppy-cock. "You can have no fears on this score, especially when you consider what 250 to 500 mercenaries have done in the Congo." In other words, when it came to fighting, blacks were no match for whites.

The arithmetic of white fighting white in Central Africa was rarely examined in public. But contingency plans were made by the British army and details of these reached the defence correspondent of *The Times* early in August 1965. His report was given a leading position in the paper, under the headline "Police Action Plan For Rhodesia Considered." The correspondent put succinctly the question occupying the minds of the military planners: "Have we the men and materials to over-power a potentially very sizeable resistance in Rhodesia, and, assuming we have the capability, would the morale of the British servicemen weather the strain of such an operation?" He said it was a widely-held assumption that full resistance would not be forthcoming, and only on that assumption was military intervention in Rhodesia conceivable. The morale of the British forces would depend on "speedy success and bloodlessness".

The report was clearly an echo of the debate taking place inside the Ministry of Defence. The correspondent – Charles Douglas-Home, nephew of the former premier – gave the latest estimate of Rhodesian strength on the ground: 3,400 soldiers, of whom nearly 1,000 were white; 6,000 white territorials and about 20,000 white police reservists; the police force was 6,500 strong, with nearly a third of it European. The defence planners had accepted that if all these men fought it would cause heavy casualties and involve a re-allocation of British resources that other defence commitments would not permit. There was a sharp reaction to *The Times* in both Westminster and Whitehall. To stay silent would be tantamount to admitting that the plans were being drawn up and chances weighed. Publicity for the report had been extensive in Rhodesia and Zambia. Wilson told Denis Healey, the Minister of Defence, that "clouds had been added" to the outlook for negotiations.

The next day, Healey held a press conference in which he did not go to the extent of denying the report in *The Times*; he called it "irresponsible speculation". However, until UDI there remained a group of senior officers who held that in the face of a swift airborne operation the Rhodesians would crumble, the African troops would disobey their white officers and casualties would be slight. Such ideas received scant encouragement from the top.

By October, Smith felt able to fly to London for talks with Wilson without the slightest fear of being arrested. His own preparations for UDI were well advanced, whereas Britain was making no counter-moves. The Commonwealth leaders' ideas, four months earlier, of a constitutional conference within three months had been jettisoned by Wilson.

Before flying back to Salisbury with his team the Rhodesian premier said flatly that his mind was made up. There had been no agreement. Wilson's response was to go on television and tell Britain that the situation was grave. He spoke in Churchillian tones, of the dangers of racial strife, of the nightmare with which he had to live. "We have tried and we have failed," said Wilson solemnly as he stared from 12,000,000 television screens.

But at the United Nations, the General Assembly made it plain on the same day that it did not hold with such defeatist attitudes. By 107 votes to two (South Africa and Portugal) it called on Britain to "use all possible measures to prevent a unilateral declaration of independence and, in the event of such a declaration, to take all steps necessary to put an immediate end to the rebellion". This contained the implication of force, which made the reaction of Lisbon and South Africa predictable. But the United States came out strongly on the side of the 42 countries who had sponsored the motion, for the Rhodesian issue was generating much heat in Africa and Russia was taking full advantage of the opportunity. Britain abstained from voting, Sir Roger Jackling being able to fall back on the well-tried contention that Rhodesia was not within the competence of the world organisation; it was a British colony and Britain would deal with it. Before long, that position would have to be abandoned.

It was now obvious to the world that UDI could occur any day. Another "Boston Tea Party" — that heady phrase so long savoured by Rhodesian politicians — was about to become reality. Ian Smith was the end-product of a long process. What marked him out was his absolute resolve to avoid being diverted from his goal, which was the acquisition of absolute power by the white Rhodesians. He had seen Welensky bamboozled and confused by the British into agreeing that they should pick to pieces their own creation, the Central African Federation. Smith had read Welensky's memoirs, where it was all told with such pathetic clarity and so many wilful misunderstandings. Smith was determined that no similar fate should overtake him. Not only did he believe in what he was doing and in the inherent superiority of the white race, but he and his wife also liked the life at the top. And Smith was trying to contain pressures within his Cabinet. Unless he got a move on, Lardner-Burke, Lord Graham and Harper might mete out to him the treatment employed on Winston Field only eighteen months earlier.

So when Wilson sent a telex to Salisbury on October 21 to say that he was flying out for yet another round of discussions, Smith was both wary and irritated. He could not refuse to receive the British premier and replied coldly that he would keep the weekend free. But he was determined that he would agree to nothing material. Wilson asked to see Nkomo and Sithole. At this stage it did not matter, so he raised no objection. The vital need was to smother any new proposal which might delay the declaration.

The expected proposal came in the second session of the talks. Wilson worked up to it after a careful preamble in which he described his meeting with Sithole and Nkomo and stressed that he had told them not to expect any British military intervention if Smith acted illegally. This undisguised attempt to win favour fell utterly flat, for Smith and his fellow listeners had long ceased to have any doubts about their physical safety. The Wilson proposal, when it finally came, was for a royal commission to test Rhodesian opinion. At the head would be the Chief Justice, Sir Hugh Beadle, aided by one British representative and one Rhodesian. Since Sir Hugh himself was

Rhodesian born and could not by any stretch of the imagination be called a liberal, the offer was generous in the extreme. It was an indication of Wilson's desperation by this stage. He was met by evasion and irrelevancies, which were sustained until late at night in the third meeting – to which Smith had invited his whole Cabinet. Towards the end, Wilson said he suspected that the Rhodesians had already decided to take independence in the very near future and wanted nothing to delay it. They were trying to make him fall in with their wishes "virtually at pistol point".

Wilson flew off frustrated from Salisbury airport. The Governor, Sir Humphrey Gibbs, wept as he said farewell. Until that moment, Gibbs had been of little account in the political scene, with only formal authority and no wish for more. He was a patrician who had settled down in Rhodesia to a quiet life of dairy farming. Now he was to be thrust into the limelight, into a role for which he was not suited either by character or intellect.

Wilson had made it clear that he would only send troops to Rhodesia if Britain were asked – from Rhodesia – to restore order. He envisaged a collapse of authority following a UDI, arising out of what he rather quaintly called "communal rioting". The white politicians would find themselves quite overwhelmed by the elements they had released by opening their Pandora's box. As they would be outlaws by this time, it would fall upon Sir Humphrey to call for help from the Old Country. This prospect appalled the Governor, who had scant interest in politics and a horror of the unknown. He had little in common with the aggressive men around Smith, but on the other hand he could not start to sympathise with African nationalism. There was a vast gulf in thinking between Gibbs and his acquaintance Sir Evelyn Hone, the radical last Governor of Northern Rhodesia, even though Hone came from early Rhodesian stock.

There was also a great difference between the powers of a Colonial Office Governor and those of Gibbs. The former had complete executive authority, the latter had almost none. When Smith appeared before Sir Humphrey on November 5, 1965 and asked him to sign the orders declaring a state of emergency throughout Southern Rhodesia, the Governor had no option. It was a patent canard that the emergency was needed because guerrillas were coming through from Zambia, although Justice Minister Lardner-Burke blandly made this claim. Everyone knew it was a prelude to UDI. According to Smith himself, he was told by Gibbs: "Well, when you want a state of emergency, even if it is for a UDI, I will sign it." Much later, Wilson was to assert that Smith had admitted lying to the Governor about the reason for the emergency, but even if Smith did so, the point is of no consequence. Gibbs had only one weapon, and that a negative one: resignation. But he could not go, because he represented the Queen and the British Government had asked him to stand firm. It was not for Gibbs to reason why; he had to obey the traditions instilled at Eton.

So by Guy Fawkes Night, all was in place. The next morning, Smith wrote to Wilson and blamed him for "finally closing the door". The Rhodesian forces were put on a full alert and a battalion was sent up to the Zambezi River with aircraft support. These moves had been planned for months by Rodney Putterill, who had now been promoted to major-general. A few weeks earlier, Putterill had sought and achieved the immediate retirement of Maurice Benoy, Secretary for External Affairs and Defence, on the grounds that this British-born civil servant had divided loyalties. It had been a show of strength and Putterill now believed that he had his officers solidly behind him. He was right, for not one resigned in the four days between the declaration of independence and the paradoxical appeal by Sir Humphrey Gibbs for all of them to stay at their posts, yet do nothing to "further the objectives of the illegal authorities".

Smith signed the proclamation, which had been printed in advance, after brushing aside a last-minute appeal from Wilson for a meeting in Malta. It had taken less than two years since the end of Federation to cross the Rubicon, but in that time countless hours had been frittered away in empty discussion. Two British premiers had been constantly diverted from their country's most urgent problem, economic malaise. At Westminster, the leaders of the nation were perplexed, but there was little sense of humiliation that Britain had been flatly defied by a small colonial community with a population less than one two-hundredth of its own. There was even less acceptance of the moral argument put forward by Kenneth Kaunda: "If a nation chooses to become a colonial power, she must accept responsibility for ensuring the rights, the interests and the future of the people of her colonies." This was dismissed as just the out-moded idealism which Kaunda had imbibed at his mission school.

CHAPTER 8

Zambia at the Threshold

A clear understanding that Britain would rely entirely on sanctions against Rhodesia had come very slowly to the Cabinet in Lusaka. In June 1965, while in London for the Commonwealth Conference, Kaunda again offered his country as a military base – a sign that Zambia had not grasped the realities of British politics. A certain lack of sophistication was understandable, for neither Kaunda nor his colleagues had held government office until 1963; their white advisers tended to be idealistic liberals capable of wishful thinking. The confusion was abetted by Wilson's remarks in private, for he assured the Zambians that he would send in troops if a breakdown of law and order occurred. But there was no mutual understanding of what would constitute such a breakdown: in Wilson's mind this was apparently frenzied "communal rioting" in which the whites were likely to be massacred because the Rhodesian army had lost its grip – roughly, he envisaged any British intervention as a more massive version of the Stanleyville operation. To despatch troops in such a circumstance would be applauded by the floating middle-class voters, on whom Labour hopes were pinned for a strengthening of the frail majority in the Commons.

The Zambians, on the other hand, thought that there would be a breakdown of law and order if the whites merely used draconian methods to suppress the blacks; they even argued that an illegal seizure of independence would, in itself, be proof of lawlessness. Wilson responded that UDI would only be a constitutional matter, which was an oblique contradiction.

Sanctions were a novel concept in Africa, apart from the vague talk of blockading South Africa after Sharpeville. The lessons of Italy and Abyssinia twenty years earlier had not been learnt, leave alone forgotten. But the Zambians understood the political forces in southern Africa and felt instinctively that sanctions would fail. They also saw themselves as hostages – they feared that a desperate Ian Smith would take suicidal action which would wreck their new nation's economy. Anxiety began with the Kariba Dam, which supplied virtually all the power for Zambia and had its generators on the south bank. The mere flick of a switch by the Rhodesians could plunge Lusaka and the Copperbelt into darkness; there would be no electricity to pump water out of the copper mines, which might flood within forty-eight hours. Ever since the building of it began in the middle fifties, the £80,000,000 Kariba scheme had had powerful political overtones. The north had always favoured the Kafue River site for a major hydro-electric project and work had begun there before Federation; but Salisbury wanted Kariba for strategic reasons. The Copperbelt mining companies had been dragooned by Lord Malvern into abandoning Kafue by the threat of punitive taxation. While Kariba was being built there had been a shooting affray between troops and primitive villagers who were being ordered from their ancestral homes to make way for the rising waters of Lake Kariba. Now there was the unforeseen sequel – the Africans of Zambia felt that Smith would have them at his mercy through the jointly-owned power corporation.

The second major area of vulnerability was the railway, which ran down from the Copperbelt to Victoria Falls and then across Rhodesia to the sea at the Mozambique ports of Beira and Lourenço Marques. Kaunda was faced with the dilemma of having his one line of communication dominated by a potentially hostile regime; more than ninety-five per cent of imports and all copper exports moved over the line, which also carried all of Zambia's coal requirements from Wankie colliery north of Bulawayo. Early in 1965, the Rhodesians had begun to apply pressure through Rhodesia Railways, which was also jointly owned by the two governments. In May, the Rhodesian Transport Minister, George Rudland, sent a confidential message to Lusaka asking for talks about dividing the system at the Victoria Falls. The Zambians did not know what to make of it and stalled. In August, there was a public complaint by Leon Dominion, a close friend of Ian Smith, about the compulsory transfer of some white railwaymen from Rhodesia to Zambia by the railway executive. Dominion was the Rhodesian Government representative on the board of Rhodesia Railways and had made something of a name for himself a few months before by loudly referring to Zambian officials as "monkeys" in Lusaka's Ridgeway Hotel.

At the end of August 1965, Smith claimed that Rhodesia was subsidising Zambia traffic on the railway at the rate of £1,000,000 a year and implied that he meant to do something to change this state of affairs. His assertion was at the least disputable, for the American Brookings Institute had just published an academic survey which examined the freight-charge structure. Although Zambian copper only accounted for eight per cent of the tonnage on Rhodesia Railways, it provided more than a quarter of the revenue.

Rudland returned to the attack by saying that Zambia was hoarding rolling stock and held 1,500 more wagons than it was entitled to – a remark with clear UDI overtones, for the Rhodesians naturally wanted to have everything they felt was theirs on the southern side of the Falls bridge when the moment came. Relations were further exacerbated in October, less than a month before UDI, when a routine consignment of equipment for the Zambian army was seized south of Bulawayo. No explanations were offered and Kaunda received scant satisfaction from Whitehall when he protested that this was a direct breach of the Rhodesia Railways agreement and demanded that Britain should call its colony to order.

Some sort of *détente* was urgent, and finally it was agreed to hold a meeting of the railways' "higher authority" – a team of ministers from each country. This began at the Victoria Falls Hotel in the first week of November. One morning the Zambians were disconcerted to find that their Rhodesian counterparts had vanished without explanation. The latter had slipped away to Salisbury to hear their leader's historic proclamation.

As it turned out, Smith was too shrewd to seek the economic ruin of Zambia; on the contrary, he maintained that he wanted to help his northern neighbours and expressed sympathy for Kaunda as an innocent tool of Wilson. He later said: "I believe that the present British Government will forever stand condemned because of its policy of fighting the war of sanctions to the last Zambian"; it was an epigram he had borrowed from a Zambian daily newspaper and turned to his own account. As sanctions turned out, Smith had no need to ruin Zambia, or even to threaten such a course.

But Kaunda could not foresee this, and one of the first steps he took was to protect the copper mines. In August 1965, it was announced that coal deposits in the Gwembe Valley, quite close to Kariba Dam, would be opened up through a crash programme. The deposit which had been proven, although known to be a quality far inferior to that of Wankie, was at Nkandabwe. It could be exploited by the opencast method and the only real difficulty would be in constructing an access road through country which included a steep escarpment. There was a higher-quality and larger deposit at Siankandoba which would take longer to develop. The company set up to begin operations at Nkandabwe was owned in equal parts by the government and the mining companies. The latter agreed to provide technical advice – which was somewhat droll in the case of the Anglo American Corporation, larger of the copper groups; Anglo also controlled Wankie, which stood to suffer by Zambia's desire to achieve self-efficiency in coal. The mining companies contracted to buy the coal at cost, so that effectively they bore the cost of the project. Development at Siankandoba was on a different basis, with 100 per cent government ownership and a French concern doing the work on contract.

The entry into coal-mining was entirely a Zambian initiative. Britain made no moves, apart from talking in general terms after Smith's election victory in May of contingency planning for an airlift from Nairobi if the worst came to the worst. Wilson was confident until October of winning a victory over the Rhodesians at the negotiating table – he regarded detailed discussions of sanctions as superfluous and defeatist. The Zambians made a confidential request for several powerful aircraft engines to be installed on the Copperbelt as emergency generators for the mines in case Kariba was out of action. The proposal was dissipated in correspondence, the essential British objection being that the arrival of the engines in Zambia could be regarded by the Rhodesians as a provocative act.

Britain's unwillingness to embark upon contingency planning was illustrated only a few weeks before UDI. A Zambian delegation arrived in London with details of what it considered the minimum aid. The list was brushed aside with an assurance that "the possibility of UDI remained remote". The British officials added that even if Smith did make his declaration, the Rhodesian economy would crumble so swiftly that laborious preparations by Zambia were simply not needed.

In this, they were expressing the views of the Department of Economic Affairs – views which prevailed in the British Cabinet against the contentions of Arthur Bottomley and his advisers at the Commonwealth Office. The DEA was also in conflict on the subject with Barbara Castle's economists at the Ministry of Overseas Development. In the book *Crisis in the Civil Service*, this clash is hinted at by Dudley Seers, who was director general of the ODM economic planning staff at the time and later became head of the Institute of Development Studies at Sussex University. Seers describes how the DEA officials had a dominant effect on policy, and goes on: "They, for example, not the economists, were made responsible (rather oddly) for the application of sanctions against the Smith regime in Rhodesia, and thus for the advice to the Prime Minister at the end of 1965 that the regime would collapse in a very few months. . . . This staff work was almost unbelievably bad. At no time was there any serious effort to search for the weak points of the regime. . . ." Seers wrote from a detailed knowledge of Central Africa.*

Well before *Crisis in the Civil Service* appeared, a similar point was made by Arthur Wina, then Zambia's Finance Minister. In a closed session of the Commonwealth Conference on September 7, 1966, at the start of his main speech, Wina said: "As the country most closely affected by sanctions, Zambia may be permitted to explain a little more explicitly why we have never been able to accept that the application of sanctions

* See Chapter 11, p. 172.

would lead to the downfall of the Smith regime. The first reason, and it saddens me to state this, is because the campaign was so unbelievably poorly prepared. Indeed, it would perhaps be more accurate to say that it was scarcely prepared at all – staggering as this may seem when one considers that the British Government, having gratuitously thrown away even the deterrent threat of force, was itself forced to rely upon sanctions as its main weapon in the conflict. I do not suppose that anyone who was not in Lusaka shortly after UDI in November last year could realise just how poorly planned the initial measures were, or just how inadequate was the understanding of the Rhodesian economy and psychology upon which those forecasts of an early success were based."

Wina could well have reminded his audience that as early as November 1964 – a full year before UDI – the British had been advised against sanctions by Zambia. On that date, Kaunda was in London on his first State Visit as President. In confidential talks, Wilson put forward the idea and Kaunda replied that quite apart from the implications for Zambia, his experience of the Rhodesian whites caused him to doubt whether such methods would make them submit.

The Zambians were justified in complaining about the lack of foresight in Whitehall. Although their own expectations – that Smith would take the offensive against them – were inaccurate, they might well have assumed that the "mother country" would have matters well in hand. After all, Britain had continually told the United Nations that Rhodesia was her affair and she did not welcome interference. The storm clouds of UDI had been growing in the sky for nearly two years, yet even less preparations were made in London than in Salisbury where the planning was lackadaisical on any reckoning.

In Lusaka there were other preoccupations, focused upon the great post-independence surge of development work. The start of 1965 had seen the launching of a transitional plan, designed to last until the middle of the following year. It is significant that this plan took little account of the possibility of a Rhodesian rebellion and its effects on the Zambian economy. Admittedly, one major item was the building of a £5,000,000 airport at Lusaka – the second biggest in Africa and capable of taking any plane then flying or on a drawing board. But the need for a new airport at Lusaka had been recognised as early as 1958; the decision to go ahead with it had been taken by Kaunda and his Cabinet colleagues in 1964. The allocation of funds for tarring part of the Great North Road from Kapiri Mposhi to Mkushi was based purely upon traffic counts and the desire to encourage farming in a promising area. The crucial importance of the road, which links Zambia with Dar es Salaam, became apparent only when the sanctions pattern was established in 1966. The team of young economists clustered around Arthur Wina's Ministry of Finance and the Central Planning Office in Lusaka were concerned with attacking the new country's deficiencies. They grudgingly allocated, out of the £35,000,000 to be spent, £2,500,000 to defence – although nearly half of this was "one-for-all" capital expenditure on new barracks.

The priorities for Zambian development had been analysed shortly before in a long survey produced by a UN/ECA/FAO team, headed by Dr Seers. Many of the warnings in the survey – especially about the need to hold down wages – were to be ignored for political reasons, but the main arguments were beyond dispute: secondary education needed immediate expansion, the rural areas had to be wooed away from primitive subsistence farming, health facilities were lamentable, feeder roads inadequate, and much more besides. With occasional mentions of Rhodesia, the leaders in Lusaka flung themselves into arousing public enthusiasm for "The Plan".

But already there were ominous signs of overstrain in the administration, for more than half of the colonial civil servants had taken their pensions and departed in 1964. Some acted hurriedly to find new careers without losing time. Others were simply not prepared to serve a Black government – the Northern Rhodesia civil service had, for geographical reasons, a high proportion of white Rhodesians and South Africans in the clerical grades. Many of the existing women typists, in particular, could not face the idea of working for Africans; emotions were fanned by the stories of a UNIP minister who had made an overture to his white secretary.

The civil service dilemma went back to the British failure

to produce enough Zambians with secondary and university backgrounds. Of 2,500 graduate posts in the civil service at independence only 200 were filled by Africans – many of them non-Zambians; of 7,000 jobs calling for school certificate, more than 6,000 were being done by whites. Ministers dashed abroad, to Britain, New Zealand and the Irish Republic, on a hunt for recruits. The government bought a computer to make long-range projections of the manpower needs, and imported experts to run it. The heads of private businesses were asked to fill in questionnaires about the educational levels of their Zambian employees. "Zambianisation" became a key word in the vocabulary and in an effort to prove that it could have a visible meaning the decision was taken by Kaunda to replace the whites at the top of the civil service at the earliest moment. It was a daring move, for a year before only seven per cent of administrative posts had been occupied by Africans. But supernumeries were appointed to the permanent secretaries in each ministry – young graduates who would spend six months looking over the shoulder of the white man before moving into his chair. The new incumbents took over as expenditure on development projects began to reach levels never dreamed of before.

This was still an exhilarating period, before the worries crowded in. Foundations were laid for new secondary schools in every corner of the land as part of the greatest drive for education ever seen in an African country. It was the start of an expansion which was to increase secondary school enrolments from 10,986 in 1964 to 35,197 in 1967. Advisers from the Economic Commission for Africa had recommended the building of thirty new secondary classrooms a year. The plan called for 120. Yet the economy was expected to grow so fast that Zambia was like a hunter pursuing a quarry which was always moving away – the "Seers Report" had projected that the country would need 49,000 school certificate holders in 1975, of whom by that date only 24,000 could be Africans. This meant a shortfall of 25,000 – as against 20,000 in 1965 when only 1,640 Africans with school certificate were available. In West Africa, education had been incomparably further advanced, so that there were enough experienced men to take over the reins at the time of independence. Even an East African country such as Uganda possessed ten times as many school certificate holders as Zambia. So Britain's omissions while in power were to be compounded by her failure to remove the threat from across the Zambezi.

CHAPTER 9

A Matter of Weeks
rather than Months

For several weeks at the end of 1965, Kenneth Kaunda felt himself to be in the midst of a nightmare, a sequence of terrifying events from which there seemed no escape and which must end in unimaginable calamity. Harold Wilson had talked of "living with a nightmare" shortly before UDI, but in his case the horror would have been at a range of 5,000 miles. Kaunda foresaw it happening all around him. From November 11, the year-old Zambia faced the prospect of being an arena for full-scale racial war. This could be a conflict not only between a pan-African army based in the country and the white Rhodesians – who would probably be aided by South African volunteers – but also between the Zambians and the 70,000 whites living among them. Stretched almost to breaking point, Kaunda said desperately on November 25: "We are certainly drawing close to a third world war."

He believed that if only Britain would use troops to put down the rebellion, fighting would be brief and limited. But Wilson showed not the slightest sign of moving from the position he had taken for more than a year. A fortnight before UDI, the Archbishop of Canterbury, Dr Ramsey, had sent a public message to the British Premier: "If you and your government should judge it necessary to use force to sustain our country's obligations, I am sure a great body of Christian opinion would support you." Wilson's response had been cold: the Rhodesian problem was simply a constitutional one and could not be solved by arms. In the emotional but unproductive Commons debates after UDI, his one aim was to carry the Conservatives with him on a sanctions policy – difficult enough despite the weakness of the measures. Any hint of force would have made Heath and his Shadow Cabinet abandon bi-partisanship.

A vote on the issue would have brought Labour to defeat, for the party had a majority of four and several of its back-benchers, led by Reginald Paget and Fred Bellenger, were ready to defy the whips. For Wilson, the retention of power was the beacon by which he steered his course.

But if Britain was reluctant, there were others ready to fill the vacuum. Most militant were the Arab countries of north Africa, led by Algeria and the Egyptians. As early as 1962, Algerian representatives at the United Nations had approached Rhodesian nationalists and offered to supply guerrilla fighters from their own army. Now Colonel Houari Boumedienne saw a chance to remove the cloud which was hanging over him through the overthrow in mid-1965 of Ben Bella; the African countries had condemned the coup, but the memory might be erased if Algeria could play a leading role in destroying the Smith regime. For his part, Colonel Gamal Nasser had on paper the most powerful military force on the continent outside South Africa. A few months earlier there had been a massive parade of armed strength in Cairo with tanks, rockets and artillery, while jets flew in formation overhead. If the Organisation of African Unity could organise a force on the Zambezi, the stage would be set for an encounter which might destroy the "white counter-attack" and simultaneously expose the feebleness of Britain. In Accra, President Nkrumah proposed that the United Nations should authorise the African states to carry out a "police action" if Britain proved incapable and should guarantee protection against any interference from the Portuguese or South Africans; mobilisation was ordered in Ghana. The Congolese offered full facilities for the transit of OAU troops through its territory.

All this was exhilarating for leaders whose borders were well away from the projected area of battle. For Kaunda it was appalling. The prospect that Rhodesia's Canberra jets would bomb all African capitals within range if Smith was pushed against the wall had already been expounded – with what seemed like excessive relish – by Malawi's Dr Banda; he had ordered his populace to "carry on working as if nothing had happened". It appeared likely, should OAU troops begin moving into Zambia, that Rhodesia would retaliate violently — Lusaka might be in ruins, the copper mines smashed, Kariba power cut off. . . . At every point, Zambia was vulnerable.

Kaunda could not even rely upon the loyalty of his own army officers if the worst happened. There was no African above the rank of captain, because in the days of Federation it was not the policy to commission non-whites. Some of the senior officers were Rhodesians or South Africans who had made little effort to disguise where their sympathies lay. They told their friends that if fighting started on the Zambezi they would merely keep on advancing until they had joined up with their former colleagues. On the other hand, it was obvious that the Rhodesian army and air force would have no hesitation about attacking Zambia if ordered to do so — not one white officer in the south had resigned his commission after UDI. In Salisbury, derision had greeted Harold Wilson's order on November 12: "Members of the armed forces and the police in Southern Rhodesia should refrain from taking up arms in support of the illegal regime, and from doing anything which would help them to pursue their unlawful courses."

Rodney Putterill, the army commander and close friend of Ian Smith, had done his job well in weeding out doubtful elements. His tactic was to ask officers whether they would be prepared to swear an oath of allegiance to Rhodesia, if this proved necessary. One man who failed this test was the air force Commander, Alfred Bentley. He was retired at short notice and went to live in South Africa. Bentley was replaced by Harold Hawkins, a man much more to the taste of Smith and Putterill. Although in 1964, Hawkins had been regarded as suspect because of his close associations with the Royal Air Force, he gradually came around. Like Putterill, he was a sportsman and President of the Rhodesian Rugby Union — the two men had often taken the field together. In long conversations at the Salisbury Sports Club, Hawkins was won over and with his appointment was promoted to air Vice-Marshal.

Kaunda's uncertainties about the Zambian police were even more acute. Ten days before UDI, Kaunda had suddenly

appointed a Zambian, Michael Mataka, to be Police Commissioner. But under Mataka were scores of senior white
officers, many of them truculent or cynical. They had worked
their way up with the Colonial Government and had a fund of
stories about the occasions in the old days when they had
arrested Kaunda and his colleagues in political round-ups.
The area of potential racial explosion – where the role of the
police would be crucial – was the Copperbelt. The white
miners had held celebration parties on the night of November
11 with toasts to "good old Smithy". The government-owned
(but largely white-run) television station at Kitwe in the centre
of the Copperbelt had blandly carried in its programme on
UDI day a series of interviews with white miners and their
wives who without exception supported the rebellion and said
they hoped it would succeed. There seemed a likelihood that
rioting could spring from arguments between the races about
events in Rhodesia; in the humid and dusty mining towns,
groups of youths watched each other, waiting for the first
move. Kaunda had given orders that UNIP officials were not to
react to provocation; they must work "day and night" to
prevent clashes. But there was little hope in Lusaka that
trouble could be avoided. If it came, the police force might be
seriously torn within itself as to the racial group it should
treat as aggressors.

Two weeks after UDI the first incident of sabotage in Zambia
occurred. A power pylon was wrecked with charges of gelignite
a few miles from Kitwe, bringing the Copperbelt almost to a
standstill for twenty-four hours. The pylon was on the line
carrying a load of more than 200 megawatts from Kariba.
Supplies from a hydro-electric station at Le Marinel in Katanga
were boosted to their maximum and thermal plant on the
Copperbelt was put into operation. But the incident had
demonstrated in dramatic fashion the frailty of Zambia. The
press speculated that the explosion might have been caused by
Smith supporters intent upon giving the Zambian authorities a
warning. The white police officers conducting investigations
reacted sharply to the theory, saying that they were more
disposed to think that the sabotage was the work of Africans –
Rhodesian nationalists "causing trouble". They brushed aside

the point that the nationalist exiles were concentrated upon Lusaka, 200 miles south of Kitwe and that white miners would have easy access to explosives. It emerged later that the explosives came from Mufulira, the mining town near Kitwe. The culprits were never found.

Some months later, Kaunda felt obliged to dismiss almost his entire white special branch, including ten men with the rank of superintendent. He was tipped off by the British High Commission that some of them might be leaking secrets to Salisbury and also deliberately withholding information from him. The officers were taken to their offices under the escort of Zambian security men to collect their belongings, and then ordered to stop working immediately. The first news of the purge was given to a Lusaka newspaper office, in an anonymous telephone call from Salisbury. Most of the sacked men went to live in South Africa or Rhodesia, after being paid off in full.

Before the end of November 1965, Kaunda knew that he must act quickly to prevent a racial conflagration in Central Africa. An emergency meeting of the Council of Ministers of the Organisation of African Unity was due to be held in Addis Ababa on December 3. The purpose would be to organise an OAU military force to invade Rhodesia — from Zambia. The quandary was acute. Kaunda had been President of PAFMECSA, the Pan-African Freedom Movement for East, Central and South Africa. If ever there was an occasion which invited joint African action, this was it. Groundwork for the Addis Ababa meeting was laid by the OAU Defence Committee, meeting in Dar es Salaam. The chairman, Oscar Kambona, said that UDI was a "deliberate affront to the dignity of the African people". It had to be met with the "greatest force".

Kambona was Tanzania's Foreign Minister and his opposite number in Zambia, Simon Kapwepwe, was in full agreement with this approach. In Kapwepwe's thinking there was no room for half measures. He did not believe that Britain meant business against Ian Smith, he had no confidence in sanctions, and the idea of an African liberation army possessed a strong romantic appeal. There was a considerable conflict between Kaunda and Kapwepwe over the former's announcement, in anticipation of the OAU Defence Committee's meeting, that he was asking Britain to send in a military force. If the British established a "presence" — in the UN terminology — it would be almost impossible for anyone else to move in. Kaunda had disclosed his anxieties to the three East African leaders, Kenyatta, Obote and Nyerere, by sending his Vice-President, Reuben Kamanga, to a hastily-arranged meeting in Nairobi. In the conflict of views in Lusaka, Kamanga was docile. So by the time the Defence Committee began talking, ground-work was already laid.

The Committee's membership consisted of Zambia itself, Kenya, Tanzania, Nigeria and Egypt. However militant Kambona might be, Nyerere had already accepted Kaunda's line of forcing Britain to take the military initiative; within eighteen months, as it turned out, Nyerere and Oscar Kambona were to be involved in a struggle of wills on other issues, which the former won easily. Both Kenyatta and Sir Abubakar Tafawa Balewa, the Nigerian premier, were against a war policy. This left only the Egyptian representative, an under-secretary named Zayat. On November 21, Zayat left Dar es Salaam unexpectedly for Lusaka with the Zambian and Kenyan delegates. The committee broke up without issuing any communiqué.

By November 23, Kaunda was holding talks in Lusaka with Malcolm MacDonald, Britain's special representative in East and Central Africa. He told MacDonald what he wanted, both in the air and on the ground, and why. Two days later he piled on pressure by announcing that offers of troops from unnamed countries were "flowing in daily". That weekend, Common-wealth Secretary Arthur Bottomley boarded an RAF Comet in London with a team of military advisers. He had a mandate to offer Kaunda what he sought, on terms.

Wilson had realised that unless he did meet the Zambian leader's demand before an OAU army moved towards the Zambezi, he would lose any semblance of control over the UDI crisis. There would be a war in which the "liberation army" might well be defeated with heavy bloodshed, the OAU would turn to Russia or China to save them, and the whole of southern Africa would become a holocaust. Leaving other considerations aside, this would mean an economic calamity for Britain, because of her vast interests in South Africa. Even if the Russians acted within the United Nations framework – which was by no means certain in view of the recent Soviet antagonism to the UN operation in the Congo – the whole balance of power politics in Africa would be altered. It was in the interest of the West that Britain should make a pre-emptive move; Kaunda's own fear of the unknown gave the perfect excuse, and it was taken with alacrity.

The first definite news of what was in the offing was presented to the Commons by Wilson on December 1. There had already been speculation, but now it was confirmed that Kaunda had asked for jet fighters and a battalion of ground troops. To forestall criticism from the Opposition, Wilson remarked that because the bulk of the Federal air force had been given to Rhodesia – when the Conservatives were in office – Zambia felt herself without effective means of defence. He also stressed: "These forces sent to Zambia will go there purely for defensive purposes." But Britain would not stand idly by if Smith cut off the power supplies from Kariba to the Copperbelt.

Pressed by Edward Heath, the Labour leader explained without equivocation what the real motives of the British offer were: "It is a fact that if we have to maintain the position that we have asserted, that Rhodesia is our responsibility, we should do everything in our power to prevent the stationing of other air forces in Zambia, wherever they may come from, as a means of providing air cover for President Kaunda." This was a good card, for as much as the Conservatives might dislike the despatch of Javelins with a defensive guarantee, they would abhor the thought of the white Rhodesians coming under attack from Ilyushins and MIGs. In response to Heath's ponderous questioning about "not standing idly by" if Smith paralysed the Zambia mines, Wilson produced the argument of Britain's self-interest: "Rhodesian copper is absolutely vital to our own industrial production, as well as to the economy of Zambia. . . ." It was somewhat revealing that he should have described the copper as being Rhodesian; but then, most people in Britain still regarded Zambia as a part of Rhodesia which had chosen to secede.

David Ennals, a Labour back-bencher earmarked for pro-
motion, asked Wilson: "Is my Right Hon Friend aware that
there is in this country a tremendous respect for the courage
and statesmanship of President Kaunda in the difficulties with
which Zambia is faced?" This was a cue for Wilson to lift a
corner of the curtain around the talks which Bottomley and
MacDonald were having in Lusaka. He said that Kaunda was
"subject to the most tremendous pressures" and suggested that
these pressures were the cause of difficulties in the discussions.
Britain was ready to consider stationing part of a battalion on
the Zambezi – but only on the north bank. Unless Smith made a
move, there was no intention of occupying the Kariba power
station. Sir Alec Douglas-Home pleaded for a clear explanation
of the government's intentions, and after being reminded
that the Conservatives and Labour had been blackmailed
for a year apiece by the threat to cut off Kariba power,
was told that it was no good talking about a deterrent unless
there was a readiness to make it effective. It appeared
that Wilson was intent upon a commando operation to cut
off Rhodesian power in retaliation, if Zambia's lines went
dead.

In Lusaka, Bottomley was arguing from another position.
He told Kaunda that if British troops moved in, Smith would
have to keep all his own forces on the alert, including the
territorials. This would create an impossible strain on the
Rhodesian economy and quickly bring the rebellion to an
end. Should Zambia's power be cut off in the closing stages, the
British troops would then be ready and waiting to cross over to
the south bank. It was a good case, but Kaunda would have
none of it. Although Arthur Wina, the Minister of Finance,
was persuaded, Simon Kapwepwe was adamant. Kapwepwe
insisted that unless the British were willing to attack, the field
should be left clear for an OAU force. The doubts and divisions
around Kaunda were hinted at in a newspaper interview he
gave just after Bottomley had flown home: "It is a terrible
problem for the Zambian Cabinet and me to decide whether
Mr Wilson is determined with sufficient single-mindedness to
carry his task through to the end. Mr Bottomley explained to
me at length the difficulties of the Labour Government with

their tiny majority. I understood that difficulty. But what is good politics in England may be bad politics in Africa."

The decision ultimately reached was an apparent compromise. Britain would send in twelve Javelins, with several hundred troops of the RAF Regiment for airport defence. In theory, this would still allow an OAU force to enter Zambia – but only with British consent. In practice it ruled out the danger of what Wilson called "an already explosive situation becoming still more explosive". He had forecast that the RAF in Zambia would help to cool the situation down; in defending an oil embargo, which he had agreed with President Johnson during a visit to Washington, he stressed that everything possible should be done to prevent a military solution being sought by anyone else. Once more he appealed to the national pride of the Conservatives by arguing that Rhodesia was Britain's responsibility and should be kept that way. All December, Heath was in a cleft stick, for if he opposed the spoiling tactics of putting in the Javelins, he might find himself accused of opening the way for the Egyptians and Ethiopians.

Kapwepwe said bleakly that the Javelins were obsolete planes which would be no match for the Rhodesian Hunters – a judgement derived ironically enough from an article in a pro-Rhodesian British newspaper. It was the only way he could find to voice his displeasure at what had happened. He knew that the British had effectively occupied Zambia's air space, and that any OAU force would need fighter cover both during its build-up and at the moment of attack. Britain certainly would not provide it. On December 2, a source close to Kaunda said that Britain's conditions for sending in the Javelins were that the RAF should have operational control over the three main airfields at Ndola, Lusaka and Livingstone; it was added that military transport planes of other nations would now find it "difficult" to use the bases. The crucial OAU meeting started in Addis Ababa on December 3.

The meeting was an unparalleled disaster for African unity and a source of much satisfaction for Ian Smith and his colleagues. Although quarrels between President Nkrumah and eight French-speaking leaders had kept the latter away from the Summit Conference in Accra the previous October, some semblance of order had then been maintained. But this time in Addis Ababa, in the very hall where the OAU had been founded, complete bewilderment ruled.

The conference opened with a solemn speech by Haile Selassie in which he called upon all African countries to sink minor disagreements, to rescue the "brethren in Zimbabwe". If called upon to act in unison, Ethiopia was ready to make whatever sacrifices were needed. The seizure of power by the Rhodesians was one of the greatest political crimes in human history. On behalf of Nkrumah, the Ghanaian minister Kojo Botsio asserted that Africa should be prepared to "die a little", and the question before the delegates was how all the continent's forces should be mobilised to install a majority government in Rhodesia. Foreign ministers from countries such as Guinea and Algeria spoke in equally militant terms.

But behind the rhetoric was a confused emotion – part frustration, part relief – born of the knowledge that there could be no expeditionary force for the Zambezi because Britain had arrived there first. Simon Kapwepwe found himself in a position of acute anguish. After two days, a communiqué was issued. It charged that UDI had been proclaimed "with the connivance of the government of Britain", and asserted that the OAU itself had decided to put an end to the illegal regime. But the methods to be employed were not revealed, apart from the hint that the Defence Committee would co-ordinate military aid to freedom-fighters inside Rhodesia. The most spectacular result was an announcement that Britain had been given an ultimatum: if she did not end the rebellion by December 15, all 35 states represented in Addis would break off diplomatic relations with her.

It was what might be called a negative threat, and evoked memories in Britain of the African boycott tactic at constitutional conferences in the early sixties. Generally it increased sympathy for Ian Smith. Moreover, whereas the gesture would be a formality for countries like Congo-Brazzaville and Mauritania, it could be painful in the extreme for the ex-British territories. They might lose a great deal of aid and technical assistance. Certain foreign ministers returned home in embarrassment and were icily received. In a speech on December 8, Kaunda helped some of his friends off the hook. He said that as President of Zambia he felt it was his duty to explain the difficult position in which he would find himself by breaking diplomatic ties. He did not define the difficulties, but one would have been the departure of the newly-arrived Javelins, with all the implications of that.

Two days later, President Kenyatta addressed his parliament in Nairobi and mentioned that Kaunda had "expressed serious doubts" about breaking diplomatic relations. President Obote of Uganda explained that several African countries had appealed to him not to take the step. Nigeria said that it would achieve nothing. Even Ethiopia turned back from the brink, although the emperor was the father-figure of the OAU. In the end, only a quarter of the African countries went ahead – and the Somalis had to borrow a guide to diplomatic practice from the British ambassador in Mogadishu to learn the way to sever relations. White Rhodesian politicians asked sarcastically how the Africans could mount an invasion if they could not even organise a diplomatic boycott.

The notable exception in English-speaking East and Central Africa to the general retreat from the militancy of the OAU resolution was Tanzania. Julius Nyerere had a devotion to principle which raised him above the ordinary forum of politics and at midnight on December 15 the break came into effect. It was to cost Tanzania £7,000,000 in British aid. Nyerere returned to his stand at the previous Commonwealth Conference. It was not a matter of the time Britain might take to end the Rhodesian rebellion. That could be argued about. "Our anger and suspicion arises from the fact that Britain is not, even now, committed to the principle of independence only on the basis of majority rule." The close personal relationship between Nyerere and Kaunda led outsiders to speculate that Tanzania had tried to persuade Zambia to follow the same course, but without success. In reality, the two leaders had agreed that while Tanzania should make the public gesture, it was essential for Zambia as the African country most involved in sanctions to keep open lines of communication to Whitehall. Nyerere also accepted Kaunda's objections to an OAU liberation army and understood the need to keep the RAF in Zambia until the pattern of events became more clear.

After the Addis Ababa debacle, Wilson realised that he had the reins more firmly in his hands. He had been given the time in which sanctions could take their toll of Rhodesia as he was sure they would. There was little cause for alarm in the Zambian gambit of sending ministerial missions to Washington and Moscow in search of support; Kaunda hoped for an offer of troops to "take out" the Kariba power station. But the Americans would not dream of interfering in a British sphere and were, in any case, sinking deeper into the mire of the Vietnam conflict. The Russians were more of a puzzle – they never missed an opportunity to give Britain a verbal thrashing at the United Nations over Rhodesia, but when asked to produce the military goods they might prove less aggressive. So it turned out. The Russians had never shown much interest in Zambia and had offered the country nothing except 2,500,000 doses of smallpox vaccine. The Soviet ambassador in Lusaka was a retired admiral, genial but ineffectual. Kaunda's emissaries to Moscow were Arthur Wina (Finance) and Elijah Mudenda (Agriculture), the two most polished and Western-orientated members of the Cabinet – the former had studied at the University of California and the latter at Cambridge. They came back empty-handed, the Kremlin even refusing to supply planes for the airlift to Zambia which was in the course of preparation. Two months earlier Kaunda had accepted an invitation to make a State visit to the Soviet Union, but it was subsequently abandoned. The mission to Washington was led by Kapwepwe and by contrast was promised US help with the airlift.

The next positive move came from the Nigerian premier, Sir Abubakar Tafawa Balewa, who was regarded as the most moderate and stable African leader in the Commonwealth. He proposed a conference in Lagos to discuss the Rhodesian crisis and Wilson agreed that he would "look in". Not all the Commonwealth premiers responded favourably – in Canberra, Sir Robert Menzies said he had no intention of being present. President Nkrumah was irritated at this show of initiative by his West African rival and said it was a time for action, not words and promises. But the planning for the conference went ahead with a scheduled date of January 11, and in the event nineteen countries were represented.

The occasion was a tactical triumph for Wilson. He confronted his critics and spoke to them with easy confidence. There were demands for force, especially from Sir Albert Margai of Sierra Leone, but Wilson undermined them by presenting the forecasts of the Department of Economic Affairs. The most significant – and subsequently most ludicrous – section of the communiqué said: "The Prime Ministers noted the statement by the British Prime Minister that on the expert advice available to him, the cumulative effects of the economic and financial sanctions might well bring the rebellion to an end within a matter of weeks rather than months." Many of the signatories had doubts, but the forecast was on record.

Wilson shook hands with his host, Sir Abubakar, and the usual platitudes were exchanged. The conference had been a success for Nigeria as well. The date was January 12. There had been a rash of military coups in French-speaking West Africa, the latest in Upper Volta, but nobody took much heed.

Before going back to London, Wilson flew south to Lusaka. It was a long and exhausting detour, but some gesture to the beleaguered Zambians was essential. At first, Kaunda was cool and reserved. He repeated the Zambian assertion that sanctions could not be effective and stressed the dire position caused by the petrol shortage; a few days earlier there had only been enough fuel left in the country to maintain essential services for thirty-six hours. Wilson was sympathetic, then waving his aides aside took the Zambian president off for a stroll around the grounds of Lusaka's State House. When the two rejoined the main party, Kaunda's attitude was transformed. He said later that Britain and Zambia were now "nearer to each other than ever before". He expressed new confidence that Smith would soon be brought down. There was astonishment among the press corps as to how Wilson could have achieved this feat. Even Bottomley seemed surprised.

Wilson had revealed to Kaunda that he was about to call a British general election which he confidently believed would give Labour a substantial majority. Armed with this, he could by the end of March pursue a new hard line against the Smith regime; even military intervention need not be ruled out, for if the experts were to be believed, the sanctions – on oil in particular – would have reduced Rhodesia to confusion and lawlessness. Moreover, just to make sure that the rebellion would crumble on time, extra sanctions would be laid on in the middle of February. Wilson described this as the "quick kill" approach.

Kaunda was considerably impressed that Harold (as he had come to call him) should reveal to him his general election plans, which were not to be made public until late in February. The whole package, as presented on the stroll around the gardens, was most convincing. Kaunda's doubts about Britain's intentions were overcome. At the next meeting of the Zambian Cabinet, he gave a résumé of the talk. He said to his colleagues: "I am sure that Harold will do the right thing at the right time." Even Kapwepwe's forebodings were stilled. Before Wilson left Lusaka he gave a press conference in which he hinted that the use of force to restore law and order in Rhodesia might still be possible. It was a high-water-mark. But only hours distant was an event which was going to change Britain's whole vision of Africa.

The more percipient of the journalists who covered the Lagos conference also reported dangerous symptoms in Nigeria's internal affairs. The Western Region had been racked by disorders since the previous October, when elections had been blatantly rigged by Chief Akintola, the regional premier. Akintola was involved in a conspiracy with the premier of the Northern Region, Sir Ahmadu Bello, to maintain power for the Muslims of Nigeria. Tribal fighting had produced more than 600 deaths since the elections and when the Commonwealth Conference began there were steel-helmeted riot police holding down trouble in the Lagos suburbs. Sir Abubakar had appeared imperturbable to Harold Wilson – who did not know that the northerners were planning to assume power while the Nigerian President, Dr Nnamdi Azikiwe, was away in London for medical treatment. Sir Ahmadu Bello was only waiting until the Commonwealth leaders had departed from the scene. The conference had delayed events.

But before Sir Ahmadu could stage his coup, a group of young army officers – mainly Ibos from the Eastern Region – went ahead with their own. They snatched Sir Abubakar from the official residence where four days before he had been chatting to his fellow premiers; thirty miles from Lagos they shot him and buried him in a shallow grave. In the north, they took Sir Ahmadu Bello from his harem and executed him against a wall. In the west they killed Chief Akintola at his desk.

Later that day, the British High Commissioner, Sir Francis Cumming-Bruce, went to the police headquarters in Lagos. He met the army commander, Major-General Aguyi-Ironsi, who was preparing to take control of the country but was himself to be assassinated six months later. Outside, the streets of the capital were crowded with people laughing and joking about the downfall of corrupt and venal politicians.

In Britain, there was only a confused idea of what had happened for several days, since all communications between Nigeria and the outside world had been cut off. Then the picture came into focus and the shock was immense. Nigeria was Africa made in Britain's image. Its lawyers had been called to the English bar, its officers trained at Sandhurst, its legislatures were carefully modelled on Westminster. Some black civil servants were so orientated towards Britain that they even called it "home" and went there when the time for long leave came around. Others played polo and rugby. Yet excessives apart, it had been a great experiment, a showpiece with a population of 55,000,000 – and British investment worth £250,000,000.

Socialists and Conservatives alike were stunned, on one hand because faith was so cruelly undermined, on the other because Africans like Balewa and Bello had seemed bastions against radicalism. The *Daily Express*,* tireless supporter of the white man's citadel, was quick to take advantage of the general dismay. It editorialised: "Those who warned that Africans were not ready for democracy have been proved abundantly right. There is little Britain can do now for Nigeria beyond offering condolences to the bereaved and moral support to the forces of

* See Chapter 16, p. 231.

law and order. But there is something Mr Wilson can do for
Africa. And that is to seek a swift settlement with Mr Smith's
government in Rhodesia. Here, at least, we can help to pre-
serve one part of Africa from chaos."

In Accra, President Nkrumah offered a different judgement.
He said that Sir Abubakar had been a martyr to a neo-
colonialism of which he was only a figurehead. "He was
deluded, perhaps, despite his personal modesty, by the applause
of Western countries who lauded Nigeria as the one true
democracy of Africa." It was a comment of some validity, but
Nkrumah himself was not without his failings. A month later
he was himself to be overthrown by a military coup. The
events in Nigeria and Ghana at the start of 1966 not only
comforted the Smith regime and weakened British policy.
They erased any lingering thoughts of an African initiative to
bring about a military showdown on the Zambezi.

CHAPTER 10

Paper Tiger and Toothless Bulldog

As Wilson parted from Kaunda in Lusaka in the middle of January 1966, it was agreed between them that sanctions should be "given time to work". Kaunda withdrew his demand for a precise time-limit, although he was thinking in terms of about two months. Asked later whether he could hold on for a Rhodesian solution until the next Commonwealth leaders' conference – proposed for July – he replied: "I do not think we will have the patience to wait until that time." He had trouble with his Cabinet and told the Commonwealth Secretary, Arthur Bottomley, that the political risks involved in Zambia must be recognised in Britain. But Kaunda was able to carry through one promise to Wilson, that he would dissuade any of his ministers from making statements which could damage the Labour Party's chances in the forthcoming general election. Kaunda told his Cabinet repeatedly: "I am sure that Harold will do the right thing at the right time." So nobody spoke out of turn. Once again, Wilson was tailoring events in Central Africa to his domestic needs.

An immediate outcome of the Lusaka talks was the despatch to Zambia of Major-General Willoughby, the officer commanding British troops in the Middle East. The ostensible reason was for Willoughby to discuss the flying in of British forces from Aden if there was a call to maintain law and order in Rhodesia. In reality, he was looking at the military possibilities around the Kariba Dam, since the Zambians were still afraid that Smith might cut off their power supplies – which could cause the flooding of the copper mines by putting underground pumps out of action, apart from causing a general paralysis in the towns. Shortly after UDI, Wilson had talked about "taking out" Kariba and the Rhodesians had spread a baseless story that the underground turbines on the south bank were already mined, so that they could be destroyed if Britain tried to seize the dam. Willoughby drove down from Lusaka to Kariba and from a lookout post on the northern side of the gorge, studied the dam. In the centre of the wall the Rhodesians had established a sand-bagged machine-gun post; on the far side there were more troops, guarding the entrance to the underground installations. Willoughby and the three other members of the British team agreed with the white officers in charge of the Zambian army (many of whom had Rhodesian connections) that any attempt to neutralise Kariba should be ruled out. The only possible mode of attack would be across Lake Kariba at night; however, the Rhodesians had armed patrol boats on the lake. It would also be essential to make an air drop to capture the airfield on the southern side. Even so, the Rhodesians would probably have time to destroy the power-house before it could be taken.

Willoughby's reconnaissance was followed early in February by a mission from the Organisation of African Unity, led by the Ghanaian chief of staff, Major-General Aferi. It expressed itself dismayed by the complexity of the military problem; moreover, Aferi was to be removed before the end of the month, following the coup which deposed Kwame Nkrumah. This was effectively the end of orthodox military approaches to the UDI dilemma. The British Javelins maintained their patrols over Zambia but never made contact with the Rhodesian Hunters watching along the Zambezi. After the first weeks of tension, Zambia withdrew her own troops from the border. The fighting, when it began, was to be of a different variety – between the Rhodesians and nationalist guerrillas. The first major clash came in April, when seven members of the Zimbabwe African National Union were killed eighty miles from Salisbury.

As the weeks went by, anxious attention was directed to the various aspects of sanctions. The British began to make a minute analysis of the rebel economy, and to all questions they offered a stock response: whatever else happened, Smith would not be able to sell his next tobacco crop, which was due to be auctioned in Salisbury during March and April. The Commonwealth Office argued that the tobacco farmers were the backbone of Smith's Rhodesian Front party, and when they found themselves facing bankruptcy, the rebellion would fold up like a house of cards. Tobacco was Rhodesia's biggest single export, worth nearly £50,000,000 a year, and Britain was the biggest buyer. In a broadcast in the middle of March, Wilson said: "Of course, we haven't yet reached the key moment of the year, when they will try to market their main crop."

The fancy that Smith would stop in his tracks if the tobacco earnings were threatened had long mesmerised the Commonwealth Office, which was advised by its High Commission in Salisbury on these lines. Nine months before UDI, Arthur Bottomley had advocated in the Cabinet that Britain should refuse to buy its normal forty per cent of the 1965 crop, as a mark of disapproval. He conceded the argument that Rhodesia would be able to sell elsewhere on the world market what Britain had denied herself. But the price would be lower.

The Bottomley plan for a "demonstration of intent" had been rejected on financial grounds: the £20,000,000 or so which Britain paid yearly to Rhodesia in sterling would still be needed to buy tobacco from somewhere, and probably in dollars. The Treasury took a bearish view and it would certainly have had the support of the parliamentary Opposition in its disapproval of self-denial for political ideals. Finally, Wilson felt that while he still had hopes of reaching a solution by talking, such aggressive tactics would make Smith even more inflexible.

The first indication of how Britain envisaged enforcing a return to legality without bloodshed had been given quickly, on November 11. The rebels would not be allowed to buy arms from Britain; financial aid to Rhodesia would be halted (there had been a £3,000,000 grant in the previous year); Britain would stop buying Rhodesian tobacco and sugar (for the latter there had previously been the guaranteed-price advantage of the Commonwealth Agreement); there would be exchange control restrictions and Rhodesia would no longer have access to the London capital market.

Finally, Rhodesian passports would not be recognised. Wilson suggested to the Commons that these moves were "harsh" and capable of bringing the rebellion to an early end. Even a month after UDI, he was proclaiming: "The government consider that quick and effective measures will involve less suffering than a long-drawn-out agony."

But Smith had also been making preparations. His own economists had for months been anticipating what Britain might do and must have been pleasantly surprised at how far removed from harshness the first embargoes really were. Starting several weeks before UDI, gold and other assets were moved from London to Switzerland. There had been no attempt to prevent this and £22,000,000 was extricated in good time. Financially-aware onlookers, who had been surprised when Treasury officials made no move before UDI were amazed at what happened later. A young Liberal peer, Lord Reay, asked a fortnight after UDI what action was being taken to safeguard funds standing in the name of the Government of Rhodesia, in the Reserve Bank of Rhodesia. He wanted to know whether their use by the rebels could be prevented. Lord Beswick, parliamentary under-secretary of State for Commonwealth Relations, conceded that the government was finding out whether "any actions along these lines were practicable".

Something did happen the following week, when Britain announced that it was taking over the Rhodesian Reserve Bank and appointing its own Governor. The man chosen for this thankless role – the horses he was meant to lock in having already fled – was Sir Sidney Caine, head of the London School of Economics. Having surveyed the assets, Sir Sydney announced bravely that no central bank or government had denied his board's claim to be the legal custodian of Rhodesia's external reserves. It had, certainly, proved possible to freeze about £9,000,000 in Britain – but the rebel Governor in Salisbury, a Mr Noel Bruce, was far from being without funds. He also ignored all orders from London, and informed the commercial banks in Rhodesia that they must obey him.

The banks were then told from their head offices in London they were "on their own". This merely meant that they continued operating as before, but could not call for money from Britain. Financial experts in South Africa estimated that the Rhodesian commercial banks held rather more than £3,000,000 in foreign currency at the time of UDI. The rebel Reserve Bank also began to prepare a list of shares owned by Rhodesian citizens, so that orders could be given for these to be sold if the foreign exchange position became desperate. *The Financial Mail* of South Africa estimated that these were worth upwards of £25,000,000. While some of the scrip was in London and so out of reach, the bulk was readily available in Johannesburg. Also in South Africa was about £6,000,000 in Rhodesian reserves – formally frozen but quietly treated by the Bank of South Africa as co-lateral security. Moreover, South Africa continued to accept Rhodesian currency at par.

Ian Smith and his Finance Minister, John Wrathall, were quick to claim that Wilson had played a "dirty trick" by setting up a rival Reserve Bank. They took retaliatory measures. All payments due to companies or individuals in Britain would be paid into blocked accounts in Salisbury, while Rhodesia would no longer service its public debt of £108,000,000 owed largely to Britain and the World Bank; Smith dryly explained that people who wanted money due to them should apply to Downing Street, which had some point since £66,000,000 in Rhodesian bonds was held in Britain.

As a positive step to bring in hard currencies, Zambia was told that she would have to pay for all future imports with US or Canadian dollars – although Swiss francs might also be acceptable. Zambian imports from Rhodesia were running at more than £30,000,000 yearly, including more than £1,000,000 for Wankie coal without which the Copperbelt would be paralysed.

Smith had long before slipped out of the corner into which Wilson was belatedly trying to pin him. The counter-punch was felt mainly by Kenneth Kaunda, whose vexation was understandable. When by late December it was plain that Sir Sydney was in a ludicrous position, more questions were asked by Lord Reay. They reflected a growing concern for

Britain's impotence. What Rhodesian assets had been located? Was any statement of the position to be issued? Would commercial banks be prosecuted for making funds available to Smith? Would the government tell the subsidiaries in Rhodesia of British companies that they must not use reserves to buy imports? Would the government tell British commercial banks in Rhodesia to call in overdrafts? Would Britain devalue the Rhodesian pound? The noble lords (many of whom had substantial interests in Rhodesia) considered this to be wild and extremist talk, not worthy of their House. From the government, there was no reply. In February, Smith said flatly: "We have won the financial war."

Yet of far more moment than all the financial shadow-boxing was the role of South Africa on sanctions. The key to the ultimate success or immediate failure of UDI was in the hands of Dr Hendrik Verwoerd in Pretoria. In diplomatic contacts the South Africans had been ominously vague, and public comments were few. One came from Dr Hilgard Muller, the South African Foreign Minister, while he was visiting Berne a fortnight before UDI, in the course of a European tour: "This is a matter which only concerns Rhodesia. South Africa's policy is not to interfere in other countries' affairs." The Swiss bankers took the point: there would be business as usual. Two days after UDI, Dr Verwoerd was more explicit: "We will continue to deal with one another in economic and other matters as before." This was the decisive statement – whoever else might join Britain in sanctions, South Africa would not; it meant that there could be no quick solution.

It was inevitable that Verwoerd should take such a line, and there seems no reason why Britain should not have been so advised by its embassy in Pretoria. Any "abandonment" of the whites in Rhodesia would have been a crucial issue in South African politics. The waning United Party, led by Sir de Villers Graaff, would have taken full advantage of this to accuse the ruling Nationalist Party of isolationism and Afrikaans bigotry. It would have destroyed Verwoerd's new-found support in Natal – always "more British than the British". Natal regarded itself as having much in common with Rhodesia – where the Union Jack still flew, rebellion or no rebellion.

In the early months of sanctions, the United Party several times accused the government of lacking sympathy for the Salisbury regime. But the facts did not sustain the accusation. The South African Government had long opposed UDI and Verwoerd had tried, unsuccessfully, to deter Smith – as he had been able to do four years before with Welensky. A Rhodesian rebellion, however it turned out, would destroy the *status quo* in southern Africa. So many dangerous possibilities could spring from it that Pretoria's long-range African strategy – still very tentative at this period – might be thrown into entire confusion. There might be a need for commitments, both economic and military, north of the Limpopo which the *platteland* wing of the National Party would instinctively resist.

But when UDI was clearly inevitable, then Verwoerd knew that above all it must not be overcome by sanctions. Much better, if the Rhodesians were to be defeated, that it should be by force of arms. The South African Government had never seriously feared a military challenge to its own position – the international force which would be needed to undertake an invasion put the idea in the realms of fantasy. But sanctions were far less improbable and if they worked against Rhodesia the stimulus to the United Nations "sanctioneers" would be tremendous. South Africa would be next on the list.

The blueprints existed in Manhattan. By 1965 more than thirty resolutions aimed directly at South Africa had been passed by the General Assembly; they were increasingly emphatic after the Sharpeville shootings of 1960. International sanctions had been proposed, not only by the Afro-Asians but also by the Scandinavian bloc. In March 1965 a committee of experts had reported to the Security Council on the possibilities of oil sanctions against South Africa; it had considered in addition the prevention of emigration from European countries to the citadel of apartheid. Britain, the US and France had refused to lend their names to such ideas, but a leading Johannesburg newspaper remarked that the committee's report was "another step forward to concerted action" and contained some "ominous features". Any prospect of losing the steady flow of immigrants from Britain, Germany and the Netherlands was undeniably ominous – for without them the expansion of the South African economy would be halted, unless the politically explosive step of advancing natives into white job categories were taken.

Thus it was that South Africa, with Portuguese co-operation, gave Smith succour at the point where he was most vulnerable. Thirty years before, Mussolini had admitted that the League of Nations could have brought him down during his conquest of Ethiopia by the effective use of oil sanctions. It would have been true for Rhodesia, and when the British added oil to the list of prohibited exports to the rebel colony there seemed to have been no understanding in Whitehall that this would be entirely futile unless the South Africans would participate. Sir Hugh Stephenson, the British ambassador in Pretoria, was not asked to seek any guarantees.

The result was fiasco. Although the 200-mile pipeline from Beira in Mozambique to Feruka refinery in Rhodesia stopped pumping (the Hon Angus Ogilvy was a director of the company which owned it), petrol and oil gushed into the rebels from Durban, Johannesburg and Lourenço Marques. South African sympathisers drove up to Salisbury in lorries loaded with drums of petrol, and were given much-publicised receptions. But the bulk needs were met by fleets of road tankers which crossed the border at Beit Bridge, while tank cars moved in over the railway through Malvernia from Lourenço Marques. For South Africa it was a small problem; she did not have to significantly increase her own crude oil imports, since Rhodesia's requirements were less than one-twentieth of South Africa's.

At Lourenço Marques there was an oil berth and the Matola refinery, run by Sonarep. The refinery had been completed in 1961 and had a capacity of 600,000 tons a year, and as Mozambique's needs were only 400,000 tons a year there was ample to spare for Rhodesia. Almost half the crude oil discharged at Lourenço Marques after the British embargo was brought by British tankers, the owners blandly explaining that they assumed these supplies were being used legally by the Portuguese. In the light of the heavy flow from farther south, Wilson's decision to impose a naval blockade of Beira was a mere facade, A hollow victory was achieved when a "pirate tanker", the *Joanna V*, docked in Beira but was prevented from discharging her cargo.

But it made little difference to the white Rhodesians, who were never seriously troubled by the petrol rationing imposed to meet the embargo. It was even argued in Salisbury that the rationing was a good thing, because it gave an air of reality to UDI, and offered the whites an excuse for working up a "Dunkirk spirit". Until then, it had all seemed like a phoney war. By the middle of February, Sir Hugh Stephenson had been told to call at the South African Foreign Ministry in Pretoria and protest to Hilgard Muller. His counterpart in Lisbon went to Dr Nogueira, the Portuguese Foreign Minister. It was stony ground and the failure of oil sanctions was now obvious. The newly-formed Rhodesian buying organisation, GENTA, was dealing from its Johannesburg offices with many major companies, British included. Yet three weeks later, Wilson was prepared to say in public: "I will admit this, that there has been a certain seepage, leakage, of oil from South Africa – perhaps from the Portuguese territories too – more than we like, although nothing on the scale that the press has been talking about. And this problem will have to be dealt with." It never was.

The principal victim of the abortive oil sanctions had been Zambia, which was faced with a sudden predicament when her traditional liquid fuel supplies from Feruka were cut off by Smith. Rescue came in the form of a costly airlift by British, American and Canadian planes, until Zambia was able to develop her own emergency road route on the "Hell Run" from Dar es Salaam, 1,000 miles away. At the start of oil sanctions, Kaunda had written directly to Wilson, asking him if Britain would build a pipeline along the route to Tanzania, suggesting that either the Royal Engineers could undertake it or a suitable British company could be encouraged to show an interest. The idea of a pipeline had first been put to Kaunda in the middle of 1965 by Lonrho, which was involved with the Beira–Feruka pipeline. Wilson's response to the appeal was cold. The reply sent to Kaunda said that the pipeline would cost £35–40,000,000, according to the advice given to the British Government; it would also take a "very long time" to complete – and by

K

mentioning that the Beira pipeline had taken two years and was 200 miles long, Wilson implied that a pipeline extending 1,000 miles could therefore take ten years. The British Premier added: "I am sorry for the disappointing nature of this reply, but this is one of those matters where it is surely of the greatest importance to take account of the facts, however stark and unpleasant they may be." Eventually, Kaunda gave the job to the Italian organisation, ENI; the total cost was £16,000,000 and the time was 17 months. When the Italians were awarded the contract, there was an outcry that British firms had been discriminated against.

Wilson's rejection of the pipeline was in accord with the "weeks rather than months" prediction given to him by the experts at the Department of Economic Affairs. When he sent Maurice Foley, a junior minister, to Lusaka to discuss emergency assistance for implementing sanctions, the conditions were that nothing agreed should extend beyond three months; it would not be necessary. The failure of the oil sanctions cast all plans into the melting-pot, in particular the "quick kill" project which at one stage was being scheduled for February 15. Only a few senior officials were informed about the "quick kill", which involved the overnight banning of all Zambian imports from Rhodesia, with a simultaneous tightening of British measures. The British advocates of this initiative accepted that Zambia could only survive under such conditions for about two months, but no longer would be needed. The Rhodesians should already be reeling from the oil sanctions, and this new blow would give them the *coup de grace*. When it was seen that the Rhodesians were nowhere near reeling, the "quick kill" was shelved, since it could only have ruined Zambia to no good purpose.

It was towards the end of March that Wilson decided, in the midst of the general election campaign, that sanctions had no hope of working within weeks rather than months. Their failure had handed a psychological advantage to Smith, and to the Tory opposition. Shortly before, there had been a visit to Salisbury by Selwyn Lloyd,* an "elder statesman" of the Conservative Party. He had returned to advise Edward Heath in a

* Lloyd went back to Rhodesia in the spring of 1969.

confidential report that sanctions were unlikely to bring down
the Rhodesian regime and Heath had tabled a motion calling
for a start to talking with Smith – a suggestion which Wilson
greeted with expressions of horror. After all, it was less than
three months since the Commonwealth Secretary, Arthur
Bottomley, had told the Commons about Smith: "He has lied
not only to me, but to others. This is one of the reasons why we
cannot deal with Smith in any way: because he is not a man to
be trusted."

In great secrecy, Wilson sent to Salisbury an assistant
under-secretary in the Commonwealth Relations Office, Duncan Watson. On his return, Watson was said to have been ex-
amining the problems of the British residual mission, two of
whose members had been accused by Smith of spying on the
workings of his economy. (It might have been assumed that
since Britain still held Rhodesia to be a dependency, the two
had every right; however, they were told to go, and left.)
Watson wrote a memorandum on his talks with the Governor,
Sir Humphrey Gibbs, and the Chief Justice, Sir Hugh Beadle;
neither of these two were Liberals, but provided Britain with a
channel of communication into the rebel hierarchy. Sir Humphrey, who wanted nothing more than to retire from his queer
position to his Rhodesian farm, urged the value of early negotiations; Watson's memorandum was also gloomily emphatic
about the strength of the Rhodesian economy.

It had become apparent that there was now no prospect of a
"moderate" white challenge to Smith's group. The business
community which in earlier years had been the mainstay of
Sir Roy Welensky's United Federal Party had always assured
the British High Commission that this challenge would emerge.
The High Commission staff had relied implicitly, almost exclusively, upon this and other assurances from the business
element, and the regular fortnightly reports to Whitehall had
done much to condition thinking there. It only became understood much later that certain of these captains of Rhodesian
industry were engaged in a deliberate Trojan horse operation
on behalf of the Rhodesian Front to make the British ideas
more confused than they already were. This was particularly
true of the forecasts that UDI would never happen. After it

did, these same people turned to sanctions-breaking with a will.

In any case, there existed no credible alternative to Smith as a white leader, around whom opposition might gather. Welensky pontificated whenever invited to do so, but was regarded as a political dinosaur. Whitehead had left Rhodesia and was living in Britain in obscurity. Field was farming quietly at Marandellas near Salisbury. One former premier, Garfield Todd, was restricted to his farm near Belingwe and was regarded by almost all the whites as a traitor because of his support for the African nationalists. The only defiance to the Rhodesian Front's policies came from Malcolm Smith, the editor of the main daily newspaper, the *Rhodesia Herald*. In spite of constant efforts to intimidate him, Malcolm Smith continued to mock the censorship regulations by bringing out his paper with large white spaces where vetoed material should have been. But if the whites had been a disappointment, the Africans had been a calamity and did nothing to produce the industrial disorder which might have helped to supplement the effect of sanctions.

On the last day of March, the British voters gave Wilson the security he had lacked for eighteen months. The Labour Party was returned with a majority of more than 100 seats. In Salisbury, Smith commented bleakly: "If the British people are happy, then I am happy." But in Lusaka, there was jubilation. Kaunda told his Cabinet colleagues: "Now you will see. Harold will do the right thing." There seemed every hope for a new, tough policy. Perhaps force could be used, after all.

Wilson had embarked, however, upon quite different preparations and a constant flow of messages between London and Salisbury led to another secret visit to Salisbury. This time the emissary was a Foreign Office man, Oliver Wright (shortly afterwards promoted to the post of British ambassador in Denmark). There was a meeting between Wright and Smith, and on April 27, all was set for Wilson's announcement to the Commons. It had been agreed that informal talks between officials should be held to see whether a genuine basis existed for negotiation. Reaction from the assembled MPs was mixed: the Tories were delighted, while most of the *soi-disant* Socialists sat mute. Wilson explained: "I make it plain that these are not negotiations. Her Majesty's Government are not negotiating with the illegal regime. These are informal talks to see whether there is a basis on which proper negotiations could take place." He added that he was able to "forget and forgive" quite a lot of what Smith had done.

Mr Wilson had not been without private difficulties before making his revelations of April 27. It represented a complete switch. No longer was the Salisbury regime to be a nest of traitors with whom bargaining was unthinkable. If not a capitulation, this was certainly a major retreat, both in principle and in fact.

Arthur Bottomley was amazed and warned Wilson that there would be a furious reaction from African leaders, who would claim that they had been misled. For his part, Wilson was irritated at Bottomley's lack of political acumen. It was a parting of the ways and three months later Bottomley was removed from the Commonwealth Office; the year afterwards he was dropped entirely from the government.

But Bottomley was right in his forecast of how the Africans would feel. The man most difficult to placate and persuade was surely going to be Kaunda — and as luck would have it, the message from Wilson to break the news before the Commons statement was sent too late. When it arrived in Lusaka an official from the High Commission was sent hurriedly with it to State House. But Kaunda had already left for the airport to take off for a tour in one of Zambia's remote rural areas. The officials drove to the airport, only to see the presidential Dakota lifting off the far end of the runway. Out in the bush, Kaunda tuned his transistor radio to a BBC news bulletin. The British–Rhodesian "talks about talks" were the lead news item — and the first Kaunda knew of them.

It would be hard to over-estimate the importance of this moment in its effect upon relations between Britain and Zambia. They were never to be restored to what they had been. The fact that Kaunda did not receive the message added to the shock he felt, but even if he had, all the faith he had placed in Wilson and the Labour administration could never have survived the conviction that he had been deceived. In

January, during the private talk with Wilson, there had been a sense of trust. What had all the promises been worth?

Kaunda hurried back to Lusaka. Waiting to meet him was Malcolm MacDonald, the British "special representative" in East and Central Africa. Instructed by Wilson to smooth matters over, MacDonald found he had been given an impossible task. Backed up by Sir Leslie Monson, the High Commissioner in Lusaka, the special representative – who was regarded by Whitehall as having a special charm for winning over awkward Afro-Asians – insisted that the forthcoming talks in Salisbury meant no change in the resolve to end the rebellion. Kaunda was not impressed and the meeting was angry. Only the day before, Smith had made a speech in Bulawayo – where the Rhodesians were holding a trade fair; he had said: "There are, I gather, some people who are wondering whether, by stipulating that we should not insist on any preconditions before going to the conference, that this means we would have to give ground. Well, I would like to assure you that it means nothing of the sort." This implied an understanding well beyond Wilson's presentation of the matter.

Any claims that Watson and Wright had not been used earlier to send up trial balloons were made unconvincing when details of the first round of "talks about talks" were released. These same two officials led the British team. The meeting began in Whitehall. The head of the Rhodesian delegation was Sir Cornelius Greenfield, an economist who was credited with master-minding the anti-sanctions manœuvres. Later it was to be disclosed by Smith that Watson had brought a message from Wilson during his visit to Salisbury in March, notwithstanding the story that he had only gone out to attend to the problems of the residual mission.

Meanwhile, Kaunda was bracing himself for a meeting of his Cabinet. In private talks with friends he seemed more bewildered than anything else. He kept repeating: "I can't understand what's come over Harold." The Cabinet gave him a painful time. Several ministers, spearheaded by Simon Kapwepwe, argued that it had been wrong to go along with Wilson. The inference was that Kaunda had been too trusting. It was pointedly recalled how members of the Cabinet had promised not to say anything which might "rock the boat" while Wilson was preparing for his general election. So he had gained the big majority he wanted – and immediately treated Zambia's views with contempt. Heightened feelings against Britain were quickly given expression when 300 students attacked the High Commission just after MacDonald had left it. Stones were flung through the windows, the Union Jack was hauled down and torn up and police carried 100 demonstrators off in trucks. The rest were dispersed by riot police armed with shields and batons.

A fury which Kaunda had never shown before began to appear repeatedly in his speeches. He called Britain's handling of the Rhodesian affair "shifty and evasive", leaving little doubt as to who he felt deserved the adjectives. His anger was increased in the middle of May when he heard that Wilson was trying to put off another Commonwealth conference until September, although it had been agreed in Lagos that the meeting should be in July if UDI had not been ended by then. MacDonald rushed around the African capitals appealing to the presidents to agree to the postponement, until it was clear to Whitehall that Kaunda had been outflanked. On May 22, Kaunda was still insisting that the conference should be held as scheduled and went to the extent of suggesting that Britain should be expelled from the Commonwealth. The idea was greeted with sneers by rightwing Tories and when later it was hinted by Kaunda that Zambia might leave the Commonwealth instead, Wilson sent him a letter warning that British assistance in implementing sanctions might be withdrawn.

A pattern had now been set, within six months of UDI, and was to last for more than two years. Wilson settled down to negotiate his way out of his predicament, hoping that sanctions would ultimately make Smith more flexible, even if they had failed to have the dramatic effect he had so optimistically forecast earlier in the year. The pursuit of this policy, with all its tedious hair-splitting, involved dozens of politicians and officials. Sometimes they went out to Salisbury in a glare of publicity, at others in great secrecy – even with false passports. Officially and unofficially, leading Conservatives joined in: Lord Alport,

Reginald Maudling, Duncan Sandys, Sir Alec Douglas-Home — each one seeking a formula which might reconcile the 200,000 Rhodesian whites with their 50,000,000 kith and kin in Great Britain. Debates were held regularly in the Lords and Commons with many notable displays of semantic skill. At the United Nations, resolutions were piled on resolutions, Britain usually abstaining; Lord Caradon, formerly Sir Hugh Foot, opposed the calls for force and doggedly defended a Rhodesian policy far less plausible than the one he had resigned over a few years earlier. Like travellers set down upon an endless plain, political observers began to lose all sense of time or direction. Yet sometimes there were hillocks, from whose tops it was possible to see mirages of the longed-for goal, the "honourable settlement".

One such hillock was the Commonwealth leaders' conference of September 1966. Kaunda refused to attend, but sent instead Foreign Minister Kapwepwe and Finance Minister Arthur Wina. In typical style, Kapwepwe accused Wilson of being a racialist and walked out; Wina apologised for him. But even without Kaunda and Nyerere, the going was hard for Britain and Wilson had to make large concessions to African attitudes. The most significant of these was that if Rhodesia did not take early steps to abandon the rebellion, Britain would withdraw all previous offers and lay it down that there could be no independence before majority rule (NIBMAR). The deadline was Christmas. If Wilson became committed to this, it would greatly reduce his chances of making a deal with Smith, but he had no alternative to promising that he would implement it if new approaches failed. As he afterwards admitted, the Commonwealth came near to collapse during the conference, and Wilson was resolved to avoid going down in history as the premier who presided over the break-up of the Commonwealth.

The comings and goings between London and Salisbury built up to a crescendo with the visit to Smith by Herbert Bowden, the new Commonwealth Secretary, at the end of November. Ostensibly he went at the request of Sir Humphrey Gibbs, who had earlier been threatening to resign but had been persuaded out of it during Bowden's previous visit in September. Although the visit lasted for only forty-eight hours, Bowden had with him fourteen officials — a sign that the stage was being set. Bowden was a dour but notably honest man, who by this time had come to distrust Wilson's handling of Rhodesia. Like his predecessor, Bottomley, he had no illusions about Smith's determination to cling to power and regarded the missions to Salisbury as degrading. He was opposed to the new formula now being developed in Downing Street, which was to leave Smith in as premier at the head of a "broadly-based" government. He clung to the view that the colony should be administered during an interim period by a British-appointed governor of progressive leanings; Sir Evelyn Hone, the Rhodesian-born last Governor of Northern Rhodesia, had been suggested for the job. Bowden's relations with Wilson were soon to become so vexatious that within a year he was given a peerage and removed completely from the political arena.

Another man who was growing increasingly unhappy was Sir Morrice James, the deputy under-secretary at the Commonwealth Office. He was also shuttling to and fro between London and Central Africa. James had a reputation for skilled negotiation, derived from his performance as peace-maker in the Rann of Kutch dispute between India and Pakistan. One of the issues which James pursued tirelessly concerned Smith's insistence that there should be a Senate to protect African interests which would contain six chiefs and six elected representatives. Even the Conservatives had refused to accept that the chiefs reflected African opinion. These tribal figureheads were appointed by the government and paid by the government; until the early sixties, chiefs had almost ceased to exist among the Africans of Rhodesia but had been artificially revived – as in South Africa – to represent "moderate native opinion" in contrast to militant nationalism. Six months before UDI, Smith had sent a planeload of fifty chiefs on a tour of South Africa, Greece, Portugal, Italy and Britain to widen their education.

On Bowden's second return from Salisbury, Wilson decided to pin all his hopes on a face-to-face meeting with Smith and put this scheme to his Cabinet. There was a strong opposition, led by Barbara Castle, who insisted that it would give Smith an exaggerated idea of his own importance. Anything he might be offered which was honourable from Britain's point of view would inevitably be rejected by the rebel regime, which would make propaganda out of the meeting by blaming Britain for refusing to compromise. But Wilson was able to muster a majority, of whom the key figures were George Brown, Denis Healey, Richard Crossman and Roy Jenkins. He was given a mandate to sign an agreement with Smith at the meeting. There was an air of urgency, for the Commonwealth Sanctions Committee was to meet on December 5. If no progress could be reported to the high commissioners sitting on the committee, Britain would be bound before Christmas to go forward to NIBMAR as the basis of any future settlement and to promote mandatory sanctions through the UN Security Council.

So Sir Morrice James was despatched hurriedly to Salisbury, to invite Smith to fly to Gibraltar for a "summit" aboard the British cruiser *Tiger*. Also invited were Sir Humphrey Gibbs and the Chief Justice, Sir Hugh Beadle – who at that time was still trusted by Wilson and referred to by him as the "lion-hearted Sir Hugh". It was handled in a cloak-and-dagger manner, but rumours were already abroad. When the party boarded an RAF Comet at Salisbury at four in the morning they were spotted by a journalist. There was a certain irony at the presence of Sir Humphrey, walking across the runway with Smith, for the two had been studiously refusing to recognise one another for a year. Smith had cut off Sir Humphrey's telephone, withdrawn his staff and tried to make him leave his official residence. Now they were re-united for the 4,000-mile flight to Gibraltar.

It was soon remarked upon that the meeting at sea upon a warship bore a similarity to events of a quarter of a century earlier. However, Wilson was no Churchill, nor Smith a Roosevelt. For all the initial melodrama, the *Tiger* talks soon degenerated into farce. Wilson was able to score debating points about the chiefs, but Smith threw him into confusion by announcing that he had no mandate; whatever proposals were reached would have to be taken back for discussion with the Rhodesian Cabinet. Wilson protested that he would not have come if he had known this. His colleagues had authorised him to meet Smith only on the understanding that the aim was to reach a final settlement. He had been put in a very awkward position. Smith made it clear that he did not care greatly about that and began demanding that he should be allowed to fly home immediately. The exchanges became exceedingly sullen and ill-tempered, the mood being in no way improved when Smith's companion, Rhodesian Information Minister Jack Howman, began to pull from his pocket a collection of newspaper clippings giving examples of racial discrimination in Britain.

In a hotel in Rome all this while was Kenneth Kaunda of Zambia. He was on his way back to Lusaka after a tour through Canada, the United States, the Caribbean and South America. To drive home his alienation from Wilson, he had flown to the Americas without touching Britain and had chartered a jet airliner from Alitalia. Asked to comment on the Gibraltar talks, Kaunda said: "Any agreement which includes majority rule before independence will have my whole-hearted support. We must be realistic, of course – majority rule in Rhodesia cannot come overnight." He went on to say that he had no quarrel with the British people, among whom he had very warm friends. It all sounded disarmingly mild, but it pinpointed the NIBMAR promise hanging over Wilson's head. It was a promise which had to be kept, with clear reluctance, in the week before Christmas 1966.

Smith and his colleagues rejected the "working document" devised in the *Tiger*, an act which gave the clearest proof of the wide gulf between the British and rebel Rhodesian positions; to the Labour Party's leftwing the proposals made by Wilson were a sell-out to racialism, and an agreement on the *Tiger* terms would have forced several rising politicians at Westminster to choose between their careers and their consciences. One who was understood to have a letter of resignation already locked in her desk was Judith Hart, the Minister of State at the Commonwealth Office. Mrs Hart had earlier in the year made two expeditions to Lusaka to discuss sanctions support costs and made no secret of her sympathy for Kaunda's views. She frequently referred to the white Rhodesians as fascists.

Rhodesia had already provoked a minor dispute inside the party. Two months before the *Tiger* meeting, Wilson had forced the removal of George Cunningham from the position of Commonwealth Officer at the Labour Party's headquarters. Cunningham's sin had been to write a Fabian Society pamphlet called "Rhodesia: the Last Chance" in which he argued that the use of force might be right and necessary.

Wilson explained failure at the summit by giving an entirely new interpretation of Ian Smith's character and position. The Rhodesian leader was a mere tool of extremists, acting under orders. In the Commons on December 22, Wilson borrowed Mrs Hart's terminology: "It is clear that he is a prisoner of some very racialistic and fascist-minded people, and that they forbade him to enter into this agreement." A month later, Wilson returned to this theme: "I regret that contrary to what Mr Smith said to me, he has not had the spunk to stand up to those extremists, despite his great confidence that he could and would do so." But the records of the *Tiger* discussions, as published in the British White Paper, give scant support to all this and it was assumed that the premier spoke in the hope of sowing dissension within the rebel ranks.

From the start of 1967 until the middle of 1968, negotiations between Britain and Rhodesia were virtually at a standstill. In Downing Street, there were other worries, more immediate and desperate. The Labour Party's support in the country had sunk so low that in one by-election after another the Conservatives scored crushing victories. The British economy had run into such trouble that Wilson was forced to accept devaluation as the only way out (Smith made it known that he felt strong enough to forego the option of following suit). It seemed at moments that Labour could not survive and that the Conservatives – who had promised to find a quick solution to the Central African deadlock – would be brought back. But Wilson clung on.

At a moment when the Rhodesian issue seemed most quiescent, a new actor had appeared upon the stage, to speak a memorable line and stir the passions and pride of Britain. Ali Simbule, an old guard Zambian nationalist, gave a press conference in Dar es Salaam after it had been announced that he was being promoted to high commissioner in Britain from the same position in Tanzania. Asked what he thought about UDI, Simbule said Britain was shirking her moral and constitutional responsibilities. To drive the point home he added: "Britain is a humbled, toothless bulldog, wagging its tail in front of Rhodesian premier Ian Smith and fearing him like hell." Set against what Zambian politicians had been saying for more than a year, this was mild; but Simbule was by way of being a diplomat. The remark was briefly reported in Britain and was noticed in the Commonwealth office. It particularly excited George Thomas, a small Welshman recently appointed Minister of State in place of Judith Hart – who had predictably been given a ministry which removed her from any connection with Central African affairs. Thomas set the wheels in motion to demand an explanation from Lusaka, insisting that if Simbule refused to retract the British Government would not accept him.

Faced with this challenge, Simbule offered his own gloss on the statement: "It is only natural that if you have teeth you can crush a bone, but if you have no teeth you cannot crush it – even if it is a soft one." This did nothing at all to mollify Thomas, and by now the "toothless bulldog" controversy was making headlines in the British newspapers. Kaunda was in a dilemma, for while he wanted Simbule in London it was politically impossible for him to make anything approaching an apology. A long statement was sent to London, reiterating Zambia's attitude to Rhodesia but offering no hint of regret. A Foreign Ministry official in Lusaka then said that there was no intention of disallowing the nomination of Simbule to London and he would leave in a few days. So at the end of May 1967, Simbule landed at London Airport. There was no representative of the British Government to welcome him and he drove direct to the high commission residence, overlooking Regent's Park.

A week later, Foreign Minister Simon Kapwepwe went even further. Simbule had been right, he told a cheering crowd on the Copperbelt. "The British Government are cowardly, toothless hyenas. They are running away." Although the world was much taken up at that moment with the Israeli–Arab war, this further insult added to the chagrin of George Thomas. Letters between London and Lusaka became more heated and in the Commons there were demands that Simbule should be declared *persona non grata*. If that had happened, Zambia would have broken off diplomatic relations. The prospect seemed so likely that a new British deputy high commissioner was told by the Commonwealth Office not to fly out to Lusaka in case he would only have to fly right back.

At last a formula was devised. Simbule said he accepted that expressions he would normally use in talking to fellow-Africans may have hurt the people of Britain; if so, he regretted it. At that, he was forgiven and went to see the Queen. But the *détente* was brief, for less than a month later Simbule was interviewed in Nairobi while in transit to Lusaka to attend the annual conference of the ruling United National Independence Party. He insisted that Britain was still toothless, or otherwise it would show its teeth to Smith. "The truth always hurts," he added. Thereupon, Kaunda resolved to look for another high commissioner who would be more likely to arouse sympathy for Zambia in Britain. For four months, Simbule stayed out of the public eye in America and at the end of the year moved quietly to West Africa to become ambassador to the Ivory Coast. His place in London was taken by Elias Chipimo, a soft-spoken ex-headmaster who wrote poetry and quoted Latin tags.

It fell to Chipimo to prepare the ground for Kaunda to visit London. The need for such a journey became more urgent, for a variety of reasons, as 1968 wore on. Kaunda felt he had to explain directly to the British public his fears about developments in southern Africa. He also had important demands to make of Harold Wilson. The two had not met for thirty months, since their private talk in the grounds of State House, Lusaka. Much had changed since then and they both had aged noticeably; only their common adversary, Smith, seemed as serene and confident as ever.

PART FOUR

Inside Zambia — The First Four Years

CHAPTER II

The Economy and Sanctions

When Kaunda arrived in London in the middle of 1968, he had a dual purpose. Firstly, he wanted to waken the British public to the dangers he saw mounting up in southern Africa. Secondly, he planned to appeal to Wilson for the renewal of financial aid to Zambia, to help her withstand the economic pressures of sanctions. It was three years since he had last set foot in Britain, and two and a half since his brief meeting with Wilson in Lusaka soon after the Rhodesian UDI. Yet it had not been easy for him to arrange the trip, which came at the end of a long tour through Scandinavia. Several members of Kaunda's Cabinet had been unhappy about his sitting down with a man so detested as Wilson; if the British wanted to talk, let them come to Zambia. It was also argued that if Kaunda came home from London without tangible results, he would have lost face. In the week before Kaunda met Wilson, a series of bitterly anti-British speeches were made in Zambia by the Vice-President, Simon Kapwepwe.

Although Kaunda spoke repeatedly on television during his weeklong visit, and was given sympathetic coverage in the national newspapers, his impassioned warnings about the prospects of a racial holocaust in Africa fell on stony ground. The British had grown intensely bored with Rhodesia, they had their own domestic racial problems and they felt that he was probably being melodramatic in the hope of manœuvring Wilson into more positive policies. Those with longer memories recalled that Kaunda had been making similar forecasts in the past. In December 1965 he had warned of "a racial war which would leave the entire southern Africa devastated". It was generally conceded, even by Conservatives, that Kaunda was a

sincere and well-meaning man. But all in all, the less one heard
of African politicians and their woes, the better it was. Leaders
of big business applauded politely when Kaunda spoke to them
at Burlington House in Piccadilly; meanwhile, the London
Chamber of Commerce was organising an important trade
mission to South Africa. As for Harold Wilson himself, he was
feeling his way towards a new encounter with Smith.

On the second purpose for his visit, Kaunda was equally un-
rewarded. Britain was still awaiting the benefits of devaluation,
and the level of aid to Commonwealth countries had been
frozen at the 1967 level. Wilson refused to do more than promise help when Britain's economy improved. Kaunda was deeply
distressed at this rebuff, even though he had received warnings
before his departure that he could expect little from Downing
Street. But none the less, Zambia had an unanswerable case, in
moral terms.

Sanctions had not "brought Smith to his senses", which was
the declared aim of the Labour Party. The Zambians, who had
long experience of white attitudes in Central Africa, had always
prophesied such a failure. But they had gone along with Britain's sanctions policy although it was to cost them dear —
realising that if they refused to co-operate it would have been
held against them afterwards; they would have been accused of
having sabotaged the whole operation through self-interest.
Regardless of his doubts, which he had first expressed to Wilson
a year before UDI, Kaunda would not contract out in the
manner of the Malawian leader, Hastings Banda. Not all the
Zambian Cabinet agreed, some of its members insisting that the
Black Rhodesians should fight their own battles and that charity
should begin at home. The leader of the opposition African
National Congress, Harry Nkumbula, put it harshly: "I would
not ask Zambians to suffer so that others could be free."

For their part, the British had pressed Zambia from the start
to reduce its imports from Rhodesia with all speed. In the year of
UDI these had amounted to £35,538,000 (more than a third
of the total import bill) and ranged from coal and fertilisers to
shirts and tinned beans. The Zambian import agencies, most
of which were subsidiaries of Rhodesian firms, resisted governmental pressure to change their sources of supply; it had been

very convenient to ring friends in Bulawayo or Salisbury to place orders. Some Zambian firms who tried to order direct from Britain were referred back to franchise-holders in Rhodesia and threatened by them with legal action. But by 1966, Zambia had been able to réduce its imports from the rebel colony to less than twenty per cent of the total and by 1967 to eleven per cent.

It was a notable achievement, but Wilson had hoped for more. In the middle of 1966 he had sent out Mrs Judith Hart, Minister of State at the Commonwealth Office, to put to the Zambians a modified version of the "quick kill" plan which had been abandoned in February. Treated as top secret and never hinted at to the Zambian public, this called for the complete stopping of all imports from Rhodesia by the end of 1966. Mrs Hart, although an outspoken left-wing socialist, well disposed towards Kaunda, had a painful time in Lusaka. The start of "talks about talks" with Smith had made the Zambians hostile and suspicious. They were not prepared to risk the destruction of their country's economy without categorical promises from Britain.

A permanent secretary, Dominic Mulaisho, read out a long statement to Mrs Hart. In it, he pointed to the hazards facing Zambia. An imports cut-off would almost certainly mean that use of the Rhodesian railway would be entirely denied; copper production would have to be slashed from 58,000 tons to 38,000 tons monthly; imports would have to be reduced from 87,000 tons a month to a maximum of 60,000 tons by the end of the year; a drop in employment by twenty per cent or more was likely, as was a fall by a quarter in Zambia's national income. If this was to be accepted, Britain would have to offer all-out help. But Mrs Hart had no such mandate – she could only talk of limited assistance with a £7,000,000 ceiling.

Mulaisho's statement put the challenge squarely: "Here we are, in support of your policy, contemplating measures that will lead to a twenty-five per cent reduction in our national income while the British Government balks at the prospect of financing projects that will not even cost one-tenth of one per cent of your national revenue. Where is the parity of sacrifice in that?" He went on to describe the Zambian schemes for using the alternative routes through Tanzania, Malawi and the Congo to the maximum, then returned to his earlier complaint: "Even more perplexing and indeed distressing to us is, while we are talking of necessary tonnages, to hear you speaking in terms of limited cash commitments and expenditure ceilings. This is like quibbling over the cost of a blood transfusion. It is more than inappropriate; it amounts to a dereliction of a proper and necessary responsibility. Once we embark, at your behest, upon full-scale sanctions it will be impossible to set a limit upon our commitment either in terms of economic loss or in terms of extra financial expenditures that will have to be incurred. What right therefore have you to insist that your proportionately small commitments in this regard should be limited to a specific sum? We cannot accept the principle that lies behind your offer – that of limited commitment. Our commitment is not limited. Our risks are open-ended. We know that you are reluctant to use force to embark upon military war to end the rebellion in Rhodesia, but we had understood you were prepared to use the weapons of economic war. But, if this is a war of any kind, let us not hear of limited commitments or we shall conclude that it is a war waged with limited determination and with limited sincerity."

Judith Hart had taken this resounding message back to Wilson, after a detour through Blantyre to represent Britain at Malawi's republic celebrations. She was followed to London by Foreign Minister Simon Kapwepwe, who called for "sterner economic measures" against Rhodesia immediately. He made derisory remarks at a meeting in Marlborough House about initial British offers of £3,600,000, partly in the form of a loan. The extent to which relations had worsened was made plain when Mrs Hart told the Commons about her long discussions with Kapwepwe.

They fully understood one another's point of view, but there was a "considerable area of political disagreement". She hoped it would be possible to avoid a departure from the Commonwealth by Zambia. Although Mrs Hart did not mention it, there had been pained reports from Lusaka that Kaunda and his colleagues had instituted a rigid boycott of British high commission functions – she had been snubbed on her visit.

Wilson meanwhile had weighed the Zambian demands, which amounted to a promise of full compensation for the effects of a full cut-off. He was not prepared to give it, and this meant a drastic revision of Britain's whole sanctions policy. The "long haul" was now a certainty. But perhaps even more important was the need to keep receiving Zambia's copper, which met almost half of Britain's needs for the metal. Zambia was in the sterling area, and the only other adequate sources were the U.S., Canada and Chile. With Britain's economy already reeling, this was a vital consideration. In the middle of 1966, copper was at a record level of more than £600 a ton on the London Metal Exchange and the Zambian producers had abandoned their fixed selling price in the wake of the Chileans. If Zambian supplies were to dwindle away, prices would rise still further, Britain would have to buy from across the Atlantic in dollars and British exports using copper would become dearer.

There was a vicious circle. Wilson had pressed the Zambians hard to stop all their copper exports by way of Rhodesia, since he did not want to be indebted to the illegal regime for giving passage to supplies for Britain. The Zambians had taken an initiative in April by prohibiting the transfer of any funds from Zambia to Rhodesia to pay for freight costs on the section of the railway south of the Victoria Falls. This amounted to about £1,000,000 a month, copper freight supplying almost a third of railway revenue. The Rhodesians retaliated by saying that all freight would be blocked unless payment was made in advance from Zambia; the currency should be dollars or Swiss francs. Complex litigation began in the courts of Lusaka and Salisbury. The hapless Sir Sidney Caine, head of the British version of the Rhodesian Reserve Bank, tried to intervene in a case in the Salisbury High Court, but was brushed aside.

By the middle of July, more than 30,000 tons of copper worth £20,000,000 had been stockpiled in Zambia, adding to the world shortage and keeping up the exorbitant price on the London Metal Exchange. The copper companies were maintaining full production, but growing more anxious by the day. The Anglo American chairman, Harry Oppenheimer, flew up from Johannesburg for talks with Kaunda. But the Zambians would not budge – saying their principles would not permit them to make payment to the rebels. It was estimated that by the end of the year, the stockpile could be worth £100,000,000; the value of such a frozen asset could change dramatically if the world price of copper slumped. There was good reason to fear an end to the Vietnam war.

Quite suddenly, a way out was devised. The mining companies in Zambia would not pay for the freight to be moved through Rhodesia, but the customers who bought the metal would meet this cost. The arrangement was given as little publicity as possible, but it was soon asked how the British buyers – taking about 250,000 tons of Zambian copper a year – could send money to Rhodesia; it was a criminal offence under the sanctions regulations. An official of the mining companies said with careful vagueness that this would be done through a European country. Then in Geneva, a firm of metal dealers revealed that it was taking instructions from London to make Swiss francs available for the Rhodesian authorities. It was also noted that Switzerland had a consulate in Salisbury. In London, Sir Sidney Caine maintained a discreet silence at this breach – worth several millions a year in hard currency to Smith – in the wall of currency laws.

Kaunda made a short and angry statement, reluctant to confess that Zambia had been saved from ruination by the "Swiss device". He said that Wilson had made promises which had proved false, so a new strategy was needed. Small amounts of copper would go over the railway in Rhodesia. In fact, to clear the stockpiles while the world price remained high, railings were an all-time record for several months. It was to take more than a year before as much as half of the copper could be diverted on the new routes being developed.

The most obvious alternative was the Benguela Railway through Katanga and Angola. But its potential was limited by the confusion in the section between Lubumbashi (Elisabethville) and the Congo–Angola border at Dilolo. It was the time of mutiny in Stanleyville and public executions in the capital, Kinshasa. The Zambians had frequent discussions with the Congolese and communiqués were issued which expressed an optimism in which nobody believed. The copper companies

discounted the possibility of moving more than 10,000 tons to
Lobito. It would not be realistic to hope to get more than
another 15,000 tons out by the three other routes: road to
Malawi and then rail to Beira; the "national route" through
the Congo; and by air to Dar es Salaam. The first trial ship-
ments by road to Dar es Salaam were just beginning. This
method was hazardous and when vehicles broke down the
precious loads of wirebars were sometimes jettisoned at the
roadside to lie there unattended for months. It took two years to
achieve 10,000 tons a month by this route.

The "Hell Run", as it was dubbed, ran from a point on the
highway from Lusaka to Ndola all the way to the Indian
Ocean, a distance farther than from London to Moscow. The
official name, the Great North Road, was more than a little
ironic, for even the section to the Zambia–Tanzania border
was untarred and became a foot deep in reddish mud in the
rainy season. Years before, a part of the Zambian section had
been improved with the help of American funds, but even so it
was not designed to withstand the pounding it was to receive
from hundreds of heavy trucks. Inside Tanzania the road
passed over a mountain range rising to 8,000 feet. From there
on the road was generally narrow and rutted, with primitive
bridges and poor drainage.

The freelance contractors who travelled the Hell Run were
often Afrikaners, earning huge profits which they piled up to
buy farms in South Africa or Rhodesia. Others were Greeks,
and on the Tanzanian side Arabs and a few African traders.
The first priority was to bring in petrol as the airlift, mounted
just after UDI, was phased out. The petrol was carried in
drums, 40,000 of which were discreetly bought from South
Africa. It was a dangerous and absurdly expensive operation,
for the banging together of the drums on the week-long trip
made them burst at the seams. Petrol seeped out over the
vehicles, which sometimes caught fire. Drivers forcing themselves along to bring in as much as possible of their vanishing
cargo sometimes fell asleep at the wheel and hurtled into the
bush. The Great North Road was strewn with wreckage and
more than a hundred men died; sometimes they died slowly,
trapped in their overturned trucks, and sometimes in a roar of

petrol flames. The money was good – as much as £220 a trip. But it was the wages of fear.

In Lusaka, the planners learned to cut by a third the amount of petrol despatched from Dar es Salaam as they worked out their likely stocks. The monthly rations for motorists varied, sometimes falling to two gallons a week. Pumps ran dry at the worst moments of the long petrol emergency and cars were abandoned at the roadside. It was almost three years before Zambia was freed from fuel rationing by the £16,000,000 pipe-line from Dar es Salaam – a project put through in the face of discouragement from Britain. In all that time the Rhodesians, who were meant to be the main sufferers from sanctions, had far more petrol than the Zambians. The financial punishment sustained by Zambia over this period was severe, involving a loss of £14,000,000 a year on fuel transport subsidies alone. Added to this was the loss of revenue through the extra freight costs on copper exports. At the start of 1968, Kaunda said that sanctions had so far cost Zambia £35,000,000 and some economists regarded this figure as extremely conservative.

The first agreement between Britain and Zambia for support costs in the sanctions campaign was not finally signed until February 1967. It was for £13,850,000 and was to run until the middle of 1967. The Zambians complained that the amount was not adequate to cover their losses on a policy which Britain had always insisted was her direct responsibility. More than £5,000,000 of the £13,850,000 was allocated outside Zambia, mainly for improvements to roads and harbours in Tanzania, and about £2,000,000 spent inside Zambia would not have been needed under normal conditions.

The mood of the Zambians was clearly shown in the confidential "Memorandum of Intention and Understanding" drawn up by the two governments. Paragraph six said that the representatives of the Government of Zambia did not believe that sanctions would work and that force should be used. Paragraph eight said that the financal support was being accepted on the basis that by furthering the permanent development of alternative routes, it would give "some recompense for exceptional economic and financial damage that had been and would

be in the future suffered by Zambia". The British signatory
was Kenneth Ritchie, the acting High Commissioner in Lusaka. He gave a commitment that the aim was to end the rebellion and then negotiate with a legal government in Rhodesia.
He repeated the promise given by Wilson in the Commons
that Rhodesia could not have independence before majority
rule. It was also agreed that the funds supplied by Britain
should never be referred to as "aid" in the conventional
sense. To the fury of the Zambians, this distinction was to be
obscured by the Ministry of Overseas Development in 1968,
when it put out a statement saying that in the previous
year more than £14,000,000 in bi-lateral aid had been
given to Zambia. Only in a footnote was it explained that
£9,900,000 was sanctions support costs; almost all the rest of
the £14,000,000 was to increase salaries for British experts
working in Zambia.

At the start of 1968, the new Finance Minister, Elijah Mudenda, had presented a budget in which he said that in the
coming year sanctions would cost the country 47,600,000
kwacha, equivalent to more than £27,000,000. He said: "I
sincerely hope that in fairness to the people of Zambia the
British Government will reimburse us this sum, which is only
part of the high cost which this young nation has to pay." He
went to the extent of basing his revenue calculations on the
assumption that Britain would pay. It was a rash assumption,
for sterling had been devalued only shortly before. The Secretary to the Zambian Cabinet, Valentine Musakanya, had been
in London to seek a renewal of the support costs, but had been
coldly received. He was warned that Britain was unable to give
any more help, however much sanctions might be hurting
Zambia's economy. Wilson knew that he had Kaunda in a
cleft stick, for if Zambia decided that it could no longer pursue
sanctions, this would now be undermining the whole United
Nations strategy on Rhodesia.

As the realities came home and it was clear that Britain had
snapped its purse shut, Kaunda appealed to his followers for
patience. "Leave this to Wilson and me," he asked, a reminder
that there should be no retaliation against the British in Zambia.
He had discussions with the High Commissioner and warned

him that it would be a disaster if no more funds were forthcoming. But by the time he reached Downing Street in July, he knew that it was a lost cause. He put the familiar arguments to Wilson, but without expectation, and received the familiar replies. It might be possible, perhaps by 1970, to "have another look" at the matter; this depended on how quickly the British economy revived. There was also the hint that Zambia was, after all, exceedingly rich as far as developing countries went. The earnings from copper had been so handsome that government revenue had surpassed £450,000,000 since 1964. It was not bad for a country of only 4,000,000. The argument that copper was a fickle commodity, and that four good years might be followed by many lean ones, made scant impression. When Kaunda returned to Zambia, he passed lightly over the financial upshot of his talks and it was officially declared that no requests had been made in London.

Weighing heavily on the Zambian Cabinet by this time was a widespread fear that the country was plunging into an economic morass. The strain of grappling with the international complexities of sanctions, while putting through a massive development programme at home, had been too much. Inflation was running wild and import costs were soaring. In the latter half of 1968 some ominous comparisons with Ghana in the last days of Nkrumah began to be made.

But in one way, Zambia's economy looked even more threatening than Ghana's had done three years before. Both countries leaned heavily on a single export – cocoa in one case and copper in the other. Yet the economic slide in Ghana had been accelerated by a slump in world cocoa prices, whereas Zambia was heading into trouble while copper was still holding a level above £500 a ton. What would happen if the price fell to £300 a ton or less, as market experts were already beginning to predict? The prospect was so appalling that senior civil servants in Lusaka did not even want to discuss it. Another comparison which gave no cause for comfort was that Ghana had always possessed a capable civil service, the product of widespread education before independence. The same could not be said of Zambia, which had reached sovereignty at a stage of educational development which Ghana had achieved in 1930.

With every year that passed, the annual report of the Auditor-General, Robert Boyd, became more swingeing. Boyd announced his resignation as his report on 1967 was tabled in the national assembly in October 1968. The *Times of Zambia* described it as "amazing", saying that it painted a picture of confusion, lack of planning, and unconstitutional spending. Millions were unaccounted for and many departments had exceeded budgets without any authority. Prestige projects had often been far more expensive than the original estimates – the national assembly itself had been expected to cost £330,000, but the final bill was £560,000. The Auditor-General's swansong was forty-two pages long and every page was an indictment of the civil service.

The Vice-President, Simon Kapwepwe, jumped in to defend the civil servants. He praised them for untiring and patriotic work: "Our civil service is second to none in the whole of Africa and possibly the whole world, considering the hardships we have gone through." But Kaunda himself did not agree. He said a few weeks later: "I must indicate how disgusted I have been in the past by the apathy, sheer lack of initiative and indiscipline which has been prevalent in the civil service." He gave a warning that he was planning severe action to put matters right.

However, there was a certain cynicism abroad about such presidential warnings. They had been made repeatedly in the past but were generally followed by little in the way of action. It had begun in 1966 when the then Vice-President, Reuben Kamanga, had successfully defied an order to spend six months at the United Nations; it was no secret that Kaunda had bowed to threats of disorder from Kamanga's home area, the Eastern Province. A series of such incidents culminated in the refusal of Ditton Mwiinga to accept an appointment as ambassador in Peking. A former Minister of Health, Mwiinga was offered the unpopular Peking posting in March 1968; he was told he would keep his Cabinet rank, but this did not mollify him. Five months later he was still in Lusaka, and Kaunda announced that Mwiinga had been demoted: he would now be Minister of State. When reporters tried to interview Mwiinga, he laughed but said nothing.

The reluctance on Kaunda's part to take a hard line at the risk of temporary conflict had also shown itself over the years in his handling of the trade unions. The result had been to add to the inflationary pressures created by sanctions. A series of strikes on the Copperbelt by African miners culminated in a total stoppage throughout the industry in March 1966. After it had lasted for a fortnight, Kaunda appealed to the 30,000 strikers to go back. He promised that a commission of enquiry would be appointed and explained that the wealth provided by copper was vital to the country's progress. More than a week passed before all the miners chose to go back.

The commission was headed by Roland Brown, one of Nyerere's closest advisers in Tanzania. Brown was a lawyer and a socialist, who in Britain had had the distinction of standing unsuccessfully for Labour in Stratford-on-Avon against John Profumo. From the start, Brown was presented with a virtual *fait accompli*. The government made it clear that it favoured a massive wage rise for the African miners, to narrow the gap between them and the Europeans. At the hearings of the commission, Cabinet ministers speaking on behalf of the ruling United National Independence Party suggested a rise that would be something above twenty per cent. When the report was published, it recommended twenty-two per cent. Had it been much less, Kaunda would have been faced with a trial of strength with the miners.

As it was, peace had been bought on the Copperbelt, at a price. The Brown Report meant that another £6,000,000 a year in spending power would be thrown into the economy. But this was only the start, for the salaries on the mines had always set the pace for the rest of the country and there followed a round of similar increases for the civil servants, railway workers, local authorities employees and even farm workers. By the end of 1966, average Zambian earnings had gone up to £240, against £191 two years earlier. Yet this trend was in defiance of the Seers Report, which in 1964 had been accepted by Kaunda and his colleagues as the Bible for national development. Seers had said: "There is no question of the country being able to afford to pay everyone the £22 a month claimed by some union officials as a basic living wage; desirable though this would be in itself, it would wreck the economy and lead eventually to far lower living standards. There is really a choice for Zambia: in the next five years it can have big increases in wages or big increases in employment, not both."

Seers had gone on to admit that Zambians moving into European jobs would expect to be paid the same salaries; but this was not a proposition for a developing country. It would mean that money would be spent on the import of cars rather that on products needed for the general advancement. The mention of car imports was highly prophetic. He had ended emphatically: "The wage and salary question is perhaps the most serious problem facing the government; its decisions on the wages and salaries it pays itself and the way it exercises its influence on wages and salaries in the private sector, may be decisive in determining whether Zambia will become during this century a modern developed country." Such subtleties were very hard for certain members of the Zambian Cabinet to grasp. They could better understand the emotive political arguments, that low wages for Africans implied inferiority and racial discrimination. Indeed, it took toughness to make a man moving into a new job accept a quarter of the wage of his predecessor, as often happened on the mines.

There were other factors which caused the ministers to say at the public hearings of the Brown Commission that Seers was out of date. The Copperbelt was the citadel of UNIP power and it had to be guarded against penetration by opponents who might exploit the miners' discontent.

After announcing the twenty-two per cent recommendation, Roland Brown said somewhat paradoxically that his commission was in no way challenging the economic reasoning of the Seers Report; a policy of wage restraint was needed for many years. "Weighing in the balance the importance of the industry on which the development of Zambia ultimately depends, we have felt justified in recommending as part of a new settlement, a general increase in wages which otherwise might be regarded as excessive in terms of the growth rate of the economy as a whole."

At one blow, Zambia had been turned irrevocably into a

high-cost country by African standards. Undeniably the copper mines could afford to give higher wages – it merely meant
that they paid less in taxes to the government: the wealth was
concentrated still more in the urban areas rather than being
spread over the country as a whole. Secondary industries merely
passed the wages on in higher prices. The upward pressure was
so fierce that by 1968, when African technicians were hired for
the Tanzania–Zambia pipeline, they had to be paid four times
as much in Zambia as in Tanzania. There was talk of a wage
freeze, but none was ever imposed.

The increase of money in the towns increased the flow of
people away from the rural areas. The Tanzanian policy of
forcing the unemployed to go back to their rural areas was not
followed. Attempts to promote increased output by the farmers
foundered amid conservatism and apathy. There were some
local successes in poultry-keeping and pineapple-growing; the
country also became self-sufficient in maize, but more than a
fifth of the country's food needs still had to be imported. Cotton
production rose after a disastrous start when the farmers could
not find labour to do the picking (in a country with nearly
1,000,000 unemployed adult males). When cotton-picking
machines had been imported this problem was solved, but by
1967 output was still only half of the requirements of a new textile mill being built south of Lusaka.

As the French agronomist, René Dumont, had pointed out to
the Zambian officials, massive injections of money into the
rural areas were not an automatic solution. Millions could soon
be frittered away. But in general the old colonial pattern remained – pockets of commercial farming surrounded by vast
tracts where women and old men followed traditional subsistence methods. In the north, the slash-and-burn method of no-
madic agriculture, known as *chitemene*, still survived – to the
amazement of visiting experts. But there were not enough
people available to launch anything different, since most of
the younger men had gone off to the towns where there
were taverns, department stores and young girls in mini-
skirts. Urban overcrowding grew more dire.

The Four-Year Development Plan, by which it was hoped
to spend the colossal sum of £434,000,000 by 1970, was in-

tended to reverse the flow from the rural areas, or at least slow it down. Yet by the end of 1968 the plan was in ruins; it had almost ceased to exist. Dr Charles Elliot, reader in economics at the University of Zambia, said it had been "grotesquely over-optimistic and over-ambitious". He showed that it had added to inflationary pressures and forced the government to alter drastically the balance between recurrent and capital expenditure. The sketchy figures available gave ample support to such arguments. The recurrent spending by the government had risen by twenty per cent a year and four-fifths of this went on the salaries of the proliferating civil service. But there was also revealing itself a shortage of money for industrial development and the hope must be for greater private investment from abroad.

Yet this hope was vain. There had been comparatively little foreign investment since independence, because of the uncertainties of Africa as a whole and the dangers created for trade in Zambia by UDI. In April 1968, the chances of maintaining even the paltry level achieved up to then were much diminished when Kaunda unveiled his "economic revolution". This involved taking a majority interest in more than twenty large foreign-owned companies in almost every sector of the economy. The reasons were fully understandable: the Zambian people owned very little in the commercial and industrial field, because they had always lacked either money or managerial skills to compete with the expatriates. Now they would have a far greater stake, through the government's Industrial Development Corporation. Kaunda complained that foreign companies had been bleeding the country by making excessive profits and sending vast sums outside. On the terms of compensation, he was blunt: "There is no such thing as business goodwill or paying for future profits as far as I am concerned. I cannot see any reason why we should pay extra for the boom we have ourselves created."

Kaunda did not nationalise the copper companies, although a limitation was imposed on the amount they could send out of Zambia in dividends. He explained to a UNIP rally: "The mines are big business, too big for us, so we let them alone, although we control their profits." He made it plain, however, that he was displeased with the level of investment by the mining companies and alleged that they had done little to expand since independence. This charge brought a detailed – but only partly convincing – report from Harry Oppenheimer, the chairman of Anglo American.

Although neither side admitted as much, events in the Congo had been closely watched. There, President Joseph Mobutu had nationalised the Union Minière mines of Katanga. It had been forecast that this piece of daring would bring him to disaster. But he was successful. It was contended by big business that a pattern had been set, and that within four or five years the Zambians would be tempted to follow suit. The "economic revolution" produced a crash in the price of Zambian copper shares and hostility in the City of London. It had certainly put paid to the estimates in the Four-Year Plan of outside invest-ment amounting to £150,000,000 by 1970.

So as 1969 began, it was apparent that Zambia was balanced on a knife-edge. The pressures created by sanctions were continuing and no further help could be expected from Britain. High wages had helped to create an inflationary spiral in which the country seemed trapped. Imports had risen by fifty per cent in two years and government controls were long overdue. Everything depended on copper, which provided ninety-five per cent of the country's export earnings. If the world price fell suddenly, Zambia could burn her way through her foreign reserves in a matter of months. For several years, world con-sumption of copper had risen by a yearly average of three per cent, while between 1969–74 output was expected to go up by almost six per cent. But the greatest dilemma was posed by the burden of recurrent expenditure, which had passed the £100,000,000-a-year level. To prune this drastically would carry the risk of widespread discontent within the country. Only the budget would reveal whether the politicians could measure up to the challenge, now that a general election was safely behind them.

When the budget was presented, at the end of January 1969, it did show that the warnings of economists were belatedly being heeded. Finance had been handed after the December general election to Zambia's "strong man" – Vice-President

Simon Kapwepwe. He announced that taxes were going up and heavier duties laid on non-essential imports. But the basic vulnerability of the economy remained; as Kapwepwe himself warned, world copper prices were likely to fall since production was overtaking demand. But Kapwepwe's austerity measures were not to the liking of Zambia's miners. They had been pressing without success for yet another wage rise and were in a truculent mood, anxious to show their strength. Reports that income tax was about to affect many of them for the first time were grounds enough. Kapwepwe had to make a hurried tour of the Copperbelt to prevent a protest strike in March 1969, after 2,000 miners had ostentatiously walked out of a meeting while the Zambian national anthem was being played.

Kapwepwe headed off the strike but in the course of his campaign accused the *Times of Zambia* of having incited the public against his budget. The paper's editor, Dunstan Kamana — previously Kenneth Kaunda's press secretary — put an angry rejoinder on his front page. One paragraph said: "There is an unfortunate trend in Zambia at the moment. A certain amount of Fascism among some of our leaders is creeping in. They have assumed a measure of arrogance which tells them that they are the only people who know."

M

CHAPTER 12

White Friends and White Spies

In trying to get to grips with their economic problems, the Zambian leaders were constantly perplexed by the role of the expatriates – whites and Asians. It was not simply that the high standard of living of the 70,000 whites had set, since long before independence, a target for the Zambian man-in-the-street which spelt economic danger to a developing country. But far more basic was the absolute control of the Zambian business arena by non-citizens. An indigenous middle class on the West African pattern had never emerged: before independence too many obstacles had been in the way and afterwards all the most able Zambians, with few exceptions, were drawn into the civil service. The whites and Asians (the latter numbering about 10,000), maintained a key position in the country, yet were not part of it. Only a few hundreds had made the commitment of seeking Zambian citizenship. There was a nagging suspicion that many of the whites in particular were just making as much money as they could, by pushing up the prices in their shops as far as they dared, until they were ready to go elsewhere.

Kaunda attacked this economic impasse during 1968 with the series of compulsory take-overs of major companies owned by foreigners; to retain their expertise, the owners were allowed to keep minority holdings. The Asian grip on the smaller retail trade was broken, as elsewhere in Africa, by refusing to give licences to non-citizens. The mining companies remained firmly in foreign hands, but the Zambians now felt they had more of a stake in their own economy. Quite a different matter, however, was the ultimate political loyalty of the large body of expatriates. Undoubtedly, most of them had contracted out of the political scene. But a number of incidents showed that others had not, and nobody could be sure how they might act if some crucial showdown occurred.

At the time of independence, more than half of the whites in Zambia had relations or business contacts in Rhodesia or South Africa. Gradually it became less common to hear Afrikaans spoken openly on the Copperbelt, as the unskilled whites on the mines were replaced by Zambians. But this was no more than a marginal change. On the day Ian Smith declared independence, there were champagne toasts in towns such as Kitwe, Chingola and Mufulira. It was the money that kept most white Copperbelters in their jobs and they made no secret of where they would travel away to when their savings seemed substantial enough. Estate agents in South Africa placed regular advertisements in the Zambian newspapers, offering farms and businesses for sale in Natal and the Cape. When the schools were racially integrated, the numbers of white children going south for their education markedly increased; special trains were put on for them at the beginning and end of the holidays. Such matters were studiously ignored by the Zambian politicians – as were the sales of Afrikaans newspapers in the bookshops or the indiscretions of roistering white miners in bars.

There had long been, of course, a small group of white sympathisers, who had openly involved themselves in the fight for independence. Among the most prominent was Andrew Sardanis, a Greek-Cypriot businessman who had stood as a UNIP candidate in 1962 and later rose to be the chairman of the Industrial Development Corporation – which acquired the foreign companies during the 1968 "economic revolution". Idealists like the Rev. Merfyn Temple had also aided UNIP's cause. Then there was the comforting aspect of an apparent change of heart among some whites who had been keen supporters of Sir Roy Welensky's United Federal Party until only a few months before independence. Some tended to over-compensate – to become, as it were, more royal than the king; they also saw no contradiction in still sending their children to schools south of the Zambezi. However, such conversions gave encouragement to Kaunda, who had an almost religious belief in the need to create a multi-racial society which could set an example to white-run countries in the south. Cynics might have said that such people were the same as ever in their hearts, that their hearty applause at dinners addressed by Zambian ministers was no more than expediency. But the presidential view was always one of charity and trust. It was pointed out that sporting organisations had bowed to governmental orders that all links should be broken with parent bodies in South Africa. That issue had been brought to the fore when a white farmer in Zambia had been chosen to play rugby for the Springboks. By 1967, cricket and hockey teams were looking to Kenya instead of to the south for their international fixtures. Among the first to take the plunge in Kenya was the Zambian national swimming team, every member of which was white.

But behind this veneer there were far more fundamental issues, such as security. As a string of explosions and fires in petrol depots had shown, Zambia was an easy target for sabotage. It was accepted that such incidents were organised by pro-Smith whites. These had made the country taut and nervous so that when in October 1966 an accidental fire occurred at a petrol depot in Kitwe, gangs of Zambians began attacking nearby whites. A South African miner's wife was stoned to death in her car while her children crouched behind the seats.

One sabotage attempt was not directly related to politics: a group of Americans concocted a scheme for blowing up a railway bridge in Zambia. They reckoned that this would halt the bulk of the country's copper exports and so force up the world price of the metal, which the conspirators would buy in large quantities before the bridge was blown. The plan was bizarre and amateur, and went no further than importing explosives from the Congo in a suitcase.

Against any such threats, Zambia's defences were pathetically weak. The army consisted of three battalions, almost entirely officered by whites whose loyalty was in some cases suspect. Several senior officers had to be quietly dismissed or retired while on leave. The anti-sabotage and counter-intelligence resources available to Kaunda were negligible. Thus, there was utter confusion when a plastic bomb blew up inside

an electric copying machine airfreighted to the Lusaka headquarters of the Zimbabwe African National Union. The explosion killed a white technician who was trying to make the
machine work, although clearly it was meant to wipe out the
ZANU leaders as they watched their new possession go into
operation for the first time. Curiously enough, the machine
had travelled from Dar es Salaam to Lusaka by way of Salisbury
and Johannesburg. This piece of intelligence was made public
by the *Times of Zambia* (which had uncovered it) in the face of
marked hostility from white investigating officers. The body
of the victim was flown to his home in Salisbury for burial,
and the affair was abandoned as an utter mystery. So if
Rhodesian spies were active in Zambia it seemed improbable
that they could be uncovered, and the opportunities for passing
information from Lusaka to Salisbury were almost unlimited.
For one thing, businessmen flew daily between the two capitals
and although Rhodesian residents were obliged on entry to
Zambia to sign a form saying that they did not support Smith,
nobody treated this regulation as anything more than a part of
the propaganda war; Smith himself remarked that if Rhodesians
signed the form, he quite understood.

When it became known in April 1967 that five whites had
been arrested and detained on suspicion of spying, there was
widespread scepticism. It was remembered that six months
earlier twenty-four people had been deported for racial
offences; it had turned out some had been victims of mistaken
identity. All the five detainees were well known in Zambia.
One, Captain John Warren, was the pilot of the Anglo American Corporation's executive jet in which Kaunda had often
flown. Another, Ian Haigh, was a solicitor. A third was John
Arnott, a former lieutenant-colonel in the army who held a
senior personnel post with Anglo American. The fourth was
Henry Nursten, a Czech-born agronomist who managed a
fertiliser company in Lusaka. The fifth was a quantity surveyor,
Cecil Swift.

The group were held at the Mumbwa prison, 100 miles from
Lusaka. Two years before, the prison had been used as the
detention centre for "holy woman" Alice Lenshina. Weeks
went by as they were interrogated; although it was known

that they were being well-treated and having lobster flown in regularly from Dar es Salaam, the resentment on the Copperbelt was intense. There was an attempt to organise a protest strike among the white miners. In Britain, the newspaper reports hinted that the arrests were part of a racialistic campaign. Three of the detainees had British passports and there were demands for action to have them freed.

Then in the middle of May the men were produced before a public tribunal. It was headed by a dour North Country judge, Tom Pickett, who was flanked by a Zambian magistrate and the chairman of the public service commission. The public gallery was packed, the families of the detainees filling the front rows of seats.

But when the detainees walked in under escort, one was missing. This was the solicitor, Ian Haigh, and a few minutes after the hearing began his legal representative stood up and left the courtroom. It later became known that Haigh had already left Zambia for good. The authorities had slipped him aboard a London-bound plane. When, during the hearing police witnesses referred to a "source" who had given them crucial information, everybody in the court knew that Haigh was being referred to; one of the lawyers for the detainees persisted in mentioning Haigh by name.

As a story unfolded, it proved both sensational and nauseating. The detainees had been involved in a network of petty spying, sending information on a wide variety of security matters to intelligence headquarters in Salisbury. The key figure in Salisbury turned out to be a Colonel Claude Greathead, who had served for several years in the army at Kitwe and Lusaka during the years of the Central African Federation. The confessions ultimately made by the detainees showed that Greathead had written to his agents in Zambia under a variety of "covers". The requests for information were sent to mail collection boxes rented in false names at the Lusaka Central post office and there was an elaborate system for reporting on the receipt of letters, which were always numbered – magazines with the relevant page numbers circled in red had to be posted to Greathead in Salisbury.

Some of the material supplied by the agents was harmless enough. It ranged from lists of names of foreign diplomats in Lusaka to the activities of leftwing Europeans. Other material was more sinister, such as the extent to which Zambian air force planes patrolling along the Angolan border were fitted with bomb racks – information which would be available to the Portuguese consulate in Salisbury. There were a variety of requests for details about the exile "freedom movements" based in Zambia. The jet pilot, Warren, admitted in his signed statement that he had investigated the possibility of installing a tape-recorder listening device in his plane. But he had had to abandon the scheme for fear of detection when the plane was inspected before VIP flights and because there were electrical difficulties. An intercepted letter produced at the hearing showed that Greathead had been enthusiastic when Warren first put up the idea.

During the hearings, the detainees sat together in the centre of the court. They were smartly dressed and suntanned, for most of their time at Mumbwa jail had been passed in sunbathing. When the hearings adjourned, the four turned and waved to friends and relatives in the public gallery. Only one, the silver-haired Arnott, agreed to give evidence on oath.

James Skinner, the Zambian Attorney-General, appeared for the State. He said the affair had "all the melodrama and trappings associated with espionage". The detainees had been part of an organisation which had been designed to spread alarm and dissension, weaken internal security and damage Zambia's relations with other powers. Skinner distributed photostats of intercepted letters sent to the detainees from Salisbury and mentioned other material which had fallen into the hands of the Zambian special branch. These included documents, which were proved to have been forged, apparently written by Zambian ministers. There were letters written to people abroad which were likely to create hostility and confusion. It was clear that only a small part of what had been going on was being uncovered.

One forged letter purported to have come from Munu Sipalo, the Minister of Labour in Lusaka, and was addressed to government and party officials on the Copperbelt. The subject was relations with trade union officials on the mines and was couched in provocative terms. At the time when the letter was written, 30,000 miners had been on strike and in desperation the government had arrested thirty union leaders and put them briefly in detention. In retrospect it seemed likely that the strike itself – which had cost £5,000,000 in lost output – had been inflamed from Salisbury.

Apart from the much publicised Colonel Greathead, other contacts in Salisbury were mentioned during the hearings. One of these was Wallace Fleming, a Rhodesian magistrate who had practised as a lawyer in Zambia until two years before; at one period in his career he had been a district commissioner. Fleming's wife had also been taken into detention. There was irony in the fact that both Fleming and Skinner, the Attorney-General, had been partners in the same legal firm before independence. But they had always been on opposite sides of the political fence, for Skinner had been among that handful of whites who had befriended the African nationalists in the early sixties.

By the time the tribunal had completed its work, there could be no doubt about the guilt of the detainees. This made a considerable impact upon the attitude of the white community in Zambia – from feeling sceptical about the allegations it swung around to a mood of disgust and shame. Any sympathy which might have been felt for the detainees was dissipated by the way in which they tried to blame one another.

The big question was what Kaunda would decide to do with the four men – and with Mrs Fleming. He could go on from the tribunal to a show trial, he could keep them all in detention indefinitely, or he could deport them. At the end of May, Mrs Fleming was released and restricted to her farm near Lusaka. She had written a letter to Kaunda admitting that she had sent information to Rhodesia and pleading for forgiveness. In any case, she had only been on the fringes of the espionage network.

The others were held in the hopes of squeezing more information out of them. The Czech-born Nursten was the hardest to crack – in his confession, Warren had described him as the "brains of the organisation". Eventually, the special branch

obtained what it wanted, clues which led on to three other
Rhodesian agents. There was a series of deportations, beginning
with Warren, Arnott and Swift. They were put on planes to
Europe and to avoid questioning at London Airport dis-
embarked in Switzerland and vanished. Not one of the people
who had been named ever made any denial of guilt after
leaving Zambia and the Rhodesian authorities made no
comments. Attempts to find the men who had been branded as
the organisers in Salisbury came up against an official wall of
silence.

Kaunda was so determined to make the facts known that
he had several hundred copies of the report specially printed
for distribution to political leaders and journalists throughout
the Commonwealth. He signed each one himself, and in a
foreword said that he had long before warned Harold Wilson
that subversion from Rhodesia was likely and had asked him to
take precautionary measures. "But he felt fit to ignore the
warning." In fact, Kaunda had asked Britain after UDI to
supply Zambia with a counter-espionage staff, but the request
had been rejected. Kaunda went on in his foreword: "I would
like to make it clear that this is only one of the many activities
emanating from UDI, ranging from psychological warfare to
actual sabotage in Zambia, but I hope that those who read this
report and are interested in good relations between nations
and the progress of man as a whole will play their part to
ensure that effective steps are taken, especially by the British
Government, to resolve UDI in the best interests of the people
of Central Africa and thus remove the most dangerous racial
time-bomb that today threatens us all."

The Zambians were well aware that although they had won a
tactical victory, they had not eliminated hostile agents in the
country. A hint of what was still going on was given in the
middle of 1968 when a European living on the Copperbelt
was given a two-year jail sentence for passing military secrets
to Rhodesia. There had also been oblique references during the
tribunal to a South African intelligence man operating in
Zambia. Pretoria is acknowledged to be highly organised for
such activities throughout southern Africa and its main interest
has always centred upon the guerrilla movements. Another

white man, Harold Boyes, was jailed in Lusaka after his car boot had been found filled with smuggled explosives – meant for blowing up the Zimbabwe African People's Union offices.

Detailed reports about guerrilla holding camps in Zambia were released in South Africa and by the middle of 1968 it was said that plans had been made for "pre-emptive strikes" against them. A cat-and-mouse game was in progress and there could be no doubt about which role Zambia was filling. One new development was the appearance over Zambia of high-flying military aircraft, identified as modified Canberras. At first they were thought to have come from Rhodesia, but later were treated as South African. The planes were assumed to be on photographic missions and it was believed that they were active not only over Zambia but also along the Tanzania–Mozambique border where guerrillas of the FRELIMO organisation were active.

These aerial penetrations so worried Kaunda that he began investigating the possibility of buying ground-to-air missiles. At the start of 1968, secret negotiations were opened with the British Aircraft Corporation for the purchase of Rapier, Bloodhound or Thunderbird missiles. The extent of Zambian knowledge was limited, so progress in the negotiations was slow. The British had decided that the mere idea of an African country setting up missile bases was unrealistic, but that if anything was to be offered the relatively uncomplicated Rapier was what Zambia should have. But the Rapier was not enough: its range was only 10,000 feet, which would be useless against the modified Canberras on their sorties at far more than 30,000 feet. The Thunderbird was what appealed to the Zambians. But each Thunderbird battery would need dozens of expensive technicians. Any incompetence would be dangerous: the Canberras flew roughly along the routes taken by civil airlines.

The spy planes and the need for a deterrent were discussed when Kaunda visited Britain in the middle of 1968. Wilson brought Denis Healey, the Defence Minister, into the talks with a group of military advisers. The Zambians said they were prepared to spend up to £20,000,000. But they would also hope for British aid to defend themselves and a supply of RAF technicians to operate the missile system. The response was cold. The British were not prepared to give any aid for the missiles and they were not willing to loan technicians for operational work. Healey pointed out that the British had no wish to shoot down Rhodesian, South African or Portuguese planes which might have crossed the Zambian border by accident.

It was also implied that Kaunda would not be confronted with so much potential expense if Zambia did not harbour guerrillas. If Zambia wanted to buy military equipment from Britain on a normal commercial basis, there would be no obstacles; but she could not expect any special help in extricating herself from a position of her own making. Kaunda said after the talks that he was "having difficulties" in obtaining the missiles he wanted, and when he was home in Lusaka, began to look around for other sources.

Within two months, Kaunda was back in Europe, this time to see President de Gaulle. Before he left, he had been asked whether the possibility of buying arms from France would be discussed. "Not publicly", he answered. In the communiqué released after the Paris talks, no mention was made of arms, but it was later learned that Zambia was thinking about buying Mystère jets. Before the end of 1968, negotiations had begun with the Italian Government and a Milanese contracting group for the building of a defence base near Lusaka.

There were other aerial intrusions to worry Kaunda — by the Portuguese from Angola and Mozambique pursuing freedom-fighters often based inside the Zambian border. Sometimes attacks were made on border villages and Zambian troops opened fire on low-flying planes. Six Labour MPs who had visited Zambia early in 1969 demanded that Britain should exert pressure on Portugal's new premier, Dr Caetano, to stop the use of Sabre jets intended for NATO defence during these missions. The MPs had a somewhat bleak response from Denis Healey, the Defence Secretary, who suggested that the remedy was in Zambia's own hands — to stop the activities of the guerrillas. It was perhaps scarcely surprising that the British, having rejected the use of force against Rhodesia, were reluctant to see anyone else trying militant methods.

In the middle of the Commonwealth Conference it was

revealed that Zambia had cancelled its eleven-month-old joint services training agreement with Britain. The reason, quite simply, was that the British officers seconded under the agreement were forbidden to engage in combat; the Zambian air force pilots were still so inexperienced that it would be suicidal for them to be pitted in their trainers against the Portuguese intruders. Although Kaunda carefully avoided using the word — which in the Congo had acquired bitter connotations — he needed mercenaries. Alluding to the cancellation of the agreement, he said: "We are now able to recruit people on our own terms. We must build up a combatant team, because of the attacks on us."

Meanwhile, the Canberra flights went on. The Zambians had a persistent fear that however hard they tried, they could keep no secrets from their enemies, with their cameras trained downwards from the skies. The country's newly-won sovereignty could easily be mocked by the white man — and it was still only the white man who could protect it. Yet the paradox must be endured, since Kaunda and his colleagues had a political mission in southern Africa — just as there had been a mission at home in the years of the independence struggle.

CHAPTER 13

Tribalism, the Wasting Disease

Zambia is so large and was so neglected in the first four decades of this century that a national consciousness can only be expected to have shallow roots. Less than sixty years ago the two "wings" of what later became known as Northern Rhodesia were still being administered separately. Until 1935 the capital was in the extreme south at Livingstone – a thousand miles from the Bemba country of the north where Kenneth Kaunda and Simon Kapwepwe were growing up together. Thirty years ago, there were very few people in this remote British protectorate who had any feeling of belonging to a country. Loyalties were to the family, the village, the clan and the tribe. Of course, this was a condition common, in a lesser or greater degree, to other colonial territories – and the colonial administrators had no reason to enlarge the political horizons or to instil national pride.

Two events helped to create in the people the sense of belonging to a country: the Second World War, in which many Africans from all over Northern Rhodesia took part, mingling together in uniform; and the creation of the Central African Federation. After the war, the first national political organisation was founded. Some of those involved were ex-servicemen. It was largely a reaction to the growth of white political movements, led by figures such as Roy Welensky. Then five years later came Federation, and the arguments which surrounded its formation made the Africans of Northern Rhodesia realise that they had a land of their own, distinct in precise ways from Southern Rhodesia. The realisation came to thousands of people, whereas only a handful had understood it ten or fifteen years before. The political ambitions of the whites had created for the Africans a national identity.

From the early fifties, the main political party in the country had a supra-tribal quality. In the African National Congress, the President was Harry Nkumbula, an Ila from the Southern Province; his Secretary-General was Kaunda, born in Bemba country. In 1958, when the short-lived Zambia African National Congress was launched, the leaders were Kaunda and Kapwepwe, Munu Sipalo (from Barotseland) and Reuben Kamanga (from the Eastern Province). The first President of the United National Independence Party – while Kaunda was in jail – was Mainza Chona, a Tonga from the south. All this would scarcely have happened if Sir Roy Welensky had not become recognised as the common enemy; to that extent he played a constructive role in the establishment of Zambia. If there had been no settler problem and the territory had moved gently towards independence in the manner of colonies in West Africa, for example, parties would almost certainly have arisen on predominantly tribal lines.

However, differences did begin to show themselves after the Nkumbula-Kaunda split in the late fifties. The conservative African National Congress ceased to be a national party. Through loyalty to Nkumbula, its stronghold became the Bantu Botatwe area of the south – the Tonga, Ila, Lenje group. Only the Mufulira area on the Copperbelt and the remote Mwinilungu district of the North-Western Province showed defiance to the militants. But the United National Independence Party always described itself as being above a tribe – and race, for that matter. In the pre-independence elections of early 1964, it was able to capture seats in all eight provinces. At that stage, Congress seemed destined to fade out quickly, for Nkumbula had become a somewhat lackadaisical political leader. UNIP enthusiasts added to the national motto – "One Zambia, One Nation" – an extra objective: "One Party."

Yet this did not happen. Kaunda refused to follow the example of Nyerere and Nkrumah to create a one-party state by legislation, for he said that he wanted Zambia to be a "liberal democracy". He agreed that a one-party state would be better in a new country, for it would allow energies dissipated in party rivalry to be harnessed to national construction. He forecast that the goal would be achieved democratically at the polls. Moreover, there was a good possibility that the hard core of Congress MPs around Nkumbula would see where their political futures lay and defect to UNIP. It was agreed in the caucus meetings of UNIP that everybody should be accommodating to the Congress diehards, in the hope of wooing them across the floor of parliament.

While this slow process was put in train, the distinction between the ruling party and the State was gradually eroded, in a fashion experienced elsewhere in Africa. Resident ministers (later upgraded to be ministers of state) were appointed for each province. They were all UNIP men – generally old guard activists who had not quite qualified for a place in the Cabinet but needed to be given some of the fruits of power. Apart from having overall charge of the civil service in the province, they were also head of the provincial party structure. Around the provincial ministers were grouped several "political assistants", who were paid salaries by the government and used government transport to move around their areas; invariably these assistants were middle-echelon party men from UNIP, even in the Southern Province where Congress held most of the parliamentary seats.

The impact of all this was immediately seen in the implementation of government policy. A new slogan was put about in 1965: "It pays to belong to UNIP." This was spelt out when political assistants on the Copperbelt began to warn at party rallies that only people who could produce party cards would be given government loans to start co-operatives. The influence went further with the intervention of UNIP in local government: mayors could only be elected with the approval of the government and in most cases the men chosen were leading local officials of the party. There was a close rapport, since most of the Cabinet ministers were in the UNIP central committee. The rural areas were administered by district secretaries, who replaced the former district commissioners. But these civil servants were less powerful than the regional secretaries of the party, who ran the local development committees.

The integration of party and government was taken a stage further when it became accepted that all schemes of major national importance should, at the outset, be presented to the party for approval. The Four-Year Plan, which envisaged an expenditure of more than £300,000,000, was unveiled at a UNIP conference and was not debated in parliament. At the start of 1967 a National Convention was held and delegates from all over the country were present. Also taking part were senior representatives of the copper-mining companies, Anglo American and RST, as well as civil servants. The African National Congress was not invited.

The National Convention operated through a series of committees, each of which presented reports on specific topics. The committee on "The Role of Youth in the Nation" was chaired by Dingiswayo Banda – Minister of Co-operatives, Youth and Social Development and also the UNIP Director of Youth. Members of the committee included Mr Michael Mataka, the police commissioner, Major-General C. M. Grigg, commander of the Zambian Army, and Group Captain Griffiths from the air force. Key paragraphs in the report said: "The committee recognised the functions of the UNIP Youth Brigade as a party wing. The brigade was effectively used during the political struggle and is still regarded as the vanguard of the ruling party. The committee recommended that the brigade should be given a positive and even better role to play in national development, especially to assist in the mobilisation of youth as a whole. The committee further recommended that the youth brigade should fully co-operate with the police and armed forces, whenever necessary, in the maintenance of law and order." In a reference to the African National Congress Youth League and Action Group, the committee recommended: "These, too, should come under the aegis of the National youth movement as re-organised and be made to understand the authority of the government."

Confronted by such relentless attitudes, the Congress might well have been expected to crumble. In Mufulira its following was liquidated by intensive campaigning in which the youths were tireless; the local UNIP regional secretary was elected mayor. In Ndola matters went out of hand when the home of a minor Congress official was petrol-bombed, killing the official himself, his wife and two children. A local UNIP leader, Mishek Kabungo — who later became Ndola's mayor — was charged with complicity but acquitted.

At the start of 1968, four Congress MPs from the Southern Province resigned the party whip and crossed the floor to UNIP. By law, by-elections had to be held when an MP left the party for which he had been elected. The four defectors stood in their own constituencies for UNIP, against new Congress candidates. UNIP made a massive effort to win and almost every member of the Cabinet from the President downwards took part in the campaigning. The government's information services were also active. Nkumbula seemed unable to offer much resistance, but the results were a shock. Congress kept all four seats and the support for UNIP was shown by the figures to be negligible. Tribalism had won the day.

One consequence of the by-elections was that both Nkumbula and Mungoni Liso, the Deputy President of Congress, were charged with insulting the President in campaign speeches. Nkumbula was acquitted, but Liso was sentenced to eighteen months' jail and automatically lost his place in the national assembly under a law which unseated any MP who had received a sentence of more than six months. On appeal, Liso had his sentence cut to exactly six months, but it was ruled that he could not reclaim his seat. It was not the only time in which Congress leaders found themselves in court: the MP for Mwinilunga was charged with treason, but after listening to submissions by a barrister flown out from London the court ruled that there was no case to answer.

UNIP's pursuit of the one-party ideal was suddenly made more difficult by the emergence of the third political organisation, the United Party. This was led by Nalumino Mundia, a Lozi who had been in the top group of UNIP militants since the early sixties. Mundia had been given a place in the first nationalist government and had moved upwards in the heirarchy to become Minister of Labour. But in 1966 he had been made to resign by Kaunda after a petty financial scandal; following a series of altercations with party colleagues, Mundia was expelled from UNIP and deprived of his parliamentary seat in March 1967. When he formed the United Party it quickly attracted a wide assortment of malcontents on the Copperbelt and in Lusaka. But its main strength was centred in Mundia's own Lozi tribe, where the party promised to restore the old power of the chiefs. Once again, tribalism was reasserting itself.

Far more serious, however, were the tribal conflicts within UNIP itself. After a party conference in August 1967, Kaunda had said that the internal power struggle had been "viciously along tribal, racial and provincial lines". He had never expected such a "spate of hate". Six months later, Kaunda left a meeting of the party's national council when some of its members came to blows. He said that he intended resigning as President of Zambia; he was not willing to watch "tribalism, the wasting disease of Africa", take its course. This action stunned his followers, who saw him stalk out of a hall on the outskirts of Lusaka and set off on foot to walk three miles to State House. His official car caught him up and the chauffeur persuaded him to step in. But when Kapwepwe and a deputation hurriedly selected from the Cabinet arrived at State House they found Kaunda packing in his bedroom. "I am returning to my farm at Chinsali and leaving public life for good." After an emotional discussion which lasted most of the night he agreed to unpack and stay at his post.

The incident was minutely analysed within the party leadership. Had Kaunda been really determined to quit, or was he intending to teach his lieutenants a lesson? What would have happened if his resignation had been accepted and a power struggle within UNIP to select a replacement launched immediately? It became clear during the course of this analysis that Kaunda had wanted to administer shock treatment, but that if it had proved ineffective he would actually have left.

There was a general agreement that any more tribal manifestations within the party must be avoided. Kaunda had given a clear warning: "We have reached the point where if you are not careful this nation goes to pieces completely." But within two months the good resolutions had fallen away. In April 1968, an official visit was made to Kasama, administrative headquarters of the Northern Province, by two senior UNIP ministers, Dingiswayo Banda and Munu Sipalo. As they stepped off the plane they were greeted by a hostile demonstration, organised by local UNIP leaders. One of the placards waved at the ministers said: "Don't confuse the country." The principal target of the demonstration was Sipalo, who was thought by the Bemba of the Northern Province to be secretly supporting the United Party. Like the dissident Mundia, Sipalo was a Lozi.

On his return from the 1,000-mile round trip to Kasama, the incensed Sipalo made the incident public. He also went to Kaunda and demanded that the UNIP officials concerned should be made to apologise; Kaunda said he would order an enquiry into what had happened. Three months later a statement was put out by Kasonde Kasutu, the Kasama regional secretary and most senior UNIP functionary in the area. He said he had given "considerable thought" and would not apologise, because the demonstrations and jeers were as the people of Kasama wished. He explained: "The actual demonstrations were not intended to include Mr Banda. We were only expecting Mr Sipalo and Mr Banda's arrival was, therefore, a bit of a surprise to us." Kasutu added that he did not like arguing with senior members of the party or having the matter discussed in the newspapers.

Observers found the portents ominous. Zambia already had enough on her plate, with UDI and the effect on her economy of sanctions. She could ill afford to fritter away energy on internal squabbles. But few fully understood how it had come about, and how inescapable it was.

The Cabinet in Zambia had always been delicately balanced between the tribal poles of the Bemba in the north and the Barotse (Lozi) in the south. There was nothing intrinsically reprehensible in making all the areas feel they had a voice at the top. But it went further. President Kaunda had found it expedient to maintain four Bemba and four Lozi in the Cabinet, however the portfolios were distributed. When two ministers, Mundia and Nalilungwe, were told to resign in January 1966 for acquiring shares in companies receiving government loans, they both happened to be Lozi. They were both replaced by Lozi. The balance was maintained.

The system seemed to work well, and the general hope and

expectation was that gradually tribalism would be forgotten. After all, Zambia again had a common enemy – Ian Smith. It was engaged in a massive task of reorientating its trading pattern away from the south and to East Africa. It had achieved great things in education during the transitional development plan, setting a pace unmatched in any other African country. There was money, for notwithstanding sanctions, the output of copper had been fairly well maintained and the direct revenue to the government was more than £150,000,000 a year – a lot for a nation of 4,000,000. The people had the knowledge that in Kenneth Kaunda they possessed a leader who was universally respected.

Finally, it seemed that Zambia must have taken on board some of the lessons of other African countries where tribalism had shown itself to be a destructive and retrograde force. In the neighbouring Congo, the example was stark; many Zambia groups – the Lamba, Lunda, Kaonde and Bemba, to name a few – had close affinities with the Congo and understood well the misery over the border.

Yet the problem was smouldering and at the centre of the hidden fire lay the question of the vice-presidency. It was always understood that whoever was vice-president of UNIP would also be vice-president of the country. Kaunda had gone on record with that promise in 1964. At the time of independence, the Vice-President was Reuben Kamanga, a veteran nationalist of Eastern Province origins. He was a man with little personal magnetism and no significant support on the Copperbelt, the political powerhouse of Zambia. The Copperbelt is a Bemba area – not originally, because it is the home of the related Lamba tribe, but ever since the thirties when the Bemba migrated across the Congo Pedicle to take jobs on the mines. The man who made the crowds roar on the Copperbelt was Simon Kapwepwe, an orator, fiery and compelling; a Bemba among the Bemba. They were ambitious for him.

Quite obviously, if Kamanga stayed as vice-president, the danger that one tribe or the other would feel slighted was likely to remain in the background. The job was as important as the man. Two years went by without elections to the central committee of UNIP; the *status quo* was maintained. But by the start of 1967, the pressures from the Copperbelt were irresistible and Kaunda announced that the elections would definitely be held that year. At once, tribal intriguing and manœuvring became acute in the middle and upper echelons of the party. There was an air of unreality for several months, because the press maintained its unwritten pledge never to mention tribalism. If they did mention it, the method was oblique. Pregnant leaders were written about the catastrophic effects of tribalism in Nigeria or such distant parts, in the hope that readers would take the point.

For the public of Zambia, January–July of 1967 was rather like standing outside a building in which two ill-defined groups of men were fighting it out to the death. They could hear the bangs and groans, the smash of breaking glass, without having any clear idea of the way the struggle was going.

It would be an over-simplification to say that Kapwepwe was pushing for power. He was drafted, and did not protest too much. The Lozi in particular felt that his elevation to the double vice-presidency would mean Bemba dominance, while the Ngoni, Chewa and Nsenga of the Eastern Province were grieved at the prospect that Kamanga was facing demotion. Nobody knew what the Tonga in UNIP – not a powerful element – were thinking; nobody greatly cared. But much arithmetic was devoted to the voting that would be done by party officials at the elections. The general agreement was that if all the non-Bemba tribes stuck together, Kapwepwe could not win.

Came the election in August 1967 and Kapwepwe did win. The Bemba and the Tonga had contrived an allegiance and at a tense conference at Mulungushi it became clear that the balance of power in UNIP was irrevocably altered. Kapwepwe became Zambia's vice-president, changing places with Kamanga, who moved down to become Foreign Minister. Sipalo was beaten by Chona for the party secretary-general and Mudenda ousted Arthur Wina from the party treasurership and consequently from the job of Finance Minister.

The pattern was repeated down through the central committee. But the unavoidable fact was that the two top Lozi – Sipalo and Wina – had taken a beating at the hands of the

Bemba. Worse still, the instruments for the beating were the Tonga colleagues, Chona and Mudenda. Only seventy years before, the Tonga had been the slaves of the Lozi.

Sipalo resigned from the party, but was persuaded back by the President and took over the portfolio of Agriculture. Arthur Wina came very close to resignation and for several weeks was absent from his new desk at the Ministry of Education. Kapwepwe made great efforts to persuade the losers that he had no designs against them and that rumours of his yearning for the presidency itself were quite unfounded. But the Pandora's box had been opened and by the middle of 1968 there was no sign that all the gruesome contents could be captured and put back. Mundia was still expanding his United Party and a UNIP official in Lusaka (a Bemba) was made to resign after he had alleged that Sipalo was backing the UP. Then Sipalo came under heavy fire after he had rebuked, in the National Assembly, UNIP officials on the Copperbelt for their strong-arm methods in dealing with suspected United Party members.

In the Eastern Province near Malawi UNIP officials began promoting a new and cryptic slogan, "Unity in the East". The President told them to drop it, which they did reluctantly. But later, the party expelled its regional secretary in the provincial headquarters of Chipata (formerly Fort Jameson). Plainly, the political life of Zambia was going through a hectic transition.

Kaunda had strengthened his position in the country in April by introducing the economic measures to give Zambia greater control over its development. This was a show of power, and no other member of the Cabinet knew the details before he spoke. Kaunda's prestige throughout the country was still accepted to be of a unique nature. Although Kapwepwe had grass-roots authority within the Bemba areas, he did not have national following. Equally, there was no non-Bemba politician who had real support on the Copperbelt or farther north.

The attitude of local activists was put frankly by Chona, as UNIP's secretary-general, in a newspaper article in May 1968. He complained that most people felt that they "got better service" from leaders who came from their own tribal areas. The whole fault did not lie at the top, but essentially in the narrow attitude of those in the middle rank. "The truth is that leaders share the greater blame for failing to resist unfair tribalistic pressure, but they are not alone to blame." Chona warned that there would never be any lasting solution unless local leaders in the villages and towns stopped being competitive against other groups and began to regard top leaders as national leaders.

In the eyes of the other tribal groups, the Bemba were the principal offenders. They always seemed to be on the advance and every appointment within the governmental or party structure was studied to see if they had made further gains since the elevation of Kapwepwe to the vice-presidency. They had a restless energy and aggression against which it was hard to stand firm.

On their side, the Bemba argued that they were the people who had fought hardest against colonialism. In the middle fifties, when the political movement was at a low ebb, they had worked through the African unions on the Copperbelt. In the early sixties, the Bemba homeland in the Northern Province had been the scene of disturbances which had forced Iain Macleod to revise his constitutional plans for the country; in the disturbances, dozens of people had died and nearly three thousand had been jailed. At that time, what were the Lozi doing? It was undeniable that for much of the pre-independence period, the Barotse Province had been taken up with squabbles between the Lozi intellectuals and feudalists grouped around the paramount chief, Sir Mwanawina Lewanika.

The characteristics of the Bemba had undoubtedly been influenced over the years by life in the Copperbelt towns, which had been the magnet for more than half of the younger Bemba. All mining communities tend to be brash and the European miners had established a typical mode of behaviour which had inevitably been taken by the Africans around them as an ideal to be copied. It was above everything materialistic – the miners, both white and black, were hard drinking and free spending. The Copperbelt laid claim to having a higher consumption of alcohol per head than anywhere else in Africa and the highest rate of road accidents in the world. For the Africans, living in the huge and characterless townships around the mines, the social consequences were more stark than for their white counterparts.

But the 40,000 African miners with their high salaries* were only a fortunate élite. The Copperbelt also supported a far greater number of unemployed, hanging around the bright lights and being maintained by relatives. Many of these unemployed were young men who had never been educated, because the schools had no room for them. Without education, they had small hopes of finding work. Yet they were urbanised, often born on the Copperbelt, and the idea of going back to farm in the family villages of the Northern Province had no appeal. The obvious outlet for their energies lay in politics. This restless, frustrated element was the material of the youth brigade.

After independence, the impetus of political struggle died away and efforts were made to organise a Zambia Youth Service to give a new sense of direction, but the first recruits refused to co-operate when they realised that it was planned to settle them on the land. In an effort to remove the discontent, the politicians made promises of jobs in the towns which proved impossible to honour. Nobody was anxious to employ the products of the youth service. Despite the efforts of experts from Sweden and Israel the service was a shambles. The original aim of recruiting and training as many as 50,000 youths – mainly from the Copperbelt – had become a fond memory.

So by 1968 the Copperbelt, the power base of the Bemba politicians, was still seething with militant discontent, waiting to be exploited and orientated. At the head of the provincial UNIP structure was the Minister of State, Peter Chanda. In his speeches at the weekend rallies, Chanda gave the youths the heady rhetoric which was calculated to make them forget for a moment their deep frustrations. All the stock objects of hatred were attacked – Wilson, Smith, Vorster, racialistic white miners, Indian traders. When Martin Luther King was assassinated Chanda said that the killing had been masterminded by "those in power in the United States". An American girl Peace Corps teacher, who had one of Kaunda's sons as a

* See Chapter 11, p. 172.

pupil, wrote to a newspaper to say that the allegation was "undiplomatic, undeserved and untrue". The girl was deported.

But the main political energies of Chanda and his junior officials were directed to rooting out the growing support on the Copperbelt for Mundia's United Party. Youths roamed the townships demanding to be shown UNIP cards. People were refused permission to board buses unless they could produce a card and stallholders were stopped from trading if their loyalty to UNIP was in doubt. Throughout the middle of 1968, there were violent clashes between rival bands, with an unknown number of deaths and injuries. One woman official of UNIP told a rally: "If you know United Party members, spear them until you find their hearts."

In the middle of August, the violence came to a head at the western end of the Copperbelt. In a township regarded as a centre of United Party support, a UNIP regional youth secretary was hacked to death with pangas and one of Chanda's assistant ministers of state was badly wounded. Immediately, Kaunda banned the United Party as a "threat to public security and peace". Mundia and five of his principal officials were arrested and sent into restriction.

In a comment on the killing of the UNIP official, Chanda was quoted as saying there was no doubt that members of the Lozi tribe were to blame. The next day a public protest was made by the Lozi members of the Cabinet, including Sipalo and Arthur Wina: "It is disconcerting to see that Mr Chanda, who is the President's personal representative should demonstrate such dismal tribalism over an issue which could set the country ablaze." The following week, Chanda made a statement in the national assembly in which he said that the press had misquoted him. He had never mentioned any tribe. A Lozi minister remarked: "You can make up your own mind."

Four weeks later an anonymous circular was distributed from the Copperbelt. Copies were sent to all the leading officials of UNIP. It demanded that certain people should be prevented from standing as party candidates in the forthcoming general election. At the top of the list were four Lozi ministers, headed by Arthur Wina and Sipalo. Kaunda put out a message saying that the circular should be ignored. He added:

"Zambia's enemies are trying to spread confusion and misunderstanding."

It was a completely different issue which brought the Copperbelt back into the news at the end of October 1968. In a speech at a rally, Chanda chose as a topic the murder of Mrs Lilian Burton on the Copperbelt in 1960. (Mrs Burton had been stopped while driving along a road with her two daughters, her car overturned and set alight with petrol. Four youths, all of them UNIP members, were hanged for the crime.) Chanda told his audience that the four were national heroes, and that anyone who did not agree should leave the country. The widower, Robert Burton, who had stayed in Zambia, immediately wrote a letter to the daily newspaper saying that Chanda's remarks had "shown the true colours of UNIP". He was leaving his job, selling his house, and going away from Zambia for good. In response, Kaunda took the unusual step, for a president, of writing an open letter to the paper, appealing to Burton to stay. It was a conciliatory letter, which avoided any outright rebuke to Chanda. It described him as "a young man I have known for a very long time". Burton agreed to stay. Chanda said nothing.

By this time, all political attention was directed to the forthcoming general election, which was expected in early January 1969. A clear victory for UNIP was certain, for the only opposition was Congress with its diehard support in the South Province. The legislature was being enlarged to 105 seats and it seemed inevitable that UNIP would capture at least ninety. If there were a few pre-election brawls in the shanty-towns around Lusaka, between UNIP and Congress, this was to be expected. What was far more in doubt was the possible explosion within UNIP itself, over the allocation of seats. How many would go to the Bemba and how many to the Lozi? Then after the election, how would the ministries be allocated?

As the election drew nearer, excitement about the slate of UNIP candidates faded away. Kaunda made the choice himself, showing considerable astuteness in doing so. Some members of the party who had fallen from grace were given seats they would have trouble in winning; such a one was

Ditton Mwiinga, former Minister of Health who had refused to take up a post as Zambian ambassador in Peking – he found himself with a strongly Congress constituency where he was in due course thoroughly beaten. The two leading Lozi members of the Cabinet had Barotse seats, which appeared safe enough: Arthur Wina was given Nalikwanda and Munu Sipalo was to contest Senanga West. But in contrast, the younger Wina brother, Sikota, was given a Copperbelt seat. The election was now to be a month earlier than expected, because Kaunda had decided that he would after all be attending the forthcoming Commonwealth Conference, along with Julius Nyerere. As he dissolved parliament, Kaunda had said: "Let us not damage the name of Zambia; let us not endanger the future of Africa; let us not disgrace the cause of the common man, for which we all stand. I pray that God may continue to smile upon Zambia; may he grant that our general election shall be conducted in a manner worthy of Zambia's greatness."

This last hope was fulfilled beyond most expectations. There was a certain amount of brutality among party gangs in Lusaka. Congress supporters in the Copperbelt towns found life hard at times, and matters were not improved for them by a string of wild allegations from Harry Nkumbula and his Congress lieutenants. Yet by African standards – even by the standards of most countries in the world – it was a remarkably democratic affair. Even Nalumino Mundia, the leader of the banned United Party, was allowed to enter his name for a Barotse seat although he was still in restriction.

As the results came in, they went much as expected in the early stages. UNIP registered massive victories in the urban centres of the Copperbelt and in most other parts of the country. It was only as the returns from remote Barotse constituencies were known that UNIP officials began to realise that something had gone awry: Congress candidates – including the restricted Mundia – had swept to victory in all eight of the Barotse "heartland" seats. Both Arthur Wina and Sipalo were crushingly defeated by obscure Congress candidates. So were three other Lozis of ministerial rank. At one blow the power balance upon which Zambian politics had been based since independence was destroyed. The only Lozi of any significance among the eighty-two successful UNIP candidates was Sikota Wina.

The result produced a wave of bitterness and recrimination inside the party. Some of the Bemba were pleased to see Sipalo and the elder Wina so humiliated, but at the same time they were chagrined by the extent of the Barotse revolt. Quite plainly, the Congress candidates had picked up the votes which would have gone to Mundia's United Party. In their Tonga stronghold also, the Congressmen had done better than they could have expected. Once again, the Tonga had been a tribal pivot – in 1967, the Tonga leadership within UNIP had done a deal with the Bemba over the central committee elections; in 1968, the Tonga had combined with the Lozi traditionalists to win again. On both occasions, Arthur Wina and Sipalo had been the victims. They were so disconsolate that they refused to accept nominated seats in the national assembly, and vanished for the moment into political oblivion.

The results increased fears that a new attempt at secession by Barotseland was being prepared. The elections had clearly shown that four years of independence had in no way removed hostility in the province towards the nationalists of the Copper-belt and Lusaka. The national motto – "One Zambia, One Nation" – was being mocked, and matters had been made far worse by a startling event almost on the eve of polling. A new Barotse paramount chief had been elected to replace Sir Mwanawina Lewanika, the aged Litunga who had died several months before. The new Litunga was none other than Godwin Mbikusita, who had been a political opponent of Kaunda and his associates for many years. It was Mbikusita who had been one of Sir Roy Welensky's African parliamentary secretaries in the time of Federation. He had encouraged Sir Mwanawina to demand secession in the early sixties and had taken Duncan Sandys (then Commonwealth Secretary) to Barotseland in March 1962 to receive a signed document calling for the region's complete separation from the rest of the country. Since the end of Federation, Mbikusita had stayed in obscurity until this sudden elevation to the most august tribal position in

Zambia. Kaunda had been present to hear the result of the deliberations by Barotse elders to choose a new Litunga. When Mbikusita's name was announced, Kaunda did not make his presidential speech of welcome; it was later explained that the rain had been too heavy. Quite quickly, a campaign was launched to have Mbikusita removed through the tribal system, on the ground that he had been improperly selected. Kaunda said he would not interfere, although under an act passed in 1965 he had the power to recognise or remove any chief in the country. He explained: "If the people are dissatisfied with the choice of the Litunga, the decision is theirs."

But for the moment, most attention was being directed towards the new-found strength of the African National Congress. For the next five years, it seemed, UNIP would be faced with a lusty opposition. The easiest solution would be to declare a one-party state and steamroller any defiance that this might provoke. Some members of the newly-formed "inner Cabinet" argued furiously for this and foremost among them was Sikota Wina, who had been appointed Minister of Information. Wina declared that Congress supporters would "get it in the neck" if they did not start to appreciate UNIP. Their shops were being closed and those who did not like it could emigrate to Malawi, Rhodesia, South Africa or Angola. Kaunda did his best to ride the tide of such attitudes – himself reviving the old slogan "It pays to belong to UNIP", while later urging that political opponents should not be persecuted.

All the time, he had to keep a close eye on the Copperbelt and the aggressions it aroused. In the post-election re-organisation he had moved Peter Chanda from the Copperbelt limelight to the Eastern Province and appointed Dingiswayo Banda as the Copperbelt's "provincial Cabinet Minister". It was Banda who had been with Sipalo in the early part of 1968 when the former was subjected to a hostile demonstration in Kasama. Without delay, Banda made it clear that he was responsive to Copperbelt feelings, during a speech to 3,000 party activists. He described himself as a new broom to sweep up all the rubbish: "I do not want any opposition and we are going to draw up plans to eliminate pockets of Congress." Banda also had a word for the Jehovah's Witnesses on the Copperbelt:

"If they want to talk to God and not to President Kaunda, then they should fly to heaven."

It is the custom for African politicians to speak in graphic and explosive terms about any opposition group. But in Zambia during the first half of 1969 this was part of the insistent pressure for some action which would seem to unify the country and help to mobilise the national will. Greater control from the top would also reduce the risk of subversion from within and without, and in April the security situation was described by Kapwepwe as having taken a sharp turn for the worse. He was speaking in support of a parliamentary motion to extend for a further six months the emergency regulations which had already been in force for five years. These regulations gave wide powers, including the right to keep in restriction one newly-elected MP – the former Cabinet colleague Nalumino Mundia.

The party leadership now had closer contacts with the rural areas, as a result of Kaunda's reshaping of the government structure to place a minister in every province. Yet this alone was not enough, and plans were put in hand for a national referendum. This would remove from the constitution a clause which decreed that certain parts of it could not be changed unless separate referenda were held on each one; the "certain parts" related to human rights. The African National Congress claimed the aim was to declare a one-party state after the referendum with the support of two-thirds of the national assembly – a majority the ruling party possessed with a dozen votes to spare. However, UNIP said that it had no such intention: the offending clause had been designed by the British and was a colonialistic relic denying Zambia its full independence.

PART FIVE

The Future Role in Africa

CHAPTER 14

Chairman Mao and the
Tan-Zam Railway

Whenever Johannes Vorster urged Kenneth Kaunda, in public and private, to eschew Communism, they both understood what was meant. Zambia should stop the freedom-fighters from making their southward incursions. But there is also a longer-term prospect: the Tan-Zam Railway. By the end of 1970, the Chinese Peoples' Republic is due to start building the line, which will run from Dar es Salaam to connect up with the existing Zambian railway from the Victoria Falls Bridge to the Copperbelt. In the middle of 1968, more than 300 Chinese technicians began making a detailed survey of the 1,000-mile route. It will point like an arrow from Dar es Salaam — which the South Africans regard as the headquarters for Communist subversion on the continent — to the south. In Pretoria there is a vision of hostile forces boarding trains in Tanzania and stepping out, ready for battle, only fifty miles from South-West Africa's Caprivi Strip.

The Tan-Zam railway can most easily be justified in terms that are political rather than economic. The West repeatedly threw cold water on the project, insisting that for a probable outlay of more than £120,000,000 it would not have a worthwhile volume of traffic. These arguments were summed up in April 1968 by Negro Senator Edward Brooke of Massachusetts, in a speech to the US Senate after a tour through Africa: "The United States has contended that a preferable alternative to construction of a costly rail connection would be improvement of the primitive highway linking the two countries." Brooke went on to argue that it was a false analogy to point to

o

the role of railroads in America in opening up the country –
"there is no basis for concluding that development should be
tied to a nineteenth-century technology". He suggested that
not only road transport, but also air freighting could be used to
carry imports and exports between Zambia and Tanzania,
and mentioned new giant aircraft such as the Lockheed C-5A.
Cynics claimed at one stage that the Americans were condemning the railway project because of pressure from the Detroit
automobile lobby, which hoped it might sell hundreds of
trucks for the road route. That had fallen away since the
Italian Fiat concern gained a dominating position in Zambia–
Tanzania road haulage. Later, a seeker after capitalist motives
could have suggested that the US hoped for a good trade in
freight planes – after all, Lockheed did sell five C-130 Hercules
for more than £5,000,000 to ferry copper to Dar es Salaam
from Ndola when Rhodesia declared its independence. It was
an ill-fated experiment, abandoned at the end of March
1969 with a loss of £1,000,000.

The Americans have been able to rely on a series of investigations which almost without exception have been highly
critical of the railway project. The concept is far from new – it
goes back to the start of the century and Cecil Rhodes's dream
of an "all-red" route from The Cape to Cairo. The railway from
South Africa was pushed across the Victoria Falls to open up
the British South Africa Company's vast possession north of the
Zambezi, but after the death of Rhodes the company lost
much of its impetus. By 1906, the line had reached Broken
Hill, where a lead and zinc mine was being developed, but
there it halted. A contemporary description by an engineer,
H. F. Varian, said: "The Cape-to-Cairo Railway came to an
end in the middle of a burnt-out vlei (swamp) without even a
buffer-stop at the rail terminus. Beside it stood a solitary tele-
graph pole, and in this atmosphere of desolation it languished
for several years."

The dream died hard. Three years later an English woman
journalist, Charlotte Mansfield, made an expedition along the
route which the Chinese were to survey sixty years afterwards
and wrote: "What would really put Northern Rhodesia on the
same footing as Southern Rhodesia would be a railway from

Broken Hill to Tanganyika." But in the next two decades the pattern changed. The railway continued, but instead of going north-east it linked up with the line from the Katanga copper mines of the Congo to Lobito Bay in Angola. Patterns of trade were established and as the Copperbelt was developed, it exported its output southwards over the Falls bridge and imports came in by the same route.

Little more was heard of Rhodes's railway until the early fifties, when the Colonial Office commissioned a survey by Sir Alexander Gibb and Partners; published in 1952, the report showed that the line was quite feasible in engineering terms but likely to prove a white elephant. The report was quietly pigeon-holed, although an Oxford University Press atlas published at the time marked the "proposed railway" with a line of dots. The matter rested for another decade, until Kaunda and his United National Independence Party edged its way into office in a coalition with the African National Congress at the end of 1962. Independence was still almost two years away, but Kaunda already planned with the confidence that power was within his grasp. His friendship with Nyerere was firm and they had been brought closer through PAFMECSA – the Pan-African Freedom Movement of East Central and Southern Africa. They had been together on the platform at the PAFMECSA conference of May 1962 at Mbeya, near the border of the two countries. In the election of 1962, UNIP had been allowed to use Radio Tanzania to broadcast propaganda and the party's election manifesto was printed in Dar es Salaam. But contact between the two countries remained spasmodic. There was no telephone link, an air service only once a week and the ironically named Great North Road was often impassable in the rainy season.

When Kaunda first began talking of a rail link to Tanzania, he knew nothing of the original plan by Cecil Rhodes. He only knew that if this could be done it would free his country from dependence on the line to the south. At the start of 1963 he said privately: "This railway is a political necessity. Even after Rhodesia wins majority rule, there will still be Mozambique and South Africa between us and the sea." He did not take much account of the possibilities of the route from the

Copperbelt to the Congo and thence across Angola to Lobito –
it was also controlled by Portugal. Nor did it seem possible to
put much trust in the *Voie Nationale* to Port Francqui on the
Kasai River and from there by river barge and rail to Matadi;
the Congo was in too much confusion. In March 1963, Kaunda
sent his closest confidante, Simon Kapwepwe, on a trip to
Dar es Salaam with instructions to discuss the possibility of the
new railway. Nyerere was interested, and sent a team to
Lusaka to have further discussions; not only would he be
politically helpful to his friend Kaunda, but it would also
provide the means for developing south-western Tanzania,
which had farming potential and was also known to possess
mineral resources.

By the middle of 1963, Kaunda was as obsessed as ever
Rhodes had been by this bold scheme. He told a rally of
30,000 members of UNIP that they all must help to build the
line – apparently having in mind the projects he had seen in
India completed by the massive use of human labour. The
Zambians cheered lustily, although any visible rush to carve a
swathe through the bush ahead of the track was lacking.
Kaunda claimed that he had found a large company "all
ready" to build the line in two years – an estimate of heady
optimism. The company was Lonrho, which at that time had
just begun to extend itself northwards from its base in Rhodesia.
Lonrho made a feasibility study in 1963, basing it largely
upon the report of Alexander Gibb and Partners, and then
offered to build the line and operate it. But there was a snag:
Lonrho wanted a guarantee that it would be given all the
copper traffic to the coast – more than 600,000 tons a year –
at rates to be agreed. The copper companies were alarmed when
they caught a whisper of this, for they regarded Lonrho as a
dangerous *parvenu* in African big business. Soon afterwards, the
Lonrho offer faded away.

However, the railway had become a platform in the policies
of UNIP. The party's manifesto for the general election at the
start of 1964 said that it would receive priority. Kaunda asked
the World Bank to carry out a survey. But the Rhodesians
had also taken note of the publicity and in the agreement for
the future operations of Rhodesia Railways, drawn up at the

break-up of the Central African Federation, a clause was inserted that any future project which drew traffic away from the traditional route would mean the payment of compensation; this compensation would be equal to the value of the traffic lost by Rhodesia Railways.

The World Bank report – prepared by A. Robert Sadove – was not made public, but it was known to be hostile to Kaunda's plan. It argued that trade between Central and East Africa was negligible, so that even if the line carried all the copper traffic outwards, the trains would have little to ‘bring back. Moreover, the harbour facilities at Dar es Salaam were not capable of taking extra cargo without expensive improvements. Finally, the gauge of the existing Tanzania railway – built by the Germans in 1912 – with which the new line would link up before reaching the coast, was different from that of the system in Zambia; so either some track would have to be relaid or goods would have to be trans-shipped.

The World Bank recommended that if it was a matter of opening up the northern part of Zambia and the adjoining regions of Tanzania a highway would be far cheaper. It would cost only £11,000,000.

These arguments were picked up by the United Nations survey team, led by Dudley Seers, which examined the economic needs confronting Zambia. The Seers Report was handed over to Kaunda in March 1964 and published at the end of the year. It argued that the reasons so far put forward for the railway were speculative "and naturally do not constitute in themselves a firm case". The existing railways in southern Africa had spare capacity in track and it was invalid to suggest that the line would stimulate agriculture in the north of Zambia – the most likely crops there were tobacco and coffee, neither of which needed rail transport. There was risk of an "expensive mistake", for the railway would need a heavy outlay of capital and it seemed that it would have to be subsidised for many years.

After Sadove and Seers, further condemnation was piled on in 1965 by Edwin T. Haefele and Eleanor B. Steinberg of the Brookings Institution, Washington. They made a survey, financed by the Agency for International Development, of railway systems in Africa south of the equator. Their discouraging analysis of the Tan-Zam link was rounded off with a paragraph on the political aspects: "No argument couched in economic terms has so far moved the Zambian Government to abandon its political goal of freeing itself from dependence on rail routes which run through countries at present dominated by white minority governments. Perhaps it is too much to expect any nation to remain vulnerable in such a fashion if any way can be found, however expensive, to avoid it."

As it happened, it seemed that a way was being found – one that had never been contemplated by anyone from Cecil Rhodes to Haefele and Steinberg. In Britain and America at the end of 1964, Kaunda had looked fruitlessly for financial backers for the railway. The Chinese stepped forward. A representative from their newly-opened mission called at State House a few weeks after Kaunda had returned from his trip and said that his country might be willing to help. That moment was the launching of the biggest aid project by mainland China anywhere in the world; and Kaunda was intensely wary at first.

The offer was taken a stage further in June 1965, when Premier Chou En-lai made a visit to Dar es Salaam. He put the suggestion in more precise terms to Nyerere and within eight weeks a twelve-man team had arrived from Peking and began surveying at Tunduma on the Tanzania–Zambia border. There were hints that Kaunda was upset. He re-doubled his efforts to arouse Western interest and the chance soon came at the 1965 Commonwealth conference in London. It was explained by Kaunda to Wilson that he was unwilling to see the Chinese come in; Zambia had already retained a British firm of railway engineers to make a preliminary study, which would cost £150,000. Wilson responded by offering to pay half of the amount, and the Canadians were brought in to pay the rest. So in the second half of 1965 there were two teams in operation, each one studiously ignoring the other.

For a variety of reasons, Kaunda was much less confident than Nyerere at that time about consorting with the Chinese. For a start, Zambia had been independent for less than a year, and was feeling its way in contacts with the outside world,

whereas the Tanzanians had been free since 1961. Although
Zambia had recognised the Chinese Peoples' Republic (following the British lead, like other ex-British territories in Africa)
Kaunda had an almost pathological fear of subversion. In
March 1965, all foreign missions in Lusaka had been told that
none of their staff could travel more than twenty-five miles
from the capital without obtaining permission. The move was
generally thought to aim directly at the Chinese, to stop them
infiltrating the trade unions on the Copperbelt. Suspicions
had been strengthened by the report that a Chinese diplomat
had been caught in the entrance to the Lusaka post office,
handing a minor trade union official a brown paper bag containing £75 in notes. In the following month, Foreign Minister
Simon Kapwepwe told the national assembly that all missions
would be limited to twelve people, although Commonwealth
missions could have up to three more. He explained that if
embassies were too large, "they would not be fully occupied
with their proper functions and might become engaged in
intrigue". Once again, it seemed that the Chinese were the
target. Ambassador Chin Li-chen had just presented his
credentials.

Antagonisms were increased in April 1965 by the appearance
of a magazine called *Revolution in Africa*. The magazine was well
produced and carried an imprint which said that its offices
were in a street in Tirana, the capital of Albania. The editor
was an African and a photograph showed him posing with
various Chinese dignitaries – including Chairman Mao – at a
conference in Peking. So far, this was all unremarkable: since
the early sixties, Africans had been visiting China in increasing
numbers and the volume of pro-Chinese literature circulating in
Africa was already large. Albania was a Chinese satellite and
seemed a logical place from which to publish an addition to the
flood. But what made *Revolution in Africa* the subject of so much
excitement was its comments upon African leaders. "The
Application of Mao's Precepts on Popular Revolution" was
the headline to an article which called Kaunda a "capitalist
agent" and branded Nyerere, Kenyatta and Obote as "nationalist reactionaries". The articles explained what would happen
when the "deceivers of the people" had been overthrown:

"Their personal aggrandisement will not be forgotten. The oppression of the people will be avenged."

Kaunda demanded angrily to know whether this was official Chinese policy. Ambassador Chin Li-chen denied that his country had any responsibility for the offending journal and the following week the Chinese called a press conference at the embassy. A prepared statement was read in which *Revolution in Africa* was denounced as "completely forged". The embassy spokesman declined to say who might have perpetrated the forgery. When it was pointed out that copies of the magazine had arrived from Tirana with Albanian stamps on the envelope, he replied: "Forgers can do anything." It was hardly surprising that no further issues of the magazine appeared. The incident had strange echoes of the "Letter from Sandy" affair several years earlier. A letter allegedly from a Conservative MP to a close friend in the British aristocracy was circulated to nationalists in East and Central Africa. It described how economic control of Africa would be retained and British interests protected, even if countries had to be given nominal independence. The British Government said that letter was a forgery, produced by one of the Communist countries.

Suspicions excited by *Revolution in Africa* were revived by Chou En-lai's visit to Tanzania in mid-1965. He publicly repeated the statement he had made in Somalia a year before: "An excellent revolutionary situation exists in Africa." In graphic terms, Chou described the liberation movements of the world as coming together in a torrent; he threw in a quotation from Mao about the continents being rocked with thunder. A number of African leaders expressed unhappiness, since they were not at all sure who the Chinese-led revolution was to be against and where the thunder might end.

The man who seemed least perturbed was Nyerere. At a banquet he turned to Chou and said that Tanzania would not accept subversion from any quarter. "At no time shall we lower our guard. . . . Neither our principles, our country, nor our freedom to determine our own future are for sale." On a visit to London soon afterwards he insisted that Tanzania was not being contaminated by Communism, and said lightly that he sometimes wondered whether the West was developing an inferiority complex about China. He made it clear that he had no such worries himself. In fact, he had already accepted the Chinese offer to build the railway to the Zambian border; the rest was up to Kaunda.

Nyerere understood that the mass of Africans were not immediately receptive to Communist ideology. Even when party officials used the stock phraseology of anti-imperialism, they did so because it was handy, a prefabricated language in which people might let off steam in a fashionable way.

This was not to say that the Africans lacked sympathy with the Chinese. They studied the illustrated magazines, such as the Swahili version of *China Pictorial*, which were so readily available. They felt an identity with these non-European people who were rather like themselves (as it seemed) and making their own way up from poverty. In the various Afro-Asian organisations dominated by the Communists, Chinese representatives made continual play with the point and used it as a weapon in the Sino-Soviet ideological war. The Russians, they contended, were not Afro-Asians any more than the American imperialists, and did not understand the needs of Africa. Admittedly, some of the African politicians who visited China came away displeased. Not only was it lacking in prostitutes, always one of the attractions of foreign travel, but moreover it displayed none of the richness of Western countries.

It was precisely these qualities which appealed to such a dedicated nationalist as Nyerere, when he made his first journey to Peking. He came back saying that he was highly impressed, that the Chinese were sober and hard-working. They were also economical; even Dar es Salaam alone might have more cars than he had seen throughout his visit. "We should learn from the Chinese. It would be unfair to receive aid from them if we cannot be frugal." Nyerere was enough of a realist to understand that despite their own poverty the Chinese might be offering aid—such as the railway—for reasons not purely idealistic. Yet it was important to make his own people accept that not all the world powers were as remote from themselves in terms of development as the United States and European countries. The example of the Chinese gave hope, because its achievements were attainable.

The response of Kaunda, when he made a visit to China in 1967 was revealingly similar. It was his first experience of a Communist country, with the exception of Yugoslavia, and on the way to Peking he had stopped in India. For almost twenty years, India had been a precious symbol to Kaunda, but this time he found it alarming in the complexity of its difficulties and the apparent impossibility of solving them. He felt the weight, in the words of V. S. Naipaul, of "a decaying civilisation, where the only hope lies in further swift decay". After this, China was exhilarating in its energy and order – notwithstanding the recent uproar of the Red Guard activities in the great proletarian cultural revolution. Kaunda was photographed visiting communes and factories, with a copy of Mao's thoughts in his hand. At a banquet he praised as a contribution to peace China's feat in exploding a hydrogen bomb – a startling tribute from a disciple of Gandhi.

At the end of the visit a long communiqué was released, recounting a range of topics on which Zambia and China agreed. It was couched in terms of careful equality, although the hosts were more than 150 times greater in population than the guests. One point not mentioned in the communiqué was the Tan-Zam railway, but Chou En-lai privately assured Kaunda that China was still waiting for a clear invitation to go ahead. Since the first group of surveyors had visited Tanzania in 1965, interest in the project had seemed to wane. In fact, throughout 1966, Zambia had been so obsessed with its emergency efforts to maintain supplies over the Great North Road that little thought had been given to any long-term communications project.

The only apparent activity had been by the British consultants, Maxwell Stamp Associates – who in 1964 were involved in the Chartered royalties affair. They had now made a detailed study of the economic prospects for the railway. Their report had contradicted those prepared earlier, by saying that the railway could pay its way. This assumed that all Zambia's copper would be exported through Dar es Salaam and that imports maintained or increased the levels in the post-independence boom period. It was also taken for granted that Zambia would cut off virtually all traffic from the south. But the Stamp report had been accepted with little interest when it was handed in at the end of 1966 and no copies had been distributed to Western governments. This was puzzling, for it had been commissioned in the hope of evoking Western support for the project. Was it that somebody had deliberately smothered the report? On the other hand, no Western embassies had asked for a copy, although it was known that the report had been finished. Even the British, who had paid their £75,000 share for the feasibility survey, displayed no concern. Possibly it was felt better to let sleeping dogs lie, for by now it was estimated that the railway would cost as much as £125,000,000.

When a firm agreement between China, Tanzania and Zambia, for construction of the line was signed in September 1967, there were cries of astonishment from London and Washington. Agency reports from South Africa said the Vorster administration was alarmed. Dr Hilgard Muller publically referred to it as a threat. Attempts to form a rival Western consortium were unavailing, for no country was willing to take the lead for fear of being left alone with the project on its hands. Seven international companies joined together and looked for finance, but none was forthcoming — earlier in the year, Tanzania had put through a wide programme of nationalisation; the region was a "bad risk". The Chinese were offering to bear all the capital costs themselves in the form of a longterm loan. Still the World Bank stood by its 1964 attitude to the railway, although it hinted it might be willing to lend a moderate amount for the improvement of the Zambia–Tanzania highway.

As it became clear that the Chinese were on their own, and there was to be no counter-bid, it began to be suggested that Chou En-lai was not really serious. There was a great distinction between signing an agreement or surveying, and actually laying the track. Could it not be, the embassies in Lusaka and Dar es Salaam started to hint, that when it came to the decisive moment the Chinese would invent obstacles or start to make demands that Kaunda and Nyerere could not accept? If the Chinese did fail to go through with their promise, their reputation would be shattered.

Such comforting assumptions took little account of China's

determined approach to Africa for almost a decade. It had begun in 1960, when diplomatic missions were established in Ghana, Guinea and Mali; simultaneously a Chinese–African People's Friendship Association was founded. The first visit to Peking by an African Head of State took place in September 1960: President Sekou Touré of Guinea was given a tumultuous welcome by 200,000 people and on his return to Conakry he described himself as "overwhelmed". By 1961, broadcasts beamed to Africa from Radio Peking had begun and amounted to about fifty hours a week. At first they were only in English, but gradually the range was extended to include French, Portuguese, Swahili, Hausa and other vernaculars. By 1968, the propaganda transmissions to Africa totalled almost 250 hours a week and Peking could be received clearly throughout the continent. Russia and the West were hard put to it to compete.

Chinese aid to Africa had expanded at a similar pace. On his visit in 1960, Sekou Touré was promised credits worth £8,000,000 and signed agreements on trade, economic co-operation and technical aid. Kwame Nkrumah went to China in the following year and was promised an interest-free loan of £7,000,000. President Modibo Keita was offered £5,000,000 for development projects in Mali. The pattern was repeated in the Somali Republic, Congo-Brazzaville and elsewhere. In the wake of the agreements came Chinese experts, some to teach rice-growing and others to build factories. It is often contended by the British and Americans that the Chinese do not fulfil their promises and that the money fails to materialise, yet there is visible evidence of their labours in many parts of Africa. The Chinese have also made a profound impression by the simple manner in which they live while carrying out an aid project. Africans repeatedly say: "They are more like us" – the implied comparison being with experts from the West who usually seem remote and tend to base themselves upon a country's luxurious tourist hotels.

By 1965, it was clear that the Chinese intended to concentrate their biggest aid efforts on Tanzania. They had in Dar es Salaam as ambassador one of their most adroit diplomats – Ho Ying. He was quick to grasp opportunities for goodwill gestures, typified by a £5,000 cheque to help the victims of flooding early in 1964. When Tanzanian ministers toured the rural areas, Ho Ying would often accompany them, and hand out money for clinics and schools as he went; it was somewhat unorthodox for an ambassador, but highly effective. A regular visitor to Dar es Salaam was Kao Liang, ostensibly a correspondent for the New China News Agency but generally regarded as far more important than that. Some years earlier he had been ordered out of India. According to a defector from the Chinese embassy in Burundi, Kao Liang was "one of the principal agents for subversion in East Africa". He is a curious-looking person with a very large head.

In 1965, China gave Nyerere an interest-free loan of £16,000,000. In 1966, there was a further loan of £2,000,000 to help finance projects which the British had been committed to until the diplomatic break over Rhodesia. A £2,500,000 "Friendship Textile Mill" was built in Dar es Salaam and at the end of 1966 a 100-kilowatt radio transmitter went into operation. The Tanzanians and Chinese set up a joint shipping line, mortars and machine guns were supplied for the Tanzanian army (which nonetheless retained Canadian instructors) and there were handsome gifts of farming equipment. The number of Chinese in Tanzania rose noticeably — at one time, Nyerere would jokingly offer Western visitors £5 for every Chinese they could spot in Dar es Salaam, but by 1967 it was felt that the going rate must have fallen somewhat.

The drive in Tanzania represented a considerable outlay for a country with urgent problems of its own at home. Admittedly, there had been some rewards, for Chinese trade with East Africa began to boom after 1965. Tanzania's imports from China doubled in a year and by 1967 had leapt beyond £4,000,000. Yet this could have been achieved without the lavish aid programme, capped by the offer to build the Tan-Zam railway.

The effort is only explicable in terms of China's view of history. Mao believes that Africa has a crucial role to play in the overthrow of imperialist forces; this was fully set out in Marshal Lin Piao's essay "Long Live the Victory of the Peoples' War". Since the cultural revolution, Lin Piao has been constantly at

Mao Tse-tung's side – they were together when Kaunda met Mao in Peking. The essay extends Mao's revolutionary strategy of the countryside encircling and ultimately capturing the cities to a global plan of action. Africa is a part of the World countryside, from which the exploited masses will overcome the rich. It may take time, but it will be done.

Echoes of this faith were apparent in the Zambian–Chinese communiqué of June 1967: "The two sides are of the opinion that the present world situation is most favourable to the peoples of Asia, Africa and Latin-America in their struggle to oppose imperialism, colonialism and neo-colonialism. . . . Imperialism and colonialism will never be reconciled to their own defeat and step down from the stage of history of their own accord, but are exerting their utmost to launch frenzied counter-attacks against the anti-imperialist revolutionary forces. . . ." There was much more in a similar ringing tone, although one sentence did admit that in some areas the struggles had suffered temporary setbacks.

The very intensity of the Chinese ideas have already frightened off some African countries. Chou En-lai's statements are not forgotten and in Africa the setbacks to revolution have often been of China's own making. Sinister motives, hiding under the cloak of anti-colonialism, are attributed to Peking – and the fact that China has ten times the population density of Africa has not been missed. President Felix Houphouet-Boigny of Ivory Coast said in 1966: "The Chinese are hard pressed by their demographic expansion. They are in search of space, and that is the reason why they are attracted by the emptiness of Africa."

The leaders of Peoples' China clearly regard the Tan-Zam railway as a great show of strength, capable of earning in Black Africa even more prestige than the Aswan Dam has brought to the Soviet Union among the Arab countries. If they hope for other immediate benefits, through the influx of technicians into Tanzania and Zambia, they have to defeat a close surveillance.

The official party newspaper in Dar es Salaam is *The Nationalist*. It rarely misses a chance to lambast the misdeeds of the capitalist countries. But in August 1968 it published an editorial entitled "Hands Off!" which was held by observers of the Tanzanian political scene to be of major significance. It was a sharp attack on interference in the country's political affairs by an unidentified member of the "Eastern bloc". It said that Tanzania wanted to be friends with all, but would not allow anyone to use that friendship for their own purpose. "We did not fight against the Western colonialists to become the playthings of any Eastern country. We do not oppose neo-colonialism only if it originates in capitalist countries." The style strongly suggested that the leader had been written by Nyerere himself; certainly, it would not have been printed without his approval. It gave a glimpse of the strains and perils for a small country, trying to cling to the ideals of non-alignment in a predatory world.

Both Nyerere and Kaunda had declared that as long as the Tan-Zam railway is built, they do not care who finances it. In a speech to the United Nations in 1964, Kaunda once said: "Too often, sometimes unknowingly, technical assistance and aid have contained tendencies towards a new type of dependence, just as difficult to throw off as the old. Therefore, we ask that countries which offer us their aid should not exploit our need in order to infringe our sovereignty. . . ." In the middle of January 1969, a picture on the front page of the *Zambia News* had a certain bearing on this point. It showed a group of Chinese surveyors with their African assistants, each holding a small book. The caption explained: "During short breaks in the hot gruelling work, the Chinese and African railway builders get together. And often, as in this picture, the Chinese discuss with the local workers the works of China's leader, Chairman Mao Tse-tung."

CHAPTER 15

Pan-Africanism on the Wane

For Kaunda the Pan-Africanist, one of the most exhilarating
moments of his career was the first All-African People's Conference at Accra in December 1958. Perhaps the most depressing
came at Algiers in September 1968, when he attended the fifth
annual meeting of the Organisation of African Unity. In
Accra, Kaunda had been a virtual unknown. He had made a
brief appearance on the platform and cried joyfully, "Freedom! Freedom!" In Algiers, Kaunda had been welcomed as
one of Africa's most distinguished Heads of State, but he had
departed in a cloud of anger – refusing an invitation to be one
of the OAU's vice-presidents.

The upset in Algiers had been caused by an opening speech
from President Houari Boumedienne on the Nigerian civil
war. As a Marxist, Boumedienne had declared that every
organisation which helped Biafra was an agent of imperialism.
He indicted equally the religious bodies who had been flying
in aid on humanitarian grounds and countries which had
recognised Biafra. Kaunda stood up and made a short speech
in which he protested: "We in Zambia seem to have been
lumped together with the imperialists because of our stand on
the Nigeria–Biafra issue."

That night Boumedienne tried to heal the breach. At two
in the morning he called on Kaunda and pleaded that his
remarks – which he had made in Arabic – had been wrongly
translated. Kaunda demanded to have the speech translated
again in front of him and to be given a written version of the
Arabic for his own records. Boumedienne did not accept the
challenge and as he left Kaunda the mood was icy. Later the
Zambian leader rubbed salt in the wound by saying publicly

that he still regarded Ben Bella – who had been deposed and put in detention in 1965 – as the legitimate President of Algeria.

It had been a lonely conference in Algiers for Kaunda. He was the only one of the four African presidents who had recognised Biafra to put in an appearance and found that the Lagos regime of General Gowon had been able to swing almost all the OAU to his side. A resolution was put to the conference calling on the Biafrans to "co-operate with the federal authorities with a view to restoring the peace and unity of Nigeria". Before the matter was debated, Kaunda had left Algiers. This saved him the pain of hearing an emotional speech by President Joseph Mobutu, with whom Zambia had been trying to foster friendship, on the evils of secession in Africa. The conference was sharply aware that the continent's arch-secessionist, Moise Tshombe, was being held in a prison only twenty miles away; Katanga's ex-leader had been there for more than a year, since his charter plane was hi-jacked over the Mediterranean and forced to land in Algeria. The Nigeria resolution was carried by thirty-six to four, only Zambia, Tanzania, Gabon and the Ivory Coast voting against.

Kaunda never made any apologies for his decision to recognise Biafra. Like Nyerere, he believed that the Biafrans were genuinely scared of being slaughtered by the federal troops and that their experiences since 1966 had given them every justification. "You cannot reassure people who are afraid through the barrel of a gun." Kaunda also turned on its head the argument from Boumedienne which had so incensed him. It was not the supporters of Biafra who were the imperialists, but the backers of the federal regime in Lagos. The British were supplying armoured vehicles, guns and ammunition to the Nigerians because they wanted to retain their oil interests. Kaunda also saw it as despicable that the British found themselves on the same side as the Russians, whom he had repeatedly criticised for their invasion of Czechoslovakia. There also seemed to him another reason for the British behaviour, in what was surely a rejection of morality and humanitarianism. They had created the Nigerian federation, and so were determined to make it survive as a matter of pride. Kaunda pointed

P

to the string of federations the British had set up in the Commonwealth: West Indies, Aden, Central Africa—all of them fiascos.

As for the French support for Biafra, the Zambian President was prepared to believe that de Gaulle was responding to the general feeling on the Continent that the encircled secessionists were the victims of oppression. After Kaunda's visit to Paris, immediately following the OAU meeting in Algiers, it was officially declared that the French and the Zambians had similar positions on the "cruel affair of Biafra". Observers never disputed that Kaunda's attitude was totally sincere. But they wondered whether de Gaulle might not have been influenced by the huge oil deposits discovered near Owerri in the Biafran heartland by the French concern SAFRAP. It also seemed possible that the General took a certain pleasure in frustrating British policies in West Africa, where France was so firmly entrenched in almost a dozen former colonies.

The Biafran decision by Kaunda had not been easy, for it had cost him the friendship of the most populous state on the African continent. Diplomatic relations had immediately been broken off. Kaunda was also distressed that one of his oldest friends, President Nasser of Egypt, had openly supported the Lagos Government by supplying pilots to fly the Soviet MIGs and Ilushyins which made daily sorties against Biafra. In the United Nations, Zambia had taken a consistently pro-Egyptian line in the votes of resolutions after the "six-day war" in the Middle East. In the early sixties, Kaunda had maintained close ties with Nasser—who had supplied him with funds when the United National Independence Party was at a low ebb. But after the events of 1967, Kaunda began to realise that Nasser had little time to spare for fostering relationships in Black Africa. For Egypt, the OAU had become a sideshow. Kaunda found it a far from ideal world when heroes like Nasser had become so heavily dependent upon the Soviet Union.

Again and again, he was disillusioned by the actions of his friends when they had to compromise with economic or political pressures. As the number of non-military Heads of State in English-speaking West Africa declined almost to vanishing point, Kaunda began to seek alliances with francophone leaders. In his spare time, he began learning French. President Alphonse Massamba-Debat of Congo-Brazzaville was invited to visit Zambia and given a rousing welcome; he was a leader whose militancy and anti-imperialism were beyond question. Massamba-Debat had been in office for more than five years, after replacing Abbe Fulbert Youlou, whose reputation was so remarkable that his mattress had been publicly burned after his ousting from office. But the friendship with Brazzaville had had little time to mature before Massamba-Debat was overthrown by a military coup. Kaunda announced defiantly that as with Nkrumah and Ben Bella, he still regarded Massamba-Debat as a president.

Before the end of 1968, there was another blow with the overthrow of President Modibo Keita of Mali. Although Mali was on the far side of Africa and its capital, Bamako, was rarely visited by Zambians, the name of Keita was part of the pan-African mythology. He had been a leading member, along with Nkrumah and Sekou Touré of Guinea, of the militant "Casablanca group". Keita had survived since 1960 and now he had been sacked in a bloodless coup by a group of junior army officers dissatisfied with the rates of pay. Mao Tse-tung's famous thought about power growing out of the barrel of a gun was being alarmingly borne out in Africa.

Surveying the continent between the Sahara and the Zambezi, Kaunda saw how diminished the band of militant pan-Africanists had become. Kenyatta of Kenya and Haile Selassie of Ethiopia hardly counted – they were father figures. Milton Obote was so pre-occupied with his own internal security difficulties that he took little interest in external affairs. It really only left Kaunda himself, Nyerere and Sekou Touré.

In such a situation, one has to make allowances. Many people in Zambia had the most severe reservations about Joseph Mobutu of the Congo-Kinshasa. It was accepted that in 1961 he had known about the orders for Patrice Lumumba, the greatest martyr of African nationalism, to be put on a plane for Katanga. It was in Katanga, only a few miles from the Zambian border, that Lumumba had been shot and killed by a Belgian mercenary officer under the eyes of one of Tshombe's colleagues.

After taking power, Mobutu had done his best to don the mantle of Lumumba. At the OAU conference in Kinshasa in 1967, he had wept as he spoke of the Congo's first leader. In a ceremony attended by the visiting heads of State he had renamed a main street in the capital "Avenue Lumumba". Yet there were some who said that Mobutu owed his survival as leader of the Congo to American support. It was even suggested that the hi-jacking of Tshombe had been organised by the Central Intelligence Agency – and certainly, Tshombe himself had repeatedly claimed that he was being harassed by the CIA. The story might have been thought even more credible had it been known that in the middle of 1966, Tshombe had put up a scheme to the Russians for staging a coup in the Congo that could bring him back to power. All he had wanted, he had told the Russians in a detailed, eight-page memorandum, was 500,000,000 Belgian francs.

The image of Mobutu in Zambia had been considerably darkened by the execution of the leftist rebel leader Pierre Mulele. For six years, Mulele had run his own revolutionary movement in Kwilu Province, south of Kinshasa. Then in September 1968, Mulele had given up the long struggle and made his way across the Congo to Brazzaville. It was announced by Justin Bomboko, Mobutu's Foreign Minister, in a national broadcast that Mulele had been granted amnesty, and was returning to Kinshasa a free man, to work with the government. Trusting in this guarantee of safety, Mulele immediately crossed over from Brazzaville to Kinshasa. He was arrested, condemned by a military court and executed by firing squad. In its ferocity, the affair was very Congolese, and recalled the public hangings that Mobutu had staged shortly after taking power.

Kaunda said nothing, but the reaction within Zambia was considerable. It was Mulele, not Mobutu, who was seen as the true heir of Lumumba. Here was a second martyr, a second victim of treachery. The mood within UNIP was well expressed in an impassioned letter to the *Times of Zambia* by Michael Chileshe, a leading party official on the Copperbelt: "Mulele participated in the Congo revolution only because he was convinced that the people who killed Lumumba could not legitimately lead the Congo to true political and economic independence; . . . Mulele has died, but his followers (me included) will carry aloft the torch of the revolution until Africa has been lit and the African masses liberated from black exploiting hands, and from political murderers."

A month later, Mobutu and Kaunda held a meeting in a remote part of northern Zambia. The Congolese leader was introduced to the crowd that gathered by Kaunda as "a great and sincere friend". Yet in many eyes it seemed a friendship that might prove expensive and end unhappily.

CHAPTER 16

The High Price of Principles

For all Kaunda's desires to play a full role in the political development of Black Africa, and notwithstanding his pursuit of alliances with countries to the north of Zambia, his mind could never escape for long from the troubles on his southern border. While the Rhodesian issue remained unresolved, there would be constant tension and danger. At the start of 1966, Harold Wilson had said it might be over in weeks rather than months. But the months dragged on into years and a settlement came no nearer.

Rhodesia had dominated Kaunda's talks in London with Wilson during July 1968. There had been suspicion at first, but the British premier's persuasive tones were able to smooth this away. Wilson said little about NIBMAR and was adamant against the use of force. But he did seem to be resolutely committed to the famous "six principles" for any settlement with Smith. It was, after all, less than four months since he had told the Commons that Smith was a liar, that the rule of law had been "perverted and subverted" in Rhodesia, and that the rebel colony was a police state. These statements had been made in the course of the heated debate on the hanging of five Africans in Salisbury in defiance of the Royal Prerogative of Mercy. Wilson had said then that there could be no profit in talking to Smith in such circumstances. He went further in his comments on some of Smith's closest aides: "I am saying that there cannot be talks with the Lardner-Burkes, with the Duponts, with racialists who rejected every settlement proposed before and after UDI, including the Tiger constitution."

It seemed that Kaunda's criticisms had been too harsh. Wilson was now standing firm. But within a fortnight of the presidential flight home to Lusaka, Wilson had invited to

Downing Street none other than Sir Max Aitken, chairman of the *Daily Express*; their talk was of Rhodesia. In the opinion of Sir Max's paper, Smith was no rebel, but a hero and brave defender of white standards in darkest Africa. If any visitor from London could expect a courteous welcome in Salisbury, it was Sir Max. So on the second weekend in August he was on his way to Rhodesia, and a few days later Smith was discussing with his colleagues the possibility of a new round of negotiations with the British. There was little enthusiasm or optimism, but Smith was given a mandate to restate the Rhodesian position to Sir Max and a mysterious "third man". This was Lord Goodman, Wilson's personal legal adviser and confidante, who had flown out in the greatest secrecy to South Africa shortly before. Goodman was invited up to Salisbury from Johannesburg and booked in at a hotel near Smith's office. He stayed away from the Governor, Sir Humphrey Gibbs, and news of this new probing exercise was kept out of the newspapers. The British High Commission in Lusaka knew nothing of it, and Kaunda was left in blissful ignorance.

Goodman and Smith had three meetings, with Sir Max in attendance, and at the end a long document was drawn up in which both sides stated their views. Smith and Goodman initialled it on every page, then the latter hurried home to report to Wilson. There was also a personal message from Smith: if there was to be a settlement, there could be no delay, for within six months he might have to contend with serious opposition within Rhodesia from both left and right.

The document produced by Goodman did little more than reiterate the *Tiger* positions of eighteen months earlier, but Wilson was possessed by a new confidence – for he had found an unexpected ally. It was the South Africans, who had kept Rhodesia going for almost three years, and now wanted a speedy end to a situation which they found irksome and dangerous. Vorster had assured Wilson that he was prepared to co-operate fully in making Smith abandon his stubborn attitudes and was ready to use powerful economic levers in the process. Hints of this were given by the South African Foreign Minister, Hilgard Muller, and the ambassador in London, Hendrik Luttig. While Goodman had been waiting in South

Africa he had talked with Vorster and been astonished by his vehemence on the need to find a compromise.

The most obvious reason Vorster had was his dislike of being the chief sanction-buster. This role had become even more uncomfortable in 1968, as in the face of United Nations pressure the countries which had maintained a thriving undercover trade with Rhodesia since UDI – West Germany, Japan and France in particular – had begun to contract out. Rhodesia was an impediment to South Africa's patient efforts to win her way back to international respectability from the nadir of the early sixties. There was another potential disadvantage, in that sanctions were gradually beginning to undermine Rhodesia. Its economy had looked buoyant in the first year of UDI as new "import-substitute" industries had been started, but the fall in export earnings and the agricultural stagnation had begun to wreak a cumulative damage. South Africa knew this only too well, since she was having to bail Rhodesia out of her foreign exchange difficulties. If sanctions went on for another year, they would bring Rhodesia to the brink of collapse, and so encourage South Africa's enemies in the United Nations to call for the same methods to be applied to her. The threat inherent in sanctions, which South Africa had seen in 1965, was belatedly showing itself again.

The second main motive for Vorster's readiness to lend his hand to finding a settlement concerned the guerrillas operating from north of the Zambezi. The groups crossing into Rhodesia from Zambia were giving Ian Smith trouble by forcing him to keep his army on the alert; the South Africans had sent up 300 men to help him, which was not only a goodwill gesture but also gave the army a chance for combat experience. Yet Vorster was less worried about what the guerrillas could do, than about the attention they drew to southern Africa. It damaged the picture of stability and peace. At the very moment while Vorster was talking to Goodman, a massive "anti-terrorist" exercise was being held in the Northern Transvaal. Known as "Operation Sibasa", the exercise involved 5,000 men, with aircraft and armoured vehicles, pitted against 700 "guerrillas" using Chinese and Russian weapons. The exercise was given maximum publicity, reputedly for its deterrent value. The English-language News/Check magazine, which had a considerable sale in Zambia, carried a detailed and heavily illustrated report on the exercise under the headline "South Africa at the Ready". The editor of News/Check, Otto Krause, is an influential figure in the National Party.

But however much South Africa wanted to deter the guerrillas, it knew that this could not be achieved while Rhodesia remained in a state of rebellion. Zambia would continue to let them cross over with impunity – illegality on one side encouraged illegality on the other. The picture would become entirely different when a recognised government had been established in Rhodesia, for even if Kaunda did not approve of its racial composition he would be under much greater pressure to prevent "unfriendly acts" against a neighbouring state. If the Rhodesian deadlock could be broken, this would open the way to a much wider *détente* throughout southern Africa.

Vorster's political aims were reinforced by the desires of big business in South Africa. One of the most powerful figures in the Afrikaner community was Dr Harry van Eck, chairman of the Industrial Development Corporation. He had been saying for months: "We absolutely must find a solution to Rhodesia." In 1967, exports of South African goods to the rest of Africa had topped the £100,000,000 mark, an increase of almost a third over the previous year. Only a very small part of this rise could be attributed to trade with Rhodesia, which had levelled off after the first year of UDI. The business was with Black Africa, a market of 280,000,000 people on the republic's doorstep. For obvious reasons, no figures breaking down the grand total were released. "We do not have overmuch to say about that," commented Muller. But South African businessmen – usually travelling on British passports – were becoming increasingly active all over the continent. There was no difficulty about buying South African peaches in French-speaking West Africa, or about ordering a South African brandy in Malawi.

Easily the most important market for South African goods was Zambia, yet it was the country with which relations were most difficult. In 1964, South African exports to Zambia had been worth £16,000,000. By 1968 they had soared to £40,000,000. This had not been Zambia's intention, for early in 1965 the Economic Commission for Africa had been told by Finance Minister Arthur Wina, that the trade agreement with South Africa had been ended and this would lead to a complete break in relations. But as Zambia had stopped buying from Rhodesia after UDI, she had been forced to look more and more to the next most convenient source. So Zambia had become a very good customer, taking almost half of South Africa's total exports to the Black states.

In political terms, Malawi had represented the greatest breakthrough, yet economically it remained insignificant – its total imports were worth only £30,000,000 and only a tenth were from South Africa. With a similar population, the Zambians were importing at a rate of £150,000,000 a year and a quarter came from South Africa. Men like Harry van Eck were keenly aware that although their country's prosperity was based on gold, it would not always be so: gold production had levelled off and would be in a permanent decline by the 1980s. The future lay with manufacturing; as van Eck pointed out, South African manufacturing had increased twenty-five times in less than thirty years. The new industries needed markets, and politics should not be allowed to stand in the way of such considerations. Rhodesia was a sideshow, and its 200,000 whites should not be allowed to mar a grand design.

Irritation had been showing itself in the comments of the leading Afrikaans newspapers, *Die Burger* and *Die Vaderland*. The latter, regarded as generally reflecting official views, had remarked coldly in July that Smith would be well advised not to base his strategy upon the assumption that in the near future he would be "dealing with a more amenable Conservative government". By the beginning of September, the South Africans and the British had begun working in close liaison to bring about a new round of negotiations with Rhodesia. Muller called on Smith in Salisbury and a week later George Thomson, the Commonwealth Secretary, flew out for the Swaziland independence celebrations. Muller, Vorster and Thomson went over the ground carefully and the South Africans were optimistic that Smith was ready to come to terms. They urged a Wilson-Smith "summit" without delay — even suggesting South Africa as the best venue.

Thomson flew home to London, to learn that Wilson had, with customary adroitness, already chosen the date for the meeting: October 9. It was when the Conservative Party's annual conference was due to begin. All that remained now was to create a sufficient number of diversions to keep Smith "on the boil" for a month. The best way would be to send him a series of visitors, and the first chosen for this task was James Bottomley, under-secretary at the Commonwealth Office. The next would be Lord Shackleton, who had a reputation for action but in this instance would be required to do no more than play out time.

Bottomley was not well received in Salisbury and the report he gave on his return added nothing to what Goodman had brought back: in view of the South African pressure, Smith was willing to talk; but he was by no means in a conciliatory mood. This was made still more apparent when, at the end of September, a message was sent to Salisbury to announce the impending journey of Lord Shackleton — who had already been briefed about his trip by Wilson. On September 27 it was reported in *The Times*: "Lord Shackleton, Leader of the House of Lords, was called to 10 Downing Street yesterday after a meeting of senior Ministers. . . . It is believed that he has now been asked to visit Salisbury to investigate the possibility of new negotiations with Mr Smith." But Smith replied that he would not receive Shackleton. He wanted no more talks about talks. On September 30, Hilgard Muller arrived in London and had a meeting with George Thomson at which the South African desire for a settlement was repeatedly stressed. London could rely on Pretoria's good offices. It was a far cry from Muller's statement four months earlier that the Rhodesian question was a matter for Britain in which South Africa had no intention of becoming involved.

By the start of October, Kaunda was making his views known. He had been able to pick up from sources in Salisbury some details of the Aitken-Goodman overture and his suspicions deepened as reports began to flow in from London that Wilson was determined to dispose of Rhodesia before the next meeting of Commonwealth leaders, due in January. Kaunda announced that he had information about Wilson's desire to do a deal "at any price". The sudden diplomatic involvement of South Africa had served to increase his anxiety. Until the last possible moment, Wilson operated behind a smokescreen of rumours, until on October 8 a messenger arrived in Lusaka with definite news: within twenty-four hours there was to be a confrontation at Gibraltar, the place where almost two years before the "*Tiger* talks" had ended in deadlock. Kaunda reacted by saying he had the greatest apprehensions. Any concessions to Smith would only legalise his "diabolical intentions" towards the majority of Rhodesia's population.

There was no doubt that Wilson was quite passionately intent on a settlement by this time. He even accepted as Smith's principal lieutenant the much-reviled Desmond Lardner-Burke, whom he had described six months before as not to be trusted to carry out any agreement. He ignored Smith's repeated statements before the meeting that he still did not expect to see African rule in his lifetime. When the Rhodesians arrived in Gibraltar they were treated with a deference and cordiality far removed from the atmosphere of the previous confrontation. Most important, the terms which Wilson offered went beyond anything suggested previously; the six principles were stretched to their limits.

"The *Fearless* proposals", as they became known, were intolerable to a large part of the Labour Party. Both Barbara Castle and Judith Hart avoided voting on them and the former Commonwealth Secretary, Arthur Bottomley, was publicly hostile. At the United Nations eighty countries supported a condemnation. The proposals were a "despicable surrender to racialism" said Kaunda, who then added his opinion of Wilson: "It is amazing that any human being could sink so low." He claimed that the show of reluctance by Smith to accept the proposals was merely part of a charade arranged between the British and the Rhodesians.

Yet by the end of November it had begun to appear that Kaunda was wrong in believing this. Moreover, Wilson had been wrong in thinking that Smith wanted a settlement; he had been carried away by the South Africans' over-confidence when they claimed they could promote one. Vorster himself had heated telephone conversations with Smith, and George Thomson made a long but completely abortive journey to Rhodesia. There was no progress, no prospect for the all-round settlement in southern Africa. The essential trait of Smith had made itself apparent – a truculence which hardened under pressure. He had always mistrusted the British, having seen how they had outwitted Welensky, and now he was suspicious of South African motives. For his own convenience, to suit his own designs, Vorster might be planning to abandon the white Rhodesians and put in their stead a complaisant Black government of the Malawian type.

By the end of November, Britain began to look around for further ways of applying pressure. Thomson called in the Portuguese chargé d'affaires, Dr José de Villas-Boas; the new Premier in Lisbon, Dr Marcello Caetano, called for an "honourable settlement to end a grave situation". It was known that Caetano's redoubtable predecessor, Dr Salazar, had urged Smith to do a deal. In Salisbury, the business community added its voice, calling on Smith to accept the *Fearless* terms without more ado; there was a note of urgency provoked by rumours from Johannesburg that the South Africans were considering a withdrawal of their support for Rhodesia's currency. Still Smith would not yield, saying that he refused to accept a "second-class independence" which involved external safeguards for African progress. He accused the British of being devious and of being obsessed with the idea of majority rule; it was an obsession that was hardly surprising, since the very first of the six principles ruled that unimpeded progress to majority rule should be "maintained and guaranteed".

It seemed that nothing was changed, that the meeting aboard HMS *Fearless* had been only the latest in an interminable series of fiascos. Yet this time, Rhodesia had acted as the catalyst for a development of far-reaching importance. Britain and South Africa had been, for the moment, thwarted in their mutual designs upon Smith – but their discussions had brought them into a much closer understanding about longterm aims. These aims were generally not of a type to win commendation from Kenneth Kaunda.

With the attainment of independence by Swaziland in September, the last of the old high commission territories clustered around South Africa had passed out of British control. It was not unrelated that the Commonwealth Office, which had absorbed the Colonial Office, was at this moment being merged into the Foreign Office. Apart from that very special case, Rhodesia, Britain no longer had any colonial possessions on the African continent – whereas a mere ten years before she had had more than a dozen. One after another, the high commission territories had been granted sovereignty on terms that were agreeable to both Britain and South Africa. Their leaders were men willing to accept the limitations of their geographic and economic dependence upon South Africa. The President of Botswana, Sir Seretse Khama, soon showed that he would give no encouragement to guerrillas trying to operate through his country. Those that were captured were either deported to Zambia or put in jail. Khama had two meetings with Kaunda and at both of them said he could not support the Zambian demand for the use of force against Rhodesia; there was no active role Botswana could play, even in the implementing of sanctions. Chief Leabua Jonathan of Lesotho and Prince Makhosini Dlamini of Swaziland were even more emphatic about their need to co-operate with the white-run countries around them. Chief Jonathan declared: "I look forward to some time in the future when we in the southern region can sit down at a round table and work out an economic community."

Britain had relinquished control in the full understanding that these countries would fall under the sway of South Africa, and form part of its ring of buffer states. In Pretoria, the three territories were commonly described in conversation as "our new Bantustans", thus placing them in the same category as the Transkei. They were attractive prospects for investment, with cheap labour and membership of the South African customs union. They did not even have currency of their own, but used the South African *rand*. A leading Cape politician, F. D. Conradie, expressed a common hope when he forecast that Afrikaans would become "the sub-continental language for southern Africa".

So by the latter part of 1968, the decks were almost cleared for a thoroughly businesslike relationship between Britain and South Africa. Although it had been regretted at the time, South Africa's resignation from the Commonwealth had proved an advantage, since it prevented acrimonious debates at Commonwealth conferences about *apartheid*. There remained only one difficulty, the arms embargo against South Africa – and even this was being overcome. Wilson had provoked considerable anger at the end of 1967 by refusing to relax the ban on sales to South Africa of military equipment which might be used for internal suppression. There had been a division within the British Cabinet on the subject with Anthony Crosland, president of the Board of Trade, and Denis Healey, Minister of Defence, arguing strongly that the embargo should be relaxed. The financial factors made a powerful appeal in the Treasury: South African defence spending was likely to be worth £50,000,000 a year, and if Britain did not win the contracts they would go to other countries such as France and Italy. Moreover, a public refusal to alter the ban would antagonise Vorster and possibly endanger Britain's ordinary trade with South Africa.

For internal political reasons, Wilson had refused to yield. The reaction from Pretoria had been exactly as had been predicted. Vorster said: "We know now, after a long time of stalling and hedging, where we stand with the Wilson Government." He threatened to stop allowing British warships to use the naval base at Simonstown. At the centre of the quarrel was the knowledge that a relaxation of the ban would have been a major political victory for South Africa, showing that she was winning her way back into the international community. The arms themselves were less important.

After the first wave of anger and disappointment had passed in South Africa, a massive campaign was mounted to force a reversal of the decision. Most vocal were the industrialists. In Britain they were marshalled under the banner of the United Kingdom–South Africa Trade Association (UKSATA), whose president, Sir Nicholas Cayzer, controls the Union Castle shipping line. The parallel body in South Africa was the South Africa–Britain Trade Association (SABRITA). The tone of the campaign was set in a message from Sir Nicholas to the Conservative leader, Edward Heath, which said that the loss of goodwill and consequent loss of trade would be extremely serious in Britain's "present economic plight". Exporters to South Africa were straining every nerve and the decision had been most demoralising. Heath responded with an assurance that when the Conservatives were in power they would cancel the arms embargo.

The Confederation of British Industry put out a statement saying that it could see no sense in handing on a plate to competitors trade which Britain so badly needed. Anthony Crosland soon made his position plain by saying that British industry was rightly determined that political differences should not affect the determination to cultivate trade opportunities in South Africa: "There is no reason why people in South Africa should hesitate to place contracts in Britain for goods which they would like to buy from us, because we can offer what they want more competitively." Crosland wrote this in a letter to John Davies, director-general of the Confederation of British Industries, before Davies left in April for a tour of South Africa. During the tour, Davies met Vorster and members of his cabinet in Cape Town; back in London he immediately reported to Crosland and Michael Stewart, the Foreign Secretary. To both he stressed the damage being done to trade prospects by the arms embargo.

One of the bodies which took a leading role in welcoming Davies was the South Africa Foundation, whose president, Major-General Sir Francis de Guingand, described the arms embargo as "monstrous". He argued that South Africa needed arms to defend herself against "Communist-inspired terrorist infiltration". Sir Francis also pointed to the strategic importance of the Cape since the closure of the Suez Canal; it had meant the diversion of thousands of ships, almost half of which had refuelled in South Africa.

The Foundation, launched in 1960 with the support of international big business, has striven in seventeen countries to improve the image of South Africa; large funds have always been available. The Foundation worked tirelessly throughout 1968 to undermine the arms embargo and had an early success when it sponsored Sir Alec Douglas-Home's visit to South Africa. He said in a radio broadcast: "You must not hold me guilty of the arms embargo, because this would not have happened if I had been a member of the British Government." There was the closest liaison in the campaign between the Foundation and British business – two members of the Foundation's London committee were Cayzer, the president of UKSATA, and William Luke, chairman of both UKSATA and the British National Export Council for Southern Africa. Luke visited South Africa in March and had discussions with Hilgard Muller and other ministers. On his return he said the arms embargo was "perplexing".

The most effective medium for developing the campaign in Britain was the Foundation's monthly journal *Perspective*, published from offices in Fleet Street. The theme constantly repeated was that South Africa offered handsome profits and Britain should not allow politics to stand in the way of obtaining them. It was a market she could not afford to lose. A statement by the Paris representative of the Foundation was quoted approvingly in the June *Perspective*: "The French are no longer getting lost in ideological ruses. They are talking economics, not politics." In the September issue, the novelist Elspeth Huxley contributed a sympathetic article, fittingly entitled "Passions versus Purses".

The figures quoted by the advocates of closer British links with South Africa were impressive enough. In 1967, trade between the two countries was a record. Exports worth £257,000,000 went to South Africa – Britain's second biggest market. In return, South Africa sold Britain goods worth £220,000,000. Every year the figures rose, and Luke of UKSATA forecast that they might well be doubled. But that was only a part of the picture, for by 1968 the accumulated British investment in South Africa amounted to £1,200,000,000; a tenth of all the capital flowing out of Britain went to South Africa. These were potent reasons why Wilson should reject African demands for any extension of sanctions; and as Britain's trade gap refused to close after devaluation the temptation of the arms contracts became still stronger.

South Africa was well aware of this. When Vorster and

Muller offered their help in finding a solution to the Rhodesian deadlock, they named their price, that Britain should abandon an expensive principle. When Muller arrived in Johannesburg from London in October, he remarked that "any talks he might have had on the arms embargo were confidential". He preferred to say nothing about them. Early in December the rumours began – fittingly enough in the *Daily Express* which a fortnight earlier had carried special supplements on South Africa for two consecutive days. British firms were preparing to sell military equipment worth £200,000,000 to South Africa. This followed confidential advice from the Ministry of Defence that the government was reconsidering the terms of its ban. A denial in the Commons by Wilson did little to counter belief that something was afoot. But moral pressures won.

The co-operation between London and Pretoria to dispose of the Rhodesian problem had ended in temporary stalemate, but it had not been without its rewards. Piet Cillie, the editor of *Die Burger*, described at the end of 1968 his findings during a visit to London. South Africa's diplomats, businessmen, and bodies concerned with good relations were patiently breaking down old attitudes and indicating new possibilities. Cillie explained: "The most important path to understanding South Africa, as far as Britain and the West is concerned, lies through Black Africa. I myself encountered official sympathy and encouragement for the moderate South African attitude to Zambia. They are no longer absolutely unbelieving about our effort to establish good relations even with that country." London was an important contact-point between South Africa and Black Africa, a place where conversation could take place. Even the BBC Africa Service was interested in the dialogue, said Cillie: "Just as an important path towards influencing Britain and the West lies through Black Africa, so one path towards influencing Black Africa lies through London. We must use it to the utmost."

In Lusaka, the growing urgency of Britain's wish for political disengagement from southern Africa was being brought home to Kaunda. It increased Zambia's sense of isolation. Kaunda still felt convinced that Wilson would concede more and more to extricate himself from Rhodesia and leave the whole region

south of the Congo as a South African sphere of influence.
There were no levers he could employ to delay this process.
The time had long since passed when the OAU could make
credible threats that countries trading with South Africa would
be boycotted. Britain and her trading rivals were confident
now that they did not have to choose between white and black.
They could do business with both. There was the perfect
example of Snam-Progetti, the Italian company which had just
completed Zambia's £16,000,000 pipeline to Dar es Salaam.
It had also been awarded a contract to build a £7,000,000
pipeline from the Natal coast to the Transvaal.

Far more revealing still was the international consortium
set up to finance the Cabora Bassa project, only 100 miles
from the Zambian border. Known as ZAMCO – the Zambese
Conscorcio Hidro-Electrico – it brought together companies
from West Germany, France, Italy, Sweden and South Africa
in a £130,000,000 venture to build a massive dam in Mozambique and exploit the region's minerals. The dam would be
completed in 1974, and would supply power to South Africa,
Malawi, Mozambique and Rhodesia. The Portuguese had
even asked Zambia if it would be interested in taking some of
the power, which would be the cheapest in Africa; Kaunda had
refused. The Anglo American Corporation, which dominated
the Copperbelt, had taken a leading part in organising the
Cabora Bassa consortium and one of Anglo's directors was its
chairman. The clearest message was that South Africa could
assume that in 1974 there would be no impediment to its
receiving power from a dam as far north as the Zambezi. It was
intended some of the power would be used by the industrial
complex to be created around Richards Bay, planned as South
Africa's biggest port. The first major development at Richards
Bay would be a £10,000,000 aluminium smelter, probably
using bauxite from Malawi. The South African journalist,
Fanie Kruger, had written: "Richards Bay is a significant
step in the process which, South Africans confidently predict,
will make their country the colossus of the African continent, a
stabilising force destined to play a leading role in the New
Africa which will emerge once some of the current attitudes in
some African quarters have surrendered to realities."

But for Kaunda there were other realities. For him, the policies of South Africa were the antithesis of all he believed in. It was a country where there was ruthless segregation on the basis of colour; where the Africans formed more than two-thirds of the population but were given only one-eighth of the land; where there were 8,000 political prisoners; where forty-seven per cent of the world's executions were carried out every year, and almost all of them on non-whites. Repeatedly Kaunda insisted: "Apartheid is ungodly."

This unyielding view of the situation in southern Africa revealed itself clearly at the Commonwealth Conference at the start of 1969. Kaunda repeated his warnings of an impending bloodbath and called on Britain to use force to bring down Smith. The conference communiqué included a paragraph saying: "Some Heads of Government reiterated their call on the British Government to use force to quell the rebellion in Rhodesia. The British Prime Minister explained the reasons why the British Government regarded the use of force as wrong and impracticable." It was only Kaunda who insisted upon inserting the paragraph, and "Some Heads" meant him alone. Despite this rebuff, Kaunda announced before leaving London that he was still ready to offer Zambia as a base for British troops. This was gallant, but starkly isolated from the resigned attitude of other Commonwealth leaders. Rhodesia did not dominate the conference as it had done in 1966 and even Nyerere devoted himself to the more limited task of holding Wilson to precise negotiating positions. The *Fearless* proposals showed that Britain was no longer thinking in terms of majority rule before independence; *The Times* said bluntly in a leader that NIBMAR was dead, and that the defence must now lie in a proper test of whether any settlement agreed with Smith was acceptable to the Africans. The communiqué stressed this as being a pledge by Wilson: "He emphasised that a settlement based on the six principles would not be possible if it were shown that there could be no genuine test of its acceptability." It this were adhered to, it could only mean for the Zambians that they must go on living indefinitely in their dangerous deadlock.

CHAPTER 17

Some Crucial Factors

In trying to assess whether Zambia will be drawn into South Africa's "sphere of co-prosperity" or will be able to maintain its militant Pan-Africanism, many imponderables must be weighed. However, there are certain points which may fairly be taken for granted. To set them down is to be realistic and does not imply moral judgements, although in some quarters they may be considered provocative.

The central reality is that South Africa's present political structure is most unlikely to be changed within the next decade. It is not necessary here to look further. The country has a powerful and flexible air force, with 300 combat planes; it has heavily-armed regular forces and can quickly muster 60,000 white militia to back them up. All organised African opposition has been broken down and a successful insurrection can be totally discounted. Nor are there any signs that guerrillas from outside the country will be available in sufficient numbers and with enough ability to destroy white minority rule. The Western powers and the Soviet Union have made it plain that they do not intend to mount a military attack upon South Africa, and in the remote event of China's doing so there is every prospect that the United States would give help on the other side.

To accept that political power will not be relinquished by the white South Africans before 1980 is not to claim that they will refuse to accommodate to a changing situation. The *apartheid* defined by Verwoerd is under pressure, especially from the business world. There are serious economic contradictions, and these slow down the progress of the country. A relaxation of *apartheid* in industry will make South Africa more acceptable to world opinion, will undermine opposition from Black Africa and reduce frustrations at home. That these are the arguments of "forward-looking" financial circles does not make them less valid.

If the outlook in South Africa is reasonably plain, what of Rhodesia? Once again surveying the next decade, it can be taken as read that Britain will not use force to bring down a white regime and that the whites will not voluntarily transfer power to the Africans. Beyond that, there is less certainty. In theory, the guerrillas should be able to make the position of the ruling five per cent untenable fairly quickly: operating from safe bases, well supplied with weapons, and moving among their own people, the freedom-fighters of ZAPU and ZANU would seem to possess every advantage. But in more than three years of spasmodic activity the guerrillas have failed to destroy a single bridge, blow up a power line or petrol-bomb a police post. To persuade the African populace as a whole that defiance to the Smith regime is feasible, they will have to do much better.

Sanctions have undoubtedly set back the Rhodesian economy and caused widespread unemployment, so increasing African discontent. But the Conservatives in Britain have already made it known that when they return to power (a matter upon which they feel quite confident), they will bring sanctions to an end. After hanging on for more than three years since UDI, the Smith regime was still showing during the first half of 1969 a dogged resolve to remain for another two. In this endeavour, it will have the reluctant support of the Vorster administration in Pretoria – since following the unnerving events of September 1968, when the South Africans showed signs of wanting to jettison him, Smith has astutely moved further right. This makes it much more difficult, even impossible, for Vorster to do a deal with Britain about the fate of Rhodesia without being accused at home of having been cynical and treacherous.

It would seem reasonable, therefore, to forecast that white rule of an uncompromising kind will survive indefinitely in Rhodesia, becoming more and more closely associated with South Africa and slowly acquiring a *de jure* status. Smith underlined his intransigence in May 1969, by steps towards a republic and a constitution entrenching white rule.

On turning to examine the Portuguese territories of Angola and Mozambique, a political analyst finds himself confronted with a somewhat different range of possibilities. Here there might easily be compromise of a type well suited to South Africa's visions of a sub-continental entente. Mozambique and Angola have witnessed far more violence than their neighbours, yet there are indications that post-Salazar Portugal hopes to win over its African opponents and strike a bargain with them. Where it cannot, the nationalists will be ruthlessly subverted – the FRELIMO organisation was woefully undermined at the start of 1969 by the assassination of Dr Eduardo Mondlane and the defection of key officials. However these tactics may work out, it can be assumed that Portugal will hold tenaciously to its southern African territories. In Angola particularly there have been dramatic mineral discoveries since the middle sixties and these represent the best hope for economic growth at home. The 100,000 Portuguese troops in the region operate in close liaison with their South African counterparts in anti-guerrilla work. Only through some upheaval in Lisbon is there likely to be a radical change in Angola and Mozambique – and there can be no guarantee that the removal of Caetano would bring a shift to the left.

Therefore it is unlikely that Zambia can look forward to any early improvement in relations with the four white-run countries with which it shares common borders – unless Zambia itself changes course politically. There are grounds, however, for looking carefully at the African countries already regarded by Pretoria as being "in the sphere". If they were to change, and adopted militant attitudes similar to Zambia's, a chain reaction might be started.

In the case of Lesotho, Swaziland and Botswana, there is scant prospect of their being allowed to deviate from the path laid down for them. The highly efficient South African espionage network in neighbouring countries has always ensured virtually complete penetration of nationalist movements; it also provides a steady flow of information back to Pretoria about political trends in the former British protectorates. Any malcontent bidding to oust such a trusted ally of South Africa as Lesotho's Chief Jonathan would encounter numerous hurdles. Even in

Malawi, which is far more remote, the South African authorities have been industriously shoring up the *status quo* and offering President Banda help in security matters. It may be imagined how precautions have been taken to ensure a co-operative administration in Malawi after Banda goes. Not that he has any intentions of going yet: in March 1969 he quietly hanged eight political opponents who had tried to kill him.

The attitudes of Malawi came in for heavy attack when the representatives of 14 East and Central African countries met in Zambia a month later. This attack was led by President Ismail Al-Azhari of the Sudan, who said he would never deal with a country which oppressed the black masses – a somewhat droll remark in the light of events in the southern Sudan. Banda had not attended the conference, but sent a delegation which sat silent and defensive in Lusaka's Inter-Continental Hotel while the invective swirled around it. The conference ended with the drawing up of a rousing communique, calling for "greater moral and material support for freedom fighters" and congratulating them upon their efforts to date. A determination was expressed to "spurn any dialogue with minority regimes."

The communiqué was followed by a document in quite different vein, a long and thoughtful manifesto calling for a change of direction by South Africa and its white-run neighbours. One paragraph may be said to encapsulate Kaunda's beliefs and determination – and his dilemma: "None of us would claim that within our own States we have achieved that perfect social, economic and political organisation which would ensure a reasonable standard of living for all our people and establish individual security against avoidable hardship or miscarriage of justice. On the contrary, we acknowledge that within our own States the struggle towards human brotherhood and unchallenged human dignity is only beginning. It is on the basis of our commitment to human equality and human dignity, not on the basis of achieved perfection, that we take our stand of hostility towards the colonialism and racial discrimination which is being practised in southern Africa."

It must be a profound disappointment to Vorster and Hilgard Muller that Kaunda maintains this hostile stance and refuses to stop the guerrillas from using Zambia. Yet a decisive moment has yet to arrive. This will come when the guerrillas show themselves to be growing more effective by doing serious damage and taking lives in Rhodesia or South Africa. Then retaliation will be demanded.

Retaliation would be carried out in a delicate way, probably by a few expert acts of sabotage, against targets chosen to make it plain to Kaunda that he was being punished for his intransigence. These targets could be reached either by agents within the country or by commando groups using military helicopters. An attack in 1968 showed the style which might be adopted: a large bridge across the Luangwa River in Zambia was blown up, after a watchman had been bayoneted to death; the bridge was only three miles from the Mozambique border and near the area where guerrillas had been making incursions. A series of major sabotage strikes would present Kaunda with a desperate dilemma. Arguments about future policy might create serious strains within the government.

Yet quite apart from the price Kaunda must ultimately expect to pay for the freedom-fighters (unless they remain quite ineffectual), he must withstand the blandishments of South Africa in economic matters. Zambia is rich now, but exceedingly vulnerable. The price of copper has stayed high longer than any experts had forecast, but it must fall within the next decade if all previous cycles in the metal markets have any meaning. When it does, Zambia will suddenly find itself short of money and unable to live in the manner to which it has grown accustomed. The South Africans will be most ready to help out, on terms: that Zambia promises to be friendly, to co-operate and join the club. It is then that Kaunda's principles will face their greatest test.

Index

ZAMBIA

48770

0   50   100

CONGO

ANGOLA

MWINILUNGA

SOLWEZ

NORTH WESTERN

•KASEMPA

•BALOVALE

•KABOMPO

MANKOYA

•KALABO

R. *Kafue*

•MONGU

BAROTSE

NAMWALA

KATABA

SOUTHERN

•SENANGA

R. *Zambezi*

KALOM

ZIMBA

SESHEKE•

LIVINGSTONE

S·W·AFRICA   BOTSWANA